Joe E. Brown

Joe E. Brown

*Film Comedian
and Baseball Buffoon*

WES D. GEHRING

FOREWORD BY CONRAD LANE

McFarland & Company, Inc., Publishers
Jefferson, North Carolina, and London

Frontispiece
Brown, ever the "sound" comedian,
during his Hollywood heyday.

LIBRARY OF CONGRESS CATALOGUING-IN-PUBLICATION DATA
Gehring, Wes D.
Joe E. Brown : film comedian and baseball buffoon / Wes D. Gehring ;
foreword by Conrad Lane.
p.   cm.
Includes bibliographical references and index.

ISBN-13: 978-0-7864-2589-1
ISBN-10: 0-7864-2589-X
(softcover : 50# alkaline paper) ∞

1. Brown, Joe E. (Joe Evan), 1892–   2. Baseball — United States —
Biography.   3. Comedians — United States — Biography.   4. Motion
picture actors and actresses — United States — Biography.   I. Title.
GV865.B76G44   2006   796.357092 — dc22   2006022234

British Library cataloguing data are available

On the cover: Joe E. Brown in uniform for his all-star baseball
team,which also played under his name (circa 1935). Inset, left
to right: Brown and his signature "monster-mouth"; Brown
in *A Very Honorable Guy* (1934); Brown, ever the "sound"
comedian, during his Hollywood heyday (circa 1925).
All photographs are from the author's collection.

Manufactured in the United States of America

McFarland & Company, Inc., Publishers
Box 611, Jefferson, North Carolina 28640
www.mcfarlandpub.com

For Grandpa McIntyre
and
Sarah and Emily

Table of Contents

Foreword

by Conrad Lane

I was recently watching a DVD of the 1937 David Selznick classic *A Star Is Born*. In one of the early scenes, aspiring actress Janet Gaynor, new to the Hollywood scene, walks into the court of the famed Grauman's Chinese Theater. She stares in wonder at the various signatures (accompanied by footprints and handprints) of famous Hollywood personalities of the day inscribed in cement blocks: Shirley Temple, Eddie Cantor, Jean Harlow and Joe E. Brown (complete with mouth print). This small bit reminded me of what a major star Joe E. Brown had been in the mid–30s. By the time *A Star Is Born* was released, he had appeared in a plethora of films and had been the star of all but a few. Between 1929 and 1936 he had done 23 films at Warner Bros. alone. He would go on to appear in many more, culminating in his scene-stealing supporting role in the classic *Some Like It Hot* (1959).

Reflecting on Brown's huge popularity in the thirties, I began to reminisce about my first awareness of this remarkable entertainer. At the time, I was a pre-schooler and I remember the endless discussions my two older brothers had about the movies. They attended about twice a week and came home with tantalizing stories about all that they had beheld. One of these films was Brown's *6-Day Bike Rider* (1934). I was full of questions about a bicycle race that could last six days. (This was the era of dance marathons and the like.) I never did quite understand the concept, but I did understand their great liking for Joe E. Brown and looked forward to the time when I could see one of his films.

The following year, 1935, I got to see my first Brown film —*Alibi Ike*. As it turned out, this was probably the best of his films for Warners and it made a decided impression on me (as did his 19-year-old leading lady, Olivia de Havilland). During the ensuing years, I recall many pleasurable matinees: *The Gladiator, Wide Open Faces* and *When's Your Birthday?* During the war years, there was a memorable guest appearance in the all-star *Hollywood Canteen* and, a few years later, a very effective non-comic role in *The Tender Years*. Brown was wisely chosen to play the pivotal role of Captain Andy in MGM's Technicolor version of *Showboat*— a mammoth hit of 1951.

It was a short time later that I finally got to see Brown in person — although at a great distance. In the fall of 1953, when I was a student at UC–Berkeley, several of us journeyed down to Los Angeles to see a football game between UC and the UCLA Bruins. The game was played on a gray Saturday afternoon at the L.A. Coliseum. Sitting across the aisle was none other than Bob Hope, who impressed us all with his quiet, dignified appearance. But the highlight of the day was when Brown sprang onto the field and led a yell. We were amazed at his agility (he would have been about 60 at the time) and also at the crowd's enthusiastic response to his appearance. He was clearly still a great favorite.

Brown had built up an enormous amount of good will with the military through his tireless entertaining of the troops during World War II. Fighting men such as my brothers who were ardent fans would be ecstatic when he appeared to entertain them. But the group in attendance at the L.A. Coliseum that Saturday afternoon were not of that age group, and their delight at his appearance seemed all the more surprising.

By the late 50s, it seemed that Joe E. Brown was on the verge of oblivion. Luckily for all of us, Billy Wilder, with canny inspiration, handed him a part in *Some Like It Hot* (voted the funniest movie of all time by the American Film Institute) that gave him that classic curtain line, "Well, nobody's perfect."

I think Brown appealed to us because he usually played a bumpkin who was forever being thrown into sticky situations and managing to come out on top, despite his very modest abilities. He proved himself a champion in boat races (*Top Speed*), football (*Maybe It's Love*), aviation (*Going Wild*), baseball (*Elmer the Great*), swimming (*You Said a Mouthful*), bike riding (*6-Day Bike Rider*) and wrestling (*The Gladiator*). As the foregoing titles attest, his pictures were especially appealing to boys and young men who were interested in the world of sports. But above all, I think we liked the Horatio Alger angle of his films in which a slight, rather homely little guy prevailed against all odds and emerged the honest and thoroughly likable hero.

Although we laughed long and loud at other popular comics of the day, it wasn't always easy to identify with them. The Marx Brothers were too fast and chaotic. Laurel & Hardy were a bit too stupid and somewhat grotesque in appearance. But Joe E. Brown was Everyman, not at all handsome, not brilliant, and not terribly imposing. In short, someone like ourselves.

Finding information on Joe E. Brown has been a problem of late. His critically acclaimed autobiography *Laughter Is a Wonderful Thing* (1956) was not a best-seller and is not easily located today. That is one reason why Wes D. Gehring's book on this fine comedian is so very welcome. To persons like myself who grew up watching the Joe E. Brown films, it is truly a privilege to read such an informed biography on a great entertainer who is now so little-known to the public. And with a writer like Gehring, whose stature among film biographers is well-known, we are assured of getting the documented truth. Upon reading this informed and respectful biography, I am certain that Joe E. Brown would have smiled very broadly.

Conrad Lane is a Ball State University emeritus professor who remains active as a film essayist and a nationally recognized Elderhostel movie history instructor. He also formerly hosted the PBS film review program Now Showing *on WIPB-TV in Muncie, Indiana.*

Preface and Acknowledgments

"Nolie, remember what I told you: smile!"
— Joe E. Brown to Kathryn Grayson in *Show Boat* [1951]

In his art, as well as in his life, Joe E. Brown always tried to put a positive spin on the human comedy. His simple philosophy could be found in the title of his autobiography, *Laughter Is a Wonderful Thing* (1956).[1] As film historian Leonard Maltin would later movingly observe, this was a title Brown knew "from long experience."[2] His decent small-town screen characters, often obsessed by sports (especially his beloved baseball), were never far from the real person.

While a biographer's normal predilection is to find new angles neglected in previous profiles, Brown has been so sadly neglected since his 1930s heyday that my first order of business was just reintroducing the reader to his gift for both comedy and life itself—secular humanism of the first order. Given that my family has always been fascinated by funny films, I was, however, well aware of Brown during my childhood. Indeed, after Laurel & Hardy, he was a special favorite of my maternal grandfather— and thus he became a favorite of mine, too.

Beyond underlining anew Brown's importance as an early sound film comedian, with a personage whose physical traits (such as the signature big mouth) remind one of the silent clowns, his legacy, if remembered, has often been wrongly chronicled. That is, the comic is frequently described as a B-picture personality, whose popularity was relegated to the small town and/or the rural market. But for much of the 1930s, Brown starred in A-films that generated solid box office numbers in large urban settings. Thus, a primary revisionist angle here is to document the broad appeal of this artist during the Great Depression.

A second angle of vision documents the Dickens-esque childhood Brown had during another depression — the economic collapse of the 1890s. Joining the circus with the blessings of an impoverished family, Joe Evan's youth reads like the difficult early years of his comedy hero and contemporary, Charlie Chaplin.[3] As novelist William T. Vollmann has observed, "Any decent biography is a work of drama."[4] And Brown's challenging childhood was his first and defining drama.

For Brown, a pivotal third angle of vision has to address how baseball was an

3

integral part of his personal and professional life. Coming of age at a time when the sport was truly the national game, the comedian's view of the American experience was filtered through both playing and savoring its microcosm of populistic tendencies.[5] Couple this with Brown's ability to parlay those real-life diamond experiences into the enrichment of his celebrated baseball trilogy, *Fireman, Save My Child* (1932), *Elmer the Great* (1933) and *Alibi Ike* (1935), and one has a better understanding of how his art was an extension of the man. Moreover, the diamond connection never went away, from a miming *Elmer the Great* pitching routine being a staple of his live stage act, to later doing play-by-play television commentary for the New York Yankees. The comedian was even a pioneering collector of sports memorabilia, with such notable items as Lou Gehrig's last glove and a Babe Ruth bat from the season (1927) in which he hit 60 home runs.

Rare is the biographer who undertakes a study without already knowing a great deal about his subject — the catalyst for those aforementioned angles of vision. Still, in gathering a mountain of research material for that task of "reassembling the dust," there are always a few surprises. What most impressed me about Brown, in the surprise category, was his consistently compassionate liberalness, back when that was still a commendable commodity. For instance, during World War II he spoke out against placing Japanese-Americans in internment camps. It is now considered a shameful chapter of the war, but few other citizens of the time (prominent or otherwise) had the courage and decency to oppose this racism. But this "colorblindness" was typical of Brown, who befriended many African American athletes and entertainers and lobbied Congress to allow Jewish-German children into the country just prior to the Second World War. Consequently, one might say, Brown led a life which not only merits chronicling, but deserves celebrating — an artist and a humanitarian.

This study was immeasurably enriched by the New York Public Library's Performing Arts Library at Lincoln Center, and the Margaret Herrick Library of the Academy of Motion Picture Arts and Sciences, Beverly Hills, California. During Brown's 1930s glory days, the most insightfully expansive critiques of his films came from the numerous New York City daily newspapers. These archives were a valuable resource for the Brown New York–related reviews, as were the microfilm "tombs" (dead newspaper) holdings of the main branch of the New York Public Library at Fifth Avenue and 42nd Street. Of additional assistance was the Joe E. Brown scrapbook kept at the Local History and Genealogy Department of the Toledo-Lucas County Public Library (Toledo, Ohio — the comedian's hometown). My Toledo Local History contact was Jim Marshall.

Numerous people helped make this project possible. Ball State emeriti professor and film historian Conrad Lane was a sounding board for me and wrote the foreword. Joe and Maria Pacino provided research assistance and a place to crash when I was doing work in the Los Angeles area. My department chair at Ball State University, Nancy Carlson, assisted by facilitating university financial help. As usual, Janet Warner logged time as my copy editor. The computer preparation of the manuscript was done by Jean Thurman.

Ultimately, however, the energy level necessary to fuel a project of this nature begins with the love and support of family: my daughters Sarah and Emily, sister Sue, and my parents. Plus, my aforementioned grandfather, Wallace McIntyre, Sr., merits a special thank you for planting that initial interest in Brown. As in the brightly colored fantasy-like imagery of *Amélie* (2001, with the delightful Audrey Tautou), my family encourages me to soar. Thank you, one and all.

— Wes D. Gehring

✦ ONE ✦

"It Takes Guts
to Be a Kinker [Acrobat]"[1]

Only thing I ever *could* do was make people laugh... And I can take only second billing for that talent. Nature met me more than halfway when it threw a handful of features together and called it a face.

—Joe E. Brown [1944][2]

While this modest man came into the world as Joe Evan Brown (July 28, 1892), the veteran performer would later answer to many affectionately comic nicknames during a career spanning nearly 70 years: "cavernous-mouthed comedian," "crater-mouthed comic," "monster-mouthed," "funny face" and "Grand Canyon." Indeed, this "fortune in a face" characteristic would dominate his comedy persona, as noted by the *New York Times* reviewer of Brown's *Wide Open Faces* (1938): "[I]t must be said with respect to that phenomenal terrain [big mouth] that the sight-seers [film fans] seem never to tire of viewing it, no matter what the conveyance may be."[3] Comic schtick associated with the Brown-esque "crater" might range from a giant bovine-like yawn, to his signature howl of dismay.

There is also a mistaken belief that "Grand Canyon" was only popular with ordinary people. But for much of Brown's career, he also found critical acclaim. And one is tempted to link that praise to the joy critics had trying to comically describe his "funny face." For instance, while a *Hollywood Reporter* reviewer would succinctly liken a Brown yawn in *Elmer the Great* (1933) to "nearly a [big screen] blackout," the *New York Times* critic expands at length upon the wonders of that "crater" in *Going Wild* (1931):

Realizing that it would always be funny to look at Mr. Brown's mouth when he's saying "Ah" [during a physical], the producers make it still funnier by giving a close-up of the Brown mouth which rather causes one to think that it would be just the place to throw used safety-razors and also that it is rather dangerous for the doctor to be leaning so near the edge of such a vast cavern.[4]

Even when a reviewer was not in the Brown camp, such as the *New York Herald Tribune* critic Marguerite Tazelaar, the uniqueness of his audience's response constituted entertainment news. Consequently, the opening to her critique of Brown's *Sit Tight* (1931) documented the comedian's grass roots popularity: "The Winter Garden [Theatre] was packed yesterday by an audience ... which howled and hooted with delight at Joe E. Brown...."[5] Of course, many of his critical fans, such as the *New York Evening Journal* reviewer Rose Pelswick, also felt compelled to report on his special bond with viewers. This is the opening of Pelswick's critique of *Local Boy Makes Good* (1931): "The moment Joe E. Brown appears on the screen there's a delighted howl from the audience. So, with the customers his from the start, Brown needs do little more than yawn [that mouth again!], blink or shuffle his feet to ensure undivided attention."[6]

Despite all these "cavernous" comments, however, it is only fair to say that there is also a certain hardy stalwartness about Brown's face. For example, *New York Times* critic Bosley Crowther stated in his *Earthworm Tractors* (1936) review, "It is true that [Brown's mug] looks like something done with mirrors, a Coney Island illusion ... and living proof that nature ... is still greater than [makeup guru] Max Factor. But, for all its irregularities, it is also a face which has about it a certain rugged beauty, like the Maine coastline."[7]

Brown and his signature "monster-mouth."

With all due respect to Brown's ability to raise funny to the level of fable, ably assisted by a puss from the gods of comedy, his initial entrance into the world of entertainment had nothing to do with laughter. Moreover, like Brown's future comedy contemporaries W.C. Fields (who began as a juggler) and Will Rogers (who began as a trick rope cowboy), *Funny Face's* show business commencement did not even involve speech: Brown was first a circus acrobat.

For children of the 1890s depression, nothing could compete with the circus coming to town. As James Whitcomb Riley, arguably then America's most popular poet, wrote in "The Circus-Day Parade," "[H]ow the boys behind [the wagons], high and low of every kind, marched in unconscious capture, with a rapture undefined!"[8] Brown would later confess in his autobiography, "I was fascinated by the gaudy [circus] colors everywhere. The sound of the band and the noise of the happy, laughing crowd was the most beautiful music I'd ever heard."[9]

Ohio-born Brown was undoubtedly aware of Indiana neighbor Riley ("The Hoosier Poet") and his celebration of the circus, since this was one of the acclaimed writer's best-loved verses. For years Riley had toured both the Midwest and the East reading his populist poetry and winning praise from such literary giants as Mark Twain and Rudyard Kipling. Plus, this was a time when memorizing verse, especially that of Riley, was a part of most elementary school educations. In addition, like young Joe's father, Riley had started his blue-collar legacy as a sign painter—an everyman foundation made much of in the poet's period literature. Regardless, for Joe Evan and his friends, the height of circus royalty were the acrobats—flying superheroes whose magic was later caught in the popular song "The Daring Young Man on the Flying Trapeze."

Born in Holgate, Ohio, Joe was the third of what would eventually be seven children for Mathias and Anna Brown. The comedian's middle name (Evan) was drawn from Evan Evans, his maternal grandfather. As a boy, young Joe most often answered to the name of Evan, especially from his beloved mother. This close and hard-working family, of Welsh and German ancestry, moved often in the 1890s, based upon the meager existence to be derived from a sign- and house-painting income. But in 1899 the Browns would come to settle permanently in Toledo, Ohio.

Joe Evan's lifelong sense of fair play and gentleness was inherited from a father who was the most conscientious and even-tempered of men. Appropriately, as noted by film historian Leonard Maltin, the future screen persona the comedian projected was that of "likability, innocence, and American stick-to-itiveness."[10] Be that as it may, times were very hard for both the Brown family and much of the country in general. The comedian later remembered:

> I began life as an undernourished baby who grew into a gaunt, too-thin little boy; it was a fact that disturbed me not the slightest. Most of the other kids in my family and neighborhood were equally thin. And if it was a hardship, it was good conditioning for the [tough acrobatic] life I later knew.[11]

Throughout his life, Brown enjoyed telling people he was the only youngster who ever ran away to join the circus ... with his parents' blessing! In truth, his family needed the modest salary the nine-year-old could earn as a circus acrobat. How fitting that a working depression-era child would eventually find film fame as an everyman comic type in America's next depression. Moreover, the movie fare of his primary studio (Warner Brothers) for most of the 1930s was often known as the "cinema of poverty," given its propensity to embrace stories of struggle.

As for most low-income families, Joe Evan's early days in Toledo, even prior to his circus sojourn, was an ongoing attempt to help his parents. The Browns' first Toledo home was in the "Smoky Row" section of town—the proverbial wrong side of the tracks. In fact, it was nearly *on* the tracks, with the name "Smoky Row" coming from the area's close proximity to the coal-burning trains being serviced at the railroad round-house. Not surprisingly, an early "job" for Joe was to make faces at the passing train firemen to get free coal thrown at him. This was the first time the youngster realized that his "cavernous" cavity could be an advantage. And in the long tradition of most rubber-faced funnymen, it was at this time that he also started to build a repertoire of zany expressions. Interestingly enough, this is something of an archetypal story for many comedians from this era. For instance, a few years later Red Skelton would play the same goofy game with passing trains in his native Vincennes, Indiana, as he also worked to help a poor, struggling family.[12] Furthermore, just as legendary director and Brown contemporary Frank Capra earned extra pennies as a sidewalk newsboy in Los Angeles, Joe Evan hawked newspapers on the downtown streets of Toledo.

While young Brown's inventiveness helped him in assorted part-time jobs, his originality also fueled his fascination with all forms of entertainment. To illustrate, Joe once climbed a telephone pole simply for a partial view, through an open window, of a vaudeville show. One is reminded of Harpo Marx's revelation of climbing a hill near the New York Giants' old baseball stadium, the Polo Grounds, in order to see a narrow slice of left field.[13]

Like Harpo (who had a passion for baseball and Giants left fielder Sam Martes), Brown was also a huge fan of the national pastime. In an immigrant-rich melting pot era in this country, playing baseball was a fun way for youngsters to embrace being an American. As period populist poet Walt Whitman observed, "America's game [base-ball] ... belongs to our institutions, fits ... into them [as] significantly as our constitu-tions [sic], [and] laws: Is just as important in the sum total of our historic life."[14] Or, more succinctly, French historian Jacques Barzun stated, "To know the heart and mind of America, one must learn baseball."[15] Plus, patriotic Brown both enjoyed and excelled at the entertainment-spectacle aspect of the game. Add to this the fact that major league baseball as we know it today, with American and National League champions meeting in an annual World Series, was born during Brown's childhood, and it is easy to see why the sport was a central defining component for him. Indeed, baseball was so indeli-bly etched on his psyche that had period Mexican painter Frida Kahlo done his por-trait, she undoubtedly would have sketched ballplaying images on her drawing of his forehead. With Kahlo's surrealistic tendencies, this was her metaphorical way of sug-gesting intrinsic truths about her subject.

Baseball surfaces throughout Brown's life and career in ten meaningful ways. First, there was simply the joy of playing, which lasted long after his youth. As late as the 1930s, his Warner Brothers film contract would necessitate that the company would fund his studio team. (Brown's friend and fellow comedian Buster Keaton, another baseball aficionado, often provided the rival diamond nine.) Second, the game was so popular in the early 1900s that semi-professional teams popped up everywhere. Con-sequently, one of young Brown's perennial part-time jobs was playing for various baseball

Brown (right) and fellow Warner Bros. baseball fan Dick Powell (1932).

clubs. Third, Brown so excelled as a ballplayer that the New York Yankees flirted with the idea of adding him to their minor league farm system.

Fourth, as a touring vaudevillian Brown frequently found himself in the company of on-the-road baseball players. Thus, like his friend Will Rogers, Brown often worked out with different major league teams at various baseball parks. Fifth, arguably the comedian's greatest films, after *Some Like It Hot* (1959), were his baseball trilogy: *Fireman, Save My Child* (1932), *Elmer the Great* (1933) and *Alibi Ike* (1935). Sixth, the comedian was so identified with the sport that when he entertained troops during World War II, popular demand required that part of his stand-up schtick be diamond-directed. Surprisingly, or maybe not so surprisingly, when one such wartime performance later involved meeting some Japanese prisoners, those "who could speak English said they had seen his *Elmer the Great* movies. [And they] wanted to talk baseball."[16]

Seventh, not only was baseball material something Brown never tired of, it was also a way of periodically recharging his batteries. To illustrate, in 1940 he returned to the stage in a production of *Elmer the Great*. And in 1947 Brown recorded a double album entitled *How to Play Baseball*, with the comedian explaining the national pastime to a youngster named *Elmer*. Eighth, the man with the famous mouth long maintained professional ties with the sport, from being a 1953 New York Yankees television announcer to doubling that same year as the president of the national Pony Leagues (for 13- and 14-year-old youngsters).[17] Ninth, the ongoing significance of the sport was such that throughout Brown's long life his conversations were peppered with baseball references. To illustrate, while facing surgery at 72, he metaphorically kidded with reporters about handling anxiety: "Get on second base and run. This is the fellow [himself] that couldn't hit a curve ball."[18] Tenth, the comic passed his passion for the game on to his beloved surviving son, Joe L. Brown, who spent his adult life in professional baseball. The 1955 capstone to that career was Joe L. becoming general manager of the Pittsburgh Pirates.[19]

For a little boy, however, the color and pageantry of the circus took precedence over even baseball. As comedy contemporary and later Brown acquaintance Kin Hubbard (creator of crackerbarrel character Abe Martin) observed, "Th' trouble with walkin' in a [circus] pe-rade is that life seems so dull an' colorless afterward."[20] Of course, Brown's flying trapeze aspirations were also assisted by a local connection. William J. (Billy) Ashe was a former circus clown turned acrobat who wintered in Toledo; his troupe, "The Marvelous Ashtons," employed youngsters. When a friend of a friend was accepted into the act, what had once seemed like a dream for Joe suddenly entered the realm of possibility. With both an amazing work ethic and a propensity to absorb pain (two traits which would serve him well in his lengthy entertainment apprenticeship), young Brown tackled an assortment of gymnastic tricks, including a back somersault.

Comically, this dedicated regimen was initially assisted by an accident of housecleaning: The family couch was moved to the side porch for several days. Like the trampoline that would later be part of his comic stage act, even after he left acrobatics behind, the old sofa helped the determined boy master the back somersault ... sort of. That is, the first few times Joe Evan attempted to replicate the trick (*sans* couch) for friends on the less friendly terra firma of the schoolyard, he landed on his face. Burned more by humiliation than the numerous cinder cuts to his face, he repeated the exercise

Brown in his first baseball film, *Fireman, Save My Child* (1932, with Evalyn Knapp).

several times until he successfully managed a back hand spring (sometimes referred to as a flip-flop) for his now-admiring friends.

Unbeknownst to Joe, Billy Ashe had witnessed the boy's display of playground persistence. Though impressed by the youngster's talent, he was more taken with his stick-to-itiveness, *á la* the courage it takes to be a "kinker" (acrobat). This accidental

13

audition led to young Joe being trained after school by Billy at Toledo's Valentine Athletic Club. Brown was to be part of a "casting act" comprised of two adults (Ashe and Otto Lowery) and three boys (George Jones, Grover McCabe and Joe). Billy would hang by his knees from a stationary bar and swing one of the youngsters beneath him. The routine, at its most basic, consisted of Ashe then throwing said boy to Otto, who was also hanging by his knees from another stationary bar. The flying child would do a single or a double somersault before being caught by Lowery. The master plan called for eventually doing a triple. This acrobatic action took place 20 feet off the ground, with a safety net 16 feet below. He would eventually be called "The Cork Screw Kid."

The most memorable moment of that lengthy training period occurred in January 1903: Joe's first successful flying somersault from Ashe to catcher Lowery. Later that winter, Billy and Joe's father signed a contract for the youngster's services in the Marvelous Ashtons. Not unlike countless other children then being "hired out" by poor families across the country, Joe's parents would receive $1.50 a week and Ashe would cover the youngster's expenses. With this simple act, the boy's life would be forever changed. Besides further fueling his entertainer tendencies, the nomadic schedule upon which he would soon embark would often be the norm for the rest of his life. And though the contract was exploitive, the boy was living a dream, a far cry from the urban sweatshop existence of many other turn-of-the-century children. Brown left with the most modest of supplies — a small bundle with a pair of patched underwear (hand-me-downs from his older brothers) and a spare shirt. With comic poignancy, his mother warned him to be careful around the elephants.[21]

With Ashe, young Joe also acquired a second father figure. Unfortunately, this was not always a good thing. Unlike the youngster's gentle biological dad, Ashe was an often angry man who was prone to strike the boys, especially the youngest and most undersized — Joe. Still, Brown was so overjoyed to be part of the circus that he blocked out this Dickens-esque quality: "Far greater than my fear of Ashe was my dread that my family might learn that my life was not the bed of roses I painted [in my letters] and order me home."[22] Young Joe's ecstatic factor reminds me of novelist Michael Chabon's later description of rapturous film fans "who climbed into a movie as into a time machine ... and set the dial for 'never come back...'"[23] Remember, Brown was a boy from such an impoverished background that he never actually attended a circus ... until he was in one!

With regard to Ashe, the youngster did come to admire both the man's showmanship and his strict work ethic. Ironically, Joe suffered more physical pain, not from beatings but from the standard wear and tear of his new profession. For instance, in the Ashe act the somersaulting boys were usually caught by their wrists, rather than their hands. Though this was a more safe and secure procedure, in a long season of constant practice and performances the youngster's wrists were soon rubbed raw. Crude cloth wrappings did little to lesson the pain. Worse yet, early in Brown's first season, an awkward fall into the net resulted in a broken jaw from a wayward knee. Naturally, there was no time for a convalescence. Circus performers were supposed to soldier through like the athletes of the then-budding new sport of football: "No pain, no gain." Brown's only assist in continuing to perform despite a broken jaw was a special cap with straps attached under his chin to keep the newly set fracture secure and to hide the bandages. Paradoxically, though the Marvelous Ashtons was an airborne act, young Brown would later suffer from bone spurs in both ankles, too. This was a result of Billy Ashe's habit of banging the boy's ankles together for timing purposes before tossing them to Otto the trapeze catcher! While treating their ankles like a pair of cymbals might have helped Billy's synchronization, it resulted in more war wounds for the boys.

An unexpected big top bonus for young Brown was the chance to interact with an assortment of circus animals, a subject the comic would return to in the films *The Circus Kid* (1928) and *The Circus Clown* (1934). Amazingly, a baby elephant he befriended during his second season with the Marvelous Ashtons (1904, as part of the Robinson Circus) later surfaced in his movie *The Circus Clown*. Given both the gentleness he inherited from his father and the strong reaction against the violence of Billy Ashe, Brown was a lifelong advocate for fair treatment of animals. Appropriately, he would later campaign for and land the lead in *The Tender Years* (1948): In a rare dramatic role for the actor, Brown movingly played a pioneering animal rights activist.

Another windfall of Joe's early entrance into the world of entertainment was travel, something most people did very little of a century ago. Thus, when the boy returned home to Toledo at the end of each season, his touring tales made him seem almost cosmopolitan to friends and family. The ambitious Ashe navigated his troupe across much of the United States as they sometimes jumped from one circus to another. Moreover, though Joe's contract was supposed to be simply a summer arrangement, each "season" continued well after the resumption of autumn classes. This overlapping was at its worst in 1905, when Ashe segued the act from circus bookings to some West Coast vaudeville dates. As luck would have it, this placed the Marvelous Ashtons in San Francisco at the time of the famous 1906 earthquake.

Though the troupe came through the tragedy unscathed, the slice-of-life surrealism of seeing city walls shake like curtains in the wind forever stayed with 13-year-old Brown. With the comic irony that sometimes accompanies a disaster, however, the boy's most vivid memory of this time was the abundance of food made available to the troupe. Most youngsters are eternally hungry. For the undersized and overworked Joe, food was a subject that now rivaled baseball in his dreams. Well, because of the fires which swept San Francisco after the earthquake, parts of the city were dynamited to create "breaks" or walls to stop the flames. Providentially, the Marvelous Ashtons then happened to be passing a large grocery which was earmarked for destruction. With the poor owner encouraging one and all to take what they wanted, young Brown and company legally looted the place.

Paradoxically, not only was the undernourished boy suddenly given free access to food at a time (an emergency) when any sustenance would normally be lacking, the grocery in question might now have been labeled a gourmet shop! The troupe's diet for the next few days largely consisted of various kinds of caviar! This comic culinary luck continued during their protracted rail journey back to Ohio. As with most disasters, Americans went out of their way to assist the victims. This included sharing a vast assortment of food with displaced persons leaving the Bay area by rail. For hundreds of miles, each whistle stop became a Thanksgiving banquet. With this adventure, Joe was to experience an entirely new phenomenon, indigestion.

Moving beyond these comic developments, Brown's actual homecoming took on the nature of a miracle for his family and friends. The individual members of the Marvelous Ashtons were never included in any of the various newspaper lists of earthquake survivors. Accountability for visitors in the disaster area was spotty to begin with, and this was further exacerbated by the mass migration of displaced people from the city. Young Joe's loved ones assumed that he and his fellow acrobats had perished in the tragedy. Thus, like Mark Twain's legendary literary figure Tom Sawyer, an especially popular character at this time, Joe was accorded the provocative privilege of a return from the grave.

The only downside to this return was the accidental revelation that Billy Ashe sometimes beat the boys. Brown's parents immediately terminated the boy's association with the troupe. Billy was lucky it was kept to a split, because Joe's older brothers John and Mike wanted, to use a popular payback expression, to "clean his clock." Despite Ashe's dark side, Brown always loyally credited his first entertainment mentor with reinforcing the importance of persistence for success. Years later, a world-famous Joe E. Brown would track down Ashe in an Ohio nursing home and share those kudos.

Back in Toledo, Joe applied his cat-quick athleticism to Trolley League baseball — games played within the city's interurban system. This was semi-pro ball, with Brown able to earn pocket money *and* play with some of his older local diamond heroes. His favorite was a bartender-outfielder named Billy Smith, whose Toledo fame was based upon a put-out that anticipated Willie Mays' later celebrated catch of a Vic Wertz blast during the 1954 New York Giants–Cleveland Indians World Series. Both of these defensive gems were predicated upon the fielder needing to turn his back to the ball in order to race to the deepest part of center field. Then, with an outfield wall bearing down upon him, he makes an over-the-back basket catch of what otherwise would have been an extra base hit.

Playing with local legend Smith meant a great deal to the baseball-obsessed Joe. Interestingly enough, second baseman Brown had earlier been acutely aware of Smith's bartending duties, too. As an undersized, underfed newsboy, Joe used to sneak into Smith's saloon and lift items from the free food section of the bar. His athletic dexterity first involved using the high bar, which overhung the footrest, as a shield from the eyesight of Smith. Once securely in place, and with the exact location of the individual items memorized (plates of boiled eggs, massive open jars of dill pickles, baskets of bread), Joe would begin the process of snitching food.

As already suggested in this chapter, many of Brown's early memories involved his constant hunger. Indeed, the boy's most vivid memory of his touring time with Ashe, after the earthquake adventure, was a pre-disaster Bay Area booking at Grauman's Unique Theatre, a West Coast vaudeville venue. (This was the same Grauman later famous for a Hollywood landmark, Grauman's Chinese Theatre, whose drawing card is still a courtyard featuring the hand and footprints of filmland's royalty.) One of the gimmicks Grauman used at his turn-of-the century San Francisco theater was an exploitive feed-the-performers segment to his program. What was unusual about his *Unique* Theatre was an L-shaped stage, so some of his patrons could not see the acts. In order to humor what punningly might be called the "feeder" section of the crowd, they were allowed to watch the various acts eating in the wings ... often with a running comic commentary from showman Grauman. This circus-like "feed the animals" scenario was a hit both with the fans and the ever-hungry entertainers, especially youngsters like Brown. With the acts not having to leave the theater for meal breaks, the ever frugal Grauman would squeeze an extra performance or two from his performers.

With all the eccentric developments in Brown's early career, I am reminded of the wry observation from Jim Knipfel's darkly comic memoir *Slackjaw*: Life had "become one long slapstick routine — like living a Marx Brothers movie, except without quite so many musical numbers."[24] And like a Marx Brothers picture, the rest of Brown's life and comic times would seldom be less than entertainingly unusual.

❖ Two ❖

Acrobat to Actor ...
But Ever the Athlete

I always played baseball the same as I do anything else. Just because there are
two men out and we are ten runs behind in the ninth doesn't make the game
finished ... no game is over until there are three men out in the ninth inning.
—Joe E. Brown (1956)[1]

Brown's gung ho athletic attitude about life once created headlines during
his favorite sporting event—the World Series. The entertainer always religiously
attended these fall classics, and not just for pleasure's sake. In the 1932 Series between
the New York Yankees and the Chicago Cubs, Brown was also there to film scenes for
the screen adaptation of Ring Lardner's baseball play *Elmer the Great*. But it was the
1934 October meeting of the St. Louis Cardinals and the Detroit Tigers that produced
comic headlines like the *New York Herald Tribune*'s "Rowe's Hand Mashed by Joe
Brown."[2] Detroit pitcher Schoolboy Rowe felt something went wrong when he shook
hands with the comedian before the game: "Joe gave Rowe a good old he-man grip and
Schoolboy was not ready for it. Rowe did not remain in the hospital after the hand was
x-rayed. There was nothing broken."[3] Of course, prior to this hospital clearance, newspapers across the country had fun with this sports story. For instance, Brown's favorite
hometown paper, *The Toledo Times*, made the comedian out to be a second Paul Bun-
yan: "Joe, an enthusiastic baseball fan, is reported to have shaken Schoolboy Rowe's
hand so lustily before today's game that he fractured several small bones in the hurler's
right hand [!]"[4]

The later consensus was that Rowe was merely looking for an excuse, not unlike
the famed Ring Lardner baseball character Alibi Ike, whom Brown would play in a movie
of the same name the following year (1935). As humorist Will Rogers wrote at the time
in his syndicated daily newspaper telegram, "My old friend, Joe E. Brown, didn't wound
anybody by a handshake. If he did he must have hit 'em."[5] While one could argue that
the Rowe-Brown handshake might have contributed to a favorable climate for the later
Brown production *Alibi Ike*, a greater catalyst would have been the 1934 World Series
star Dizzy Dean. The screwball Cardinal pitcher was a combination of both Lardner

characters, the supremely confident Elmer and Alibi Ike. To illustrate the former trait, here is Dean's take on his dominating pitching during the 1934 Series:

> Boy, you know what I told you when I came up here [to the Major Leagues].
> If I was right they didn't have no chance ...
> I let them [Detroit] Tigers have a couple of base hits [today] and then I throwed strikes at 'em. Boy, there was nothing to it.[6]

Conversely, Dean was also quick to alibi about his performances, even when he won. Thus, after an earlier pitching victory against the Tigers in that same 1934 Series, Dizzy told reporters, "I'm telling you I was lousy in there today. That old curve ball of mine just wouldn't work. I couldn't do a thing with my fast one ... [and] as a result I had to pitch my head off."[7]

Not surprisingly, the period parallels between Dean and Lardner characters were not missed by baseball fans. Brown's friend Paul A. Schrader, sports editor of the *Toledo Times*, called Dizzy the "actual personification" of Elmer the Great, a verdict later seconded by the comedian in his autobiography.[8] Brown had long been fascinated with Lardner's baseball fiction. Thus, he was immediately drawn to a character (Dean) who seemed to have just stepped out of a Lardner story. After all, baseball was life itself to Joe. (As *Time* magazine later observed of the comedian, "He says that he did not get into show business until he was nine but he was a confirmed baseball fan at four."[9]) Moreover, like the Elmer-playing Brown, Dean often simply played the clown. For instance, after being knocked unconscious by a relay throw at second base in the fourth game of the 1934 Series, Dizzy always claimed that the "next day's paper supposedly read 'X-RAYS OF DEAN'S HEAD SHOW NOTHING.' ... [But] no St. Louis newspaper ran such a headline."[10]

As luck would have it, Brown was sitting with the Cardinals' general manager, Branch Rickey, when the Dean accident occurred. The comedian later recalled, "Rickey wouldn't look up. Tears streamed down his cheeks. He couldn't be comforted until x-rays proved Dizzy's head was harder than the ball and required fewer stitches."[11] Rickey and Brown had been friends for several years, a position further cemented by the fact that the comedian had played a St. Louis Cardinal pitcher in the 1932 film *Fireman, Save My Child*. (Rickey is most famous now for his 1947 integration of baseball. As the Brooklyn Dodgers' president–general manager, he handpicked Jackie Robinson to break baseball's color barrier. And, like Rickey, Brown was "color-blind" in life, too.)

Dean was not only back to normal almost immediately after the accident, his sense of humor never faltered. He supposedly told the ambulance personnel, "Make this look good." Then after the Cardinals beat the Tigers in the Series, Brown's eccentric friend Dizzy met the press "carrying a big, rubber inflated tiger, painted yellow with brown stripes. [Next, in a move reminiscent of Joe,] Dean took the tail of the tigers in his teeth and shook it like a dog chokes a bone."[12] Later he would add four knots to the tiger's tail ... one for each Cardinal Series win. And Dizzy's "pet" tiger was with him during the victory parade the following day back in St. Louis.[13] Brown would later explain his fascination with athletes like Dean "[Y]ou don't run up against so many phonies in sports. I don't know why it is, but the percentage is much lower."[14] One might add that, like Brown, or the fictional title character of Daniel Wallace's much later novel *Big Fish* (adapted so inventively for the screen by Tim Burton), Dean was always about telling a better story ... even if this involved getting creative with the facts. For instance, when this Cardinal "Big Fish" came up to the Major Leagues, he gave various life stories to an assortment of reporters — so they all could have exclusives!

Depression era students of baseball and the movies had yet another reason to link Brown and Dean. The film star was a pioneer in the collecting of sports memorabilia. Just as the comedian's ties to the 1934 Series started to fade into yesterday's news, press reports described his then-unusual hobby acquisition: "Mr. Brown's sport trophy room in his Beverly Hills home will be considerably enriched through its owner's attendance at the recent world series ... Dizzy Dean presented him with the Cardinal uniform he wore while he was blanking the Tigers in the final and deciding contest...."[15] A Dean uniform was already a pre-established flashpoint of interest in 1934. Earlier that season, Dizzy had made headlines by tearing up both his home and away jerseys after being fined. Ever the entertainer, he then further shredded one of these uniforms for the benefit of a newspaper photographer who had missed the earlier performance.

Brown's memorabilia take from the 1934 Series was not limited to Dean's uniform. The comedian was also able to acquire the Navin Field (later renamed Tiger Stadium) pitching rubber from which Dizzy hurled the clinching game for the Cardinals. It is no wonder that Brown's name was synonymous with baseball, especially during his 1930s heyday.

Consistent with this, the comedian would later reveal that as a "little fellow" his two heroes were "Ty Cobb, whom I still consider the greatest baseball player of all time, and 'The Great Commoner' [populist politician] William Jennings Bryan."[16] Cobb was the early twentieth-century superstar of baseball, winning an unprecedented *ten* batting titles (between 1907 and 1919) on his way to what is still baseball's highest lifetime batting average (.366). And it was not until 1985 that Pete Rose finally topped Cobb's 4000-plus career hit total. Thus, it makes perfect sense that young Joe would be a fan of the Detroit Tigers star outfielder nicknamed "The Georgia Peach."

An added wild card factor for Brown's fascination, however, was that Cobb always "insisted that he was not superbly endowed as an athlete, only that he had greater desire."[17] As previously established, despite Brown's obvious talent as a multi-faceted entertainer, he also felt that his success was directly linked to a blue collar mentality. Naturally, the controversial footnote to this philosophy is that Cobb's drive to win at any cost resulted in his having more than a few detractors. As another diamond hitting legend, Ted Williams, diplomatically observed, "Cobb was the fiercest competitor who ever walked onto a baseball field."[18] So how does one reconcile the populist Brown with the often abrasive Cobb? While Joe, like his father, was the most egalitarian of people, the trait he admired most was the driving discipline of persistence, *á la* Cobb.

Remember, Brown is the depression era boy who could not only look beyond the childhood abuse of his first entertainment mentor, Billy Ashe, but also even revere this man for his tenacious perseverance. Joe would have appreciated the later observation of another famous comedian, Woody Allen: "Eighty percent of life is just showing up." Moreover, Cobb never rested on his laurels. Celebrated baseball author Red Smith quoted Hall of Fame player-hitter Al Simmons on "The Georgia Peach," "Of all the guys I have known, Cobb was the only one who played as hard after he got rich as he ever did when he was hungry."[19] Simmons might just as well have been describing Brown. Consequently, Cobb was the most fitting of heroes for the future comedian. Besides, this old-school ballplayer excelled at Joe's favorite sport ... when it was unquestionably the *national* game.

As a major Cobb fan, Brown would undoubtedly also have been aware of a period publication that has since been largely forgotten — Cobb's baseball book, *Busting 'Em and Other Big League Stories* (1914, a collaboration with an uncredited John N. Wheeler). Through both humor ("The names that the occupants of the bleachers call the outfielders could not be printed on asbestos paper"[20]) and shocking revelations (playing through a death threat[21]), Cobb's chip-on-one's-shoulder attitude is made more understandable. And a budding comedian like Brown would also have been attracted to the book's entertaining cartoon illustrations.

A final footnote to the Brown-Cobb connection concerns a story told about the Georgia Peach in the 1960s. Attributed to various veteran contemporaries of the baseball legend, this now-celebrated anecdote has a young reporter asking the Cobb crony how the Hall of Famer would do now in the Major Leagues. When the journalist is told that the Detroit star would probably bat about .320, he is not impressed. After all, isn't Cobb supposed to be baseball's greatest player? "Well," replied the veteran, "you have to remember, he's in his seventies now." Joe E. Brown loved that story.

The fact that another childhood hero of Brown's was William Jennings Bryan speaks volumes about the youngster. "The Great Commoner" was the late nineteenth century's greatest champion of the poor. Plus, given that he was the Democratic Party candidate for president in 1896, 1900 and 1908, dates that covered Brown's formative years, the comedian would have known few other political representatives of the disenfranchised. The low-income Brown household was so strongly in the Bryan camp, they were not even dissuaded by the fact that President William McKinley, the winning Republican candidate in both 1896 and 1900, was a popular former governor of their own home state of Ohio!

Besides the populist nature of Bryan's various presidential races, another component of this man's legacy which would have resonated with a future entertainer like young Brown was Bryan's campaign style. This politician was arguably the most theatrically effective orator of his time. Historian C. Vann Woodward later described the

A young Brown and his acrobatic partner–friend Frank "Pre" Prevost, circa 1909.

conclusion of Bryan's famous "Cross of Gold" speech (1896): "You shall not press down upon the brow of labor this crown of thorns, you shall not crucify mankind upon a cross of gold"—as a "thrilling peroration."[22] (Bryan felt going off the gold standard, coupled with the free coinage of silver, would help jumpstart America out of the 1890s depression.)

Even Bryan's nickname, "The Great Commoner," had a theatrical ring to it. He campaigned like an entertainer, crisscrossing the nation by rail and giving over 600 speeches. This was an unprecedented approach to presidential politics for the time—the first modern campaign. In sharp contrast, McKinley conducted a "front porch" candidacy, staying home in Canton, Ohio, with trainloads of supporters being brought in to hear him speak. Underdog Bryan made the 1896 race interesting, but Brown's hero was ultimately no match for McKinley's big business–driven campaign. Bryan's subsequent presidential races (1900, 1908) were not as competitive. Comically, Joe would also later link his two early heroes, Bryan and Cobb, in a tongue-in-cheek manner. When asked to explain why he did not make it to the Major Leagues he would observe, "Naturally, I tried to play baseball like Ty Cobb, but actually I played it like Bryan."[23]

Comic modesty notwithstanding, when Joe broke with Billy Ashe in 1906, baseball was his way of reconnecting with his Toledo roots. Fittingly, when Joe returned to acrobatics later that year, his unofficial hometown agent was baseball friend Ollie Pecord. Through Pecord, the youngster was able to become part of the acrobatic Bell-Prevost Trio. Brown comically observed later, "I was Trio."[24] As when he was a member of the Marvelous Ashtons, Joe was still waiting for marquee recognition. But at least he had moved from a five-member act to a trio. Moreover, he was now suddenly performing in fast company. To illustrate, a New York vaudeville booking later that year (1906) also included W. C. Fields and comic actor Victor Moore on the same bill.

Unfortunately, one thing did not change for Brown. The nominal leader of the Bell-Prevost Trio, Tommy Bell, was abusive to young Joe. The most memorable incident of Bell aggression occurred during an on-the-road Christmas Eve in 1907. The desperately homesick boy felt completely isolated during his favorite holiday. Sitting in the hotel lobby, the feeling of loneliness was made worse by the festive nature of all the late shoppers on the downtown main street. As with many vaudevillians, people-watching was normally something Brown enjoyed doing. Like the later Red Skelton, Joe would eventually see this as comic research. But *not* this Christmas Eve. Brown was finding that sometimes the loneliest place is in the midst of a crowd.

Then, however, something positive happened. The boy discovered a lost silver dollar on his lobby chair. This would now enable him to buy presents for his partners and feel part of the season. Purchasing a pipe for Bell and a pair of slippers for Prevost, Brown raced back to the hotel to arrange the gifts in their room before that evening's performances. Throughout the act that night, Joe excitedly looked forward to his partners finding the presents. But while Prevost was appreciative, Bell's response gave the poor boy the shock of his life. The youngster had just said "Merry Christmas!" when his personal persecutor yelled, "Merry Christmas, hell," painfully jerking Brown from bed and accusing him, "Where did you steal the money from, anyway? Don't you know you're liable to get the whole act in trouble *stealing*?"[25]

Decades later, this disturbing memory would come to haunt Brown as he prepared to meet President Franklin D. Roosevelt; this childhood low point (the Bell incident) bubbled to the surface on the eve of an adult White House high. Given the callousness of Bell, it should come as no surprise that Joe's later failure to finish an acrobatic routine resulted in his leg being broken. Part of their act consisted of the boy standing upon the shoulders of one partner and then, by way of a small trampoline, performing several airborne flips on the way to another pair of shoulders. But during a 1908 booking in Hudson, New York, Bell and Brown were performing a new bit, with the former throwing the boy high into the air ... only to catch him on his shoulders after a somersault. However, for sinister reasons known only to Bell, he proceeded to take a powder with Joe still in the air.

Naturally, this terrible incident curtailed the run of the Bell-Prevost Trio, but there was a plus side to the "accident." Brown's other acrobatic partner, Frank Prevost (who the boy affectionately knew as "Pre"), had always made a point of protecting Joe when Bell got out of line. He rose to the occasion here. Instead of simply shipping the injured boy back to Toledo, Pre took him home to Cedar Manor, New York. There, with his wife Greta, they cared for Brown until his leg healed. More importantly, with regard to Joe's future career as an entertainer, Pre would encourage the youngster to add comedy to the acrobatic act they created after Brown's recovery. But prior to any show business comeback, the teenager was accorded the joy of some old-fashioned nurturing, as Pre and Greta gifted him with all the attention of an adopted son. Like good "parents," they also encouraged his every interest. Thus, before Joe and Pre returned to the vaudeville life, the youngster was taking classes at an area high school and playing baseball for a local semi-pro team. Indeed, baseball for a time would continue to rival the stage as a possible career path for Brown.

While Pre felt Joe had a natural knack for comedy, adding funny embellishments to the duo's new acrobatic act served two additional purposes. First, at this point in time, neither vaudeville nor burlesque accorded a great deal of respect to acrobats. Their acts were often used as a final "closer" to an entertainment bill; when the acrobatic act came on, people knew the show was all but over and often began to leave. An exiting audience was hardly the greatest incentive for a performer. So, adding comedy might generate more respect for Pre and Brown from both management (better billing) and the public (cutting down on early departures). Sadly, Brown later revealed that a darkly comic curse of curses during this era was, "May your children be acrobats!"[26]

Adding humor to Pre and Brown's new act served a second, equally practical purpose. Joe's partner was now in his late forties and the physical demands of acrobatic routines often left him winded. Periodically giving the act's junior partner some funny schtick would allow Pre stage time to catch his breath. Though the full transformation of their act would not occur overnight (they would spend roughly a decade together *after* the 1908 breakup of the Bell-Prevost Trio), the new duo of Prevost & Brown began comically tweaking things immediately.

Their initial approach to the subject of funny was the most obvious: dress Brown in a comic costume. Just as Charlie Chaplin (a comedian Joe later admired for his acrobatic skills) would use baggy pants for his now immortal Tramp figure, Pre and Brown felt that a baggy outfit would be a formula for funny, too. There were limitations to how baggy the costume could be, given that the youngster was still primarily an acrobat whose somersaulting airborne antics, courtesy of a trampoline, necessitated that Pre be able to catch Brown on his shoulders.

The new team had better luck with laughter simply by dressing Brown as a junior version of his well-attired partner. The comic incongruity went beyond the physical contrast of an adult and an undersized teenager. Joe also had that comic ability, as the old punchline goes, "to make a $1,000 suit look like $60." Therefore, any Brown costume had the potential to be a comic costume. Despite a minimum of formal education, the youngster was slowly working his way towards a metaphorical doctorate in humor.

A key development in the creation of Brown's future comedy persona occurred when he, in his own words, "developed an expression of super-idiocy that fascinated our audiences...."[27] (During this same era, Harpo Marx would also create a bizarre trademark facial contortion nicknamed the "Gookie.") In Brown's later films, the comedian would fluctuate between two small town–rural characters, the milquetoast antihero and the egotistical rustic, *à la Elmer the Great*. But both figures are predicated upon Brown not being the sharpest tool in the shed. And the beauty of Joe's initial development of this "super-idiocy" character was that it complimented the comic dichotomy already established with Pre — an older parental type and a goofy, childlike variation of the adult, anticipating the later team of Laurel & Hardy.

The Brown–Stan Laurel analogy works on an additional level, beyond the childlike simpleton. Early in Joe's teaming with Pre, the teenager developed the periodic use of a high-pitched squeaky voice, too, something Laurel's later character was also synonymous with.[28] The catalyst for Brown's first stage use of this squeaky verbal schtick was a particularly difficult acrobatic routine. After noticing that audiences really appreciated this bit, he milked the moment by topping it with his super-idiocy expression — as if the routine was the easiest thing in the world. Later, he found himself pushing the high-pitched comedy envelope by suddenly blurting out, "Did you see that?"

While this memorable moment is lost to time, a semblance of it survives in what is now considered the comedian's signature verbal routine — his "Little Mousie" story. Brown chronicles the tale of a mouse that falls in a vat of whiskey and is rescued by a "big pussycat" that then makes an appointment with said rodent to eat him on the following morning. But the little mousie does not show for a long time. When he finally arrives, the cat takes him to task for keeping him waiting. The mouse laughs and laughs, then explains, "I was so darn drunk I didn't know what I was saying." The comic beauty of the routine is that while Brown plays both parts, as well as an amusing commentator (who commiserates with the cat's anger over being laughed at — "As you can well imagine"), Joe delivers all lines in the high-pitched squeaky voice of a less than bright youngster. This *tour de silly* is preserved in the comedian's brilliant film *Bright Lights* (1935).

Joe's initial telling of the "Little Mousie" story dates from the early days of Prevost & Brown; it was a direct outgrowth of a need to give Pre a momentary on-stage breather. The exact origins of the bit are unclear, though it appears to be one of those archetypal comic routines tied to the nineteenth century beginnings of vaudeville. That being said, the young Brown's distinctive rendering of "Little Mousie," with his enthusiastic squeakiness, soon made it his own. Plus, the close association of the blotto rodent with Joe was further sealed by the comedian being the first to preserve the material on film.

As was typical of vaudeville and burlesque performers early in the twentieth century, Prevost & Brown proceeded to tour the country for years with essentially the same act, since no one market would see them more than once or twice a year. Granted, Joe continued to tweak the act with new comic embellishments, often involving an out-of-sight orchestra pit trampoline. For example, he would back off stage and casually bounce back ... never looking behind him. Two inspired variations of this surreal silliness were later committed to film in *Top Speed* (1930) and *Bright Lights*.

Tinkering notwithstanding, Prevost & Brown were able, as with most established stage performers of that era, to hone their routines into crowd-pleasing slickness. This would be in marked contrast to the 1950s repercussions of television. Though sometimes satirically referred to then as "vaudeville in a box," a more telling description of the new medium was the "glass furnace." That is, there was a constant need for new material. Once used on the small screen and simultaneously seen coast to coast, the entertainer had to create fresh material. Needless to say, there was a certain shock factor for veteran performers no longer able to trade upon proven material.

Romance came into the life of the young comic acrobat in the fall of 1914. Prior to this, Joe had led a rather monkish existence. He focused on the stage act nine months a year and then played semi-pro baseball every summer off-season. But in 1914 he met his future wife, Kathryn McGraw, on a Canadian National train trip to the West Coast.

The young lady was traveling with her mother, and Brown was wise enough to know that relationships, at least in that era, often began by "courting" one or both of the parents. That is what he proceeded to do with Kathryn's mother. But he had an unexpected assist from the fact that the young woman was already a fan of Prevost &

Brown — especially Joe's "Little Mousie" routine, which she had seen him perform in her hometown of Duluth, Minnesota. As it turned out, the personable Joe further impressed both mother and daughter on the long train trip, and the two youngsters agreed to correspond. They parted in Seattle, where Prevost & Brown were booked for a vaudeville engagement, with the McGraws going on to their new home in Oakland, California.

After exchanging many letters over the next few months, the couple reconnected in January–February of 1915 when Prevost & Brown played several Bay Area theaters. By the time Joe and Pre had to head east for other vaudeville dates, the shy young man, without actually proposing, had made his permanent intentions clear to Kathryn. The only thing which gave Brown pause, romantically, was that he had hardly arrived professionally. In fact, he was still flirting with a career in baseball. And that summer he would again play semi-professional baseball, this time in his hometown of Toledo.

Nineteen hundred and fifteen was also the year that Joe would stumble onto one of his defining bits of comedy. This iconic moment would occur at Toledo Beach on Lake Erie. Brown was sharing a cottage on the water with a baseball buddy. After an early morning swim, he yelled at his friend, without benefit of getting anywhere near their bungalow. Nothing. He tried again — still nothing. Finally, Brown uncorked a "cavernous-mouthed" yell so long and drawn out that people up and down the beach, not to mention neighboring areas, stopped everything to check out the source of the disturbance. Thus was born the yell that would later be a staple of his comedy persona. And while both the mouth and the yell would take time becoming part of Joe's act, he would forever date the comic potential of his siren-like vocal chords to that summer.

In the fall, Prevost & Brown were back on the vaudeville circuit in the East, with Joe and Kathryn continuing their coast-to-coast correspondence. By December the lovesick young man wrote a lengthy proposal letter. Ironically, the always painfully straightforward Brown actually made a better case for *not* marrying him! He chronicled everything from his lack of formal education to the uncertainty of show business, especially if one's act involved the dangers of acrobatics. However, like his hero Ty Cobb, Joe promised to be unrelenting in his perseverance to succeed. Plus, the letter had a sense of romantic populism: If Kathryn could accept these honest terms, he felt they could have a wonderful life together.

At a time of truly "snail mail" correspondence, Joe's letter took nearly a week to reach Kathryn. Naturally, he agonized every moment of the time, though Pre continually assured him she would accept. Joe's partner's prediction was correct. In fact, Kathryn not only accepted Joe's terms, her telegram stated that she was immediately coming East. The two would be married on Christmas Eve day (1915) at New York City's Municipal Building (City Hall). Pre and his wife Greta were witnesses for the financially strapped couple, with Brown telling his bride, "It looks like our wedding journey will have to be a subway ride. But some day we'll have a real wedding, in a church."[29]

Flash forward 25 years to the day (December 24, 1940); the now movie star Brown and wife Kathryn would remarry at Hollywood's St. Thomas' Church. Don, their oldest child, would give the "bride" in marriage. Joe L. Brown, their second son, was best man. Daughters Mary Elizabeth and Kathryn Frances were the flower girls. The ceremony was the feel-good story of the 1940 Christmas season.[30]

But in 1915 such fame and attention would have seemed like a fantasy. Joe just hoped he could support a young wife.

THREE

A Solo Stage Star

There was a line in Edna Ferber's *So Big* that I shall never forget because it just about sums up my personal philosophy. The line is: "Just remember that everything that happens to you is sheer velvet."

— Joe E. Brown (1956)[1]

Joe E. Brown anticipated counseling's "reframing" technique by decades. This philosophy allows no time for harboring bitterness or anger. The comedian's predisposition for this Ferber mantra had served him especially well in his early career, given that he had labored for *years* in the middle echelons of vaudeville and the circus world. But Brown's late 1915 marriage to Kathryn McGraw almost derailed his life in show business.

Soon after that simple New York City courthouse ceremony, Kathryn became pregnant and Joe suddenly worried about everything related to his wife, from basic health concerns, to the fact that her family was on the West Coast. When vaudeville obligations took him and partner Frank "Pre" Prevost on the road, Joe was wracked with guilt over leaving Kathryn alone in their tiny New York apartment. Kathryn was nothing but supportive of her husband's entertainment career, but Joe's anxiety would not go away, and eventually he convinced her they should relocate to his hometown of Toledo. Brown's parents would be able to help them through the pregnancy. Moreover, the comedian had been given a good business opportunity — managing two friends' new bowling and billiard emporium. Thus, Joe called upon all his acting skills and convinced Kathryn this was what he wanted.

Initially, all went well, including the Christmas Day (1916) birth of their first child, Don Evan. (Evan was the comedian's middle name.) Joe was ecstatic to be a father, and he enjoyed reconnecting with Toledo friends and neighbors. But when business dropped off at the emporium, he felt compelled to take a blue collar factory job at a local automobile light company. This business was also owned by a friend. When Joe proved less than adept at his first "Auto Lite" position, it was easy enough to be assigned elsewhere in the factory. Unfortunately, Brown's heart was just not into any of several subsequent light company jobs. As he later wrote with an insightful play on words in his autobiography, "The only lights that ever had, or ever would mean anything to me were footlights, or, impossible dream, my name in big lights over a theatre on Broadway."[2]

Several frustrating months into 1917, Brown's old friend and vaudeville partner Pre came to the professional rescue: He had a chance to profitably revive their comic acrobatic act. Since it both paid more than his "Auto Lite" position and was truly what he wanted (to be back in show business), Brown, with the full support of Kathryn, returned to the stage.

Joe's reconnection with Pre was for vaudeville's 1917–18 season. But their comeback was only a temporary thing. The much older Pre was ready to retire, and he saw this as his swan song season. Along related lines, Brown felt that, as an acrobat in vaudeville, "he had gone about as far as he could."[3] And to reach that aforementioned "impossible dream" of Broadway stardom, embracing comedy full-time seemed the best bet. Plus, Joe wanted the financial security of being a headliner. Kathryn was pregnant again, and Brown had his growing family to think of.

Sometimes, however, one must take a step back to prepare for a step forward. With the encouragement of his fatherly friend and partner Pre, Joe became a burlesque comic after the end of that season. Brown took a cut in salary, but he also had the opportunity to make a name for himself as a funnyman, which would then ideally lead to better pay and more prominent stage venues. The fact that Pre had always encouraged Joe's comic embellishments of their acrobatic act made Brown's transition to comedian easier. Indeed, unlike a newcomer, Joe even had some pre-established comedy schtick, such as his "Little Mousie" routine (see Chapter Two).

In his 1918–19 season in burlesque, Brown made only one demand of management: He would do no off-color material. But as long as he could produce laughs, this did not constitute a problem. Moreover, the format of burlesque in 1918–19 was as much defined by parodying popular entertainment properties as sexual innuendo. As a period example of burlesque's room for non-controversial comedy, part of Joe's new solo act was simply a carryover of his acrobatic schtick. Brown kept a trampoline hidden in the theater's orchestra pit and he would regularly, but ever so casually, walk and/or dance off stage only to bounce back with a sporty, nonchalant air. The audience's enjoyment of the trick had a three-part payoff, all connected to comic surprise. First, there was the amusing shock of this seemingly random stage exit. Second, there was astonishment that this danger seemed not to register with said performer — which further complicated Joe's persona of not being very bright. And third, there was the immediate gravity-defying wonder of him unexpectedly bouncing back on stage, without ever looking back (and thus giving away) the source of this "magic."

Fittingly, given Brown's humor headstart, he did well in burlesque and was soon making more than in his team days with Pre. Couple this with the fall 1918 birth of a second son, Joe LeRoy, and Joe's world could not have seemed brighter. But the wattage was about to go up again. In late 1919, Brown was given a small part in the road company of a Broadway play — *Listen Lester*. Like many musical comedies of the time, it was short on plot, with more of a vaudeville–variety show format. Joe's primary turn was an "eccentric dance" which again utilized his hidden trampoline. Consequently, not unlike the Marx Brothers (whose first Broadway play, *I'll Say She Is!*, opened in 1924), Brown found high profile success by performing a variation of something he had done in vaudeville.[4] (Two inspired examples of Joe's eccentric dancing, with the hidden trampoline, were later showcased in the films *Top Speed*, 1930, and *Bright Lights*, 1935.)

A memorable new *Listen Lester* development, however, was a bit of schtick involving Brown's soon-to-be-signature "cavernous" mouth. Joe had few actual lines in the production. To maximize these moments, as well as guard against any audience distractions (such as the random sneeze), he came up with the comic notion of opening his mouth extremely widely ... only to pause ... and pause. Once Brown had the crowd's total attention, he made "the smallest sound [with the line] I could. It was the contrast that made the difference."[5] Thus was born a key component of the comedian's persona. This technique is apparent in countless later Brown routines preserved on film, such as his 1935 rendition of "Little Mousie" in *Bright Lights*.

Joe's ability to amplify his small part in the road company of *Listen Lester* soon paid dividends. In 1920 he was given a featured part in the Broadway musical comedy *Jim Jam Jems*, which opened to critical acclaim on October 4. Brown and Harry Langdon were immediately heralded by critics as the production's comedy stars. The *New York Herald* observed, "Most of the fun was provided by Joe E. Brown, as Philip Quick, a butler, and Harry Langdon as James, a chauffeur."[6] The *New York Tribune* added, "And then there is Joe E. Brown, the busy butler of the play, who is screamingly funny. Harry Langdon, with his trick automobile and his 'vacant stare,' brings a bit of vaudeville's very best into a new [Broadway] realm...."[7]

As the latter review suggested, *Jim Jam Jems*, like *Listen Lester*, was essentially a repackaged vaudeville variety show; the loosest of storylines involved the New York nightlife adventures of a wealthy divorcé and his cloistered, at-home, naïve niece. The play's comedy was driven by both the niece and Brown's butler deciding to also explore the New York nightclub scene. But the most pivotal component of *Jim Jam Jems*, with regard to Joe's evolution as a comedian, was no doubt tied to Langdon's recycling of his vaudeville automobile sketch. This famous routine, called "Johnny's New Car," was something the then 36-year-old Langdon had toured with for nearly 20 years. The act would find Harry "driving" on stage with his wife in a self-destructing car. Langdon's milquetoast character would then be doubly frustrated by both this breakaway auto and a shrewish spouse.

How, then, did Langdon, soon to become one of silent film's most celebrated comedians, impact Brown?[8] Joe's later screen roles fluctuated between two small-town types, an endearingly anti-heroic rustic, and a likable, athletic smart aleck. When playing the former, Joe's character often has the boy/man mannerisms of Langdon. Legendary director Frank Capra, who would later collaborate with Langdon on his best films, would insightfully tell famed film critic James Agee, "If there was a rule for writing Langdon material it was this: his only ally was God."[9] And this divine humor intervention was never better showcased than in the Capra-directed Langdon picture *The Strong Man* (1926), when the sexy maneater Gertrude Astor all but comically rapes the elf-like Harry. Capra would later take much of the credit for orchestrating the Langdon persona. However, revisionist criticism would now suggest that much of Harry's comic mask was in place when Harry co-starred with Brown in *Jim Jam Jems*.[10] But whether Joe's own comedy persona was impacted by Langdon in 1920 (which is most likely, given the Broadway contact and the evolving nature of Joe as a comedian), or by the mid–1920s Capra-Langdon high-profile screen collaborations, Brown's later small-town anti-hero is reminiscent of Harry. For example, in *Riding on Air* (1937) Joe's child-like spying on another character, with his awkward little boy's hopping gait, is pure Langdon. And in *Wide Open Faces* (1938), Brown finds himself in a comic near-rape, á la *The Strong Man*, where an innocently elfish Joe is all but running from another hot-blooded woman.

This in no way diminishes the Brown legacy, since most personae are something of a composite phenomenon. In fact, the screen mask of pantheon comedian Stan Laurel borrows more than a little from Langdon, too.[11] I am reminded of a passage from Mark Twain's time-tripping novel *A Connecticut Yankee in King Arthur's Court* (1889). At one point in the title character's travel to the distant past, he must sit through the humorous speech of the court comic, Sir Dinadan. The Yankee amusingly observes:

> I think I never heard so many old played-out jokes strung together in my life ... It seemed peculiarly sad to sit here, thirteen hundred years before I was born and listen again to poor, flat, worm-eaten jokes that had given me the dry gripes when I was a boy ... It about convinced me that there isn't any such thing as a new joke possible.[12]

Twain's implied tongue-in-cheek message here, besides the lack of anything really new in humor, is that comedy success is equated with inspired variations on similar material and/or characters. As this text will demonstrate, such was the case with Brown, who made his anti-heroic vulnerability more distinctly his own with that iconic mouth, whether he broadcast an epic yell for help, or a surprisingly soft-spoken squeak. Moreover, Joe's other future screen character type, the small-town athletic smart aleck, was totally unrelated to Langdon.

Little information has survived about Brown's relationship with Harry, beyond Joe's great admiration for the inventive idiocy of Langdon's character in the "Johnny's New Car" sketch. But given their similar backgrounds (from beginning to perform as children, to logging time with circuses), the two funnymen would have had a lot to talk about. Of course, although Langdon was more the show business veteran, 12 years Brown's senior, one could argue that *Jim Jam Jems'* Joe was on the verge of usurping Harry. For instance, one pivotal reviewer, the *New York American's* Allan Dale, only had critical eyes for Brown. Over a quarter century later, the comedian's autobiography would include a lengthy excerpt from Dale's critique of *Jim Jam Jems*:

I think I should have starred a certain Joe E. Brown ... Joe was a scream from start to finish, and with a whole bag of tricks. Joe had a funny face, an amusing diction, and a wonderful activity ... The quaint things he did, he did in a legitimate manner ... You clamored for more all the time.[13]

Just as *New York World* critic Alexander Woollcott's later rave review of the Marx Brothers' first Broadway production, *I'll Say She Is!*, put them on the A-list, Dale's enthusiastic critique of Brown's initial foray on the "Great White Way" had a comparable impact on Joe's career.[14]

One of the first payoffs for Brown was receiving regular attention from the movies. Over the next several years he would make numerous screen tests at the New York studios of various film companies, including Paramount and Fox. Though two of Joe's *Jim Jam Jems* co-stars, Langdon and Ned Sparks, would find cinema popularity first, Brown is the one who would eventually have the most sustained screen career. Still, Joe's film fame was nearly a decade off. For whatever reason, he did not initially register with movie producers, though his ongoing stage success during the 1920s kept him under consideration.

While Brown's potential for film was yet to be realized, his success in *Jim Jam Jems* effectively closed the door on any lingering thoughts about a career in baseball. This was not without a certain degree of irony, since his greatest diamond accomplishment had occurred the same year (1920) *Jim Jam Jems* opened. That season, Boston Red Sox manager and Brown fan Ed Barrow had signed Joe to play in some exhibition games for the team. The comedian was always self-deprecating about his baseball skills and felt Barrow just had him around for team morale. Or, one could just call it good marketing. As a minor-league executive, Barrow had once used heavyweight champion John L. Sullivan as an umpire, and on another occasion heavyweight legend Gentleman Jim Corbett played first base. Still, there was often wisdom behind the novelty. To illustrate, manager Barrow was the one who converted Boston pitcher Babe Ruth into a full-time outfielder! Legend has it that future Hall of Famer Harry Hooper had encouraged Barrow in the Ruth decision. Fittingly, there is a Hooper connection to Brown's Boston day in the sun, too. Joe would pinch-hit for Hooper in an exhibition game and stroke a double. Though the modest comedian always felt the rival outfielder, former Braves star Joe Connolly, had merely misplayed him, it still said two-bagger in the following day's box score. *Time* magazine would later describe the double as "what may have been the happiest moment of his life."[15]

Recognition of Barrow's innate baseball skills were underlined further after the memorable (for Brown) 1920 season. New York Yankee owner Col. Jacob Ruppert hired Barrow as the most knowledgeable of baseball general managers. While Boston's earlier loss of Ruth to the Yankees is now famous for allegedly causing the "Curse of the Bambino" (finally exorcised in 2004), the Yankees' immediate dominance had a great deal to do with the acquisition of Barrow, too. Not surprisingly, Brown's longtime association with the Yankees would also date from Barrow becoming their general manager. Granted, it helped that Broadway gave Brown, a fan and sometimes player, a great deal of visibility in 1920s New York. But the comedian's friendship with Barrow would cement his Yankee connection, as well as the lingering flirtation with playing ball professionally. Regardless, team owner and Brown fan Col. Ruppert always felt that while many alleged players turned out to be jokes, Joe was a comic who could hit! (Brown regularly watched the Yankee games from the New York bench during 1921 and 1922, and he went south with the team for spring training in 1926.[16])

While budding Broadway star Brown was a confirmed baseball fanatic, no one would ever have confused him with a literary light. *Variety*, the show business bible, was his favorite reading material. Years later, when he was part of Warner Brothers' ensemble cast in *A Midsummer Night's Dream* (1935, for which Joe garnered the best reviews), he was embarrassed for never having been a student of Shakespeare. Paradoxically, however, Brown approached life in a manner which was the embodiment of renowned French novelist Gustave Flaubert's famous approach to art — live as bourgeois a life as possible and put your wildness in your work. Joe was a fiercely loyal family man to both Kathryn and his two young sons (a family which would grow to four children in the early 1930s), as well as his extended family back in Toledo, Ohio. Fame never got in the way of being a husband and father, and fame was clearly knocking on his Broadway door in the early 1920s.

The magic began late in Brown's *Jim Jam Jems* run (1921), when he realized a dream — his name in lights on a Broadway marquee. Through an ongoing series of hit stage productions, "Joe E. Brown" would remain a New York marquee fixture for much of the decade. Starting in the autumn of 1921, he was the comic headliner in three successive seasons of the *Greenwich Village Follies*, a popular variation of the *Ziegfeld Follies* — a revue featuring beautiful, stately women in arty tableaus interspaced with comedy sketches. Brown's most memorable routine was entitled "The Cop," an adaptation of O. Henry's short story "The Cop and the Anthem." The tale involves a tramp trying to get arrested at Christmas in order to receive a free holiday meal and a warm bed. If that sounds familiar, Charlie Chaplin included a variation of the story in *Modern Times* (1936). And Red Skelton, as his star character Freddie the Freeloader, did several small-screen versions of the sketch during his lengthy television career. Along more darkly comic lines was a 1923 Greenwich Village Follies Brown routine in which he was lost at sea. *The New York Times* called it "a hilarious episode aboard a raft — dealing with the serious business of starving to death."[17]

Another important Brown *Greenwich Village Follies* bit, though only used briefly at the start of the revue's 1923–24 season, was called "The Gob." Originally authored by Paul Gerard Smith, the sketch involved a smart-aleck sailor with an unexpected gift for making time with the ladies. Significantly, the character anticipates Joe's egotistical but likable screen athletes of the 1930s. In fact, Joe later utilized a variation of "The Gob" in *Son of a Sailor* (1933, in which his seaman doubles as a blowhard boxer). On shore leave he finds a pair of baby shoes in his pocket, part of a shipboard prank. But he soon discovers that when talking to attractive young women, baby shoes are often the perfect romantic ice breaker, as long as he had an effective story (which includes being single) to go along with it. (Modern variations of this idea still persist in romantic comedy, such as the single male using a baby or a cute pet to break down the resistance of good-looking female strangers.) Ironically, management for *Greenwich Village Follies* would neither pay the rights for "The Gob," nor other new material, for Brown's involvement in the 1923–24 edition of the revue. Consequently, Joe resigned from the production and put together a vaudeville troupe that successfully toured with the O. Henry sketch "The Cop," which later received critical kudos when it played New York's legendary Palace in October of 1923.[18] As a lark, Brown's wife Kathryn was even given a small part in the company — her first and last experience as a "working actress." Along more serious lines, the comedian also included former vaudeville partner Frank Prevost in his "Cop" company, after Joe discovered that Pre had fallen on hard times.

The following season (1924–25) Brown was back on Broadway starring in the musical comedy *Betty Lee*. Strangely enough, the minimalist plotline had a component that anticipated some of Joe's later sports pictures. One of Brown's co-stars (Hal Skelly) plays an allegedly unathletic character who needs to masquerade as a gifted runner. Though Joe was just as likely to play talented sports figures in his 1930s films, such as the baseball trilogy of *Fireman, Save My Child* (1932), *Elmer the Great* (1933) and *Alibi Ike* (1935), he did occasionally essay parts that involved pretending to be a great athlete. For example, in *You Said a Mouthful* (1932) Brown plays the part of a renowned long-distance swimmer, yet would sink like a rock without his special swimsuit. And in the following year's *Son of a Sailor*, he pretends to be a tough seaman-boxer. Given that a great deal of Joe's stage schtick tends to turn up in his later movies, such as his proclivity for inspired novelty dance numbers, one can assume that the hit *Betty Lee*'s anti-heroic sports subplot probably influenced the comedian's subsequent pictures.

Of course, this musical comedy's greatest claim to fame, with regard to Brown's career, was that it showcased the comedian's first professional unveiling of what would become his signature yell ... to go with that large mouth. Fueled by that seismograph of sound, *The New York Times* would say of *Betty Lee*'s Joe "[this] wide-mouthed, impish-looking comedian ... is quite fascinating to watch."[19] Moreover, the *New York Herald Tribune* would focus its whole review on Brown and the aforementioned Skelly: "Their success was instantaneous, and we have seldom heard an audience laugh longer or louder than that of last night...."[20]

By fall 1925, having a hit Broadway musical comedy was getting to be old hat for Brown. Fittingly, that autumn he would score his greatest stage triumph with *Captain Jinks*, a loose reworking of the play that gave celebrated actress Ethel Barrymore her first starring role in America (*Captain Jinks of the Horse Marines*, a turn-of-the-century popular success). Brown's new rendition of this story about a bet to win the heart of a beautiful New Jersey girl pretending to be an international prima donna, was a critical and commercial hit. *The New York Post* said, "*Captain Jinks* is a joy to the ear and a delight to the eye in every way ... Joe E. Brown and his horse Annie proceeded to make things lively. Particularly amusing was Mr. Brown, while Annie played up to him in a most human manner. These comedians were a pleasing pair."[21] The *New York Herald Tribune* added:

> The burden of the comedy was carried by Joe E. Brown and Arthur West and by both of them carried with every evidence of popular success. The audience seemed to thoroughly enjoy itself, and ... we believe and hope that *Captain Jinks* will remain a popular visitor in our midst for a long time.[22]

But the *pièce de résistance* was the critical praise Brown received from the *New York Evening Graphic's* much acclaimed Walter Winchell: "Mr. Brown, whom I have enjoyed in other musical comedies, was never better than he was last night, and if space permitted I would like to go on applauding him."[23]

Adding to the validation of *Captain Jinks* was the opening night appearance in the audience of an obviously pleased Ethel Barrymore. Accompanied by her daughter, the actress was gifting her child with a "time capsule" look-back at a production which had made Barrymore a star nearly a quarter century earlier. Appropriately, *Captain Jinks* would later be recognized as the best musical of the 1925–26 season.

Comedically, the 1920s Broadway scene anticipated the Hollywood humor heyday of the 1930s. Besides Brown's non-stop stage successes during the proverbial "Roaring Twenties," the Marx Brothers were equally prolific on Broadway: *I'll Say She Is!* (1924), *The Cocoanuts* (1925) and *Animal Crackers* (1928).[24] W. C. Fields, a regular with the *Ziegfeld Follies* and the similar *George White Scandals* (first cousins to the *Greenwich Village Follies*), scored a Broadway musical comedy triumph in *Poppy* (1923). Eddie Cantor, another *Ziegfeld Follies* regular, had Great White Way hits with *Kid Boots* (1926) and *Whoopee* (1930). Bert Wheeler and Robert Woolsey were yet two more *Ziegfeld Follies* comedy stars of the 1920s who were teamed in the Broadway musical comedy *Rio Rita* (1927). Though less well-known today than Brown, the Marx Brothers, Fields and Cantor, Wheeler & Woolsey were then major comedy players. And all of these comedians were slingshot into 1930s cinema immortality by their New York stage successes of the 1920s.

Continuing his Flaubert-like philosophy of limiting the wildness to the arts, Brown maintained a low profile private life during the Broadway days. This was nothing like the period's poster child for the out-of-control artist, novelist F. Scott Fitzgerald, whose drunken misadventures with wife Zelda, in both New York and abroad, rivaled his fiction. Of course, Brown had a friendship with one of the signature free spirits of the "Roaring Twenties"—Babe Ruth. But that was largely a Yankee Stadium relationship, given that Joe continued his love affair with baseball during these years both by working out with the team and regularly attending games. Fittingly, however, his closest Yankee friend would soon come to be the low-profile blue collar star Lou Gehrig, who joined the team in the mid–1920s. Like most New York sports fans, though, Brown had followed Gehrig's earlier high-profile successes in baseball and football at Manhattan's Commerce High School, succeeded by more athletic accomplishments at the City's Columbia College.* He helped support Anna, who had been widowed in 1919. And when the funnyman began to find major Broadway success in 1921, he bought his mother a house. Ever the dutiful son, there were always regular visits home, too.

Despite the comedian's ongoing obsession with family and baseball, stage work paid the bills. In the autumn of 1926, Brown opened on Broadway in yet another hit musical comedy — *Twinkle Twinkle*. Ironically, for a performer who kept failing at assorted screen tests during the 1920s, this play was a satire of Hollywood. A movie star (Ona Munson) walks away from a train full of film people in Kansas to see how the other half lives — only to be tracked down by a comic correspondence school detective (Brown). By this point in his career, Joe's rave theater reviews document a persona that sounds remarkably like the later screen legend. For example, *The New York Times* said, "The comedy is mostly in the hands of the open-faced, expansive-mouthed and vastly amusing Joe E. Brown, and hence particular care is taken of it."[25] In fact, as with Joe's later movie reviewers, who often doubled as humorists in their celebrations of the entertainment potential of the comedian's large mouth (see the opening of Chapter One), *The New York Post* critic expanded at amusing length on that "cavernous" cavity in *Twinkle Twinkle*:

> Once upon a time, in the dim ages, Billy Birch told the story of a girl who asked Charlie Backus, "Is that your natural mouth, or do you use glove-stretchers?" And again, there was Emily Soldene, whose mouth resembled, it was said at the time, the Mammoth Cave. All these were cast into the shade by the cavernous depths of Mr. Brown's face. And he worked it for its full value as a comic asset. It was not, however, his only stock in trade, for he can dance and make a lot of fun not only for the audience but for his fellow-players, who were highly amused at his antics.[26]

And as the *New York Herald Tribune* much more succinctly put it, Brown's inspired comedy came with a "minimum of effort."[27]

Paradoxically, for a play whose heroine would walk away from films and even utter the comment, "I never want to see another movie as long as I live," when *Twinkle Twinkle* went on the road after a successful Broadway run, it was a hit in Hollywood.[28] More specifically, Joe again received special critical acclaim, with one Los Angeles newspaper noting, "There may be funnier things than Brown's burlesque of a picture sheik in a big love scene, but it's hard to imagine anything more laughable."[29]

While Joe's many failed screen tests had had him giving up on the movies, the industry was about to come calling yet again. But this time it would be a stereotypical "Hollywood happy ending."

Brown's quiet family ways also included remembering his beloved mother back in Toledo, OH.

❖ Four ❖

Making It in the Movies

> Never let your audience walk out on you — show ... your stuff.
> — Joe E. Brown, via a title card in the silent film *The Circus Kid* (1929)

Brown's road to movie stardom was a compendium of ironies. As a New York stage star of the 1920s he had frequently been given screen tests in the East, including at Paramount's Astoria, Long Island, studio, but never with any success. Paradoxically, when he went to Hollywood in 1927 with a road company production of his hit play *Twinkle Twinkle*, which satirized the film capital, movieland finally went gaga over Brown. However, Hollywood wanted to star the *comedian* in a *tragic* part about the theater, where he dies at the end of the picture! As fellow comic W. C. Fields said after his arrival in the movie mecca, "It's hard to tell where Hollywood ends and the DTs begin."[1]

Brown's breakthrough was to come in the FBO Studio (later RKO) backstage story *Hit of the Show* (1928). Credit for casting the comedian went to the picture's director, Ralph Ince (1887–1937), brother of film pioneer Thomas Ince. While Brown was flattered by the opportunity, he told Ince, "I didn't feel that I should be thrown into such an important [dramatic] part in my first try in pictures."[2] Ince, who also both acted and produced for the low budget FBO, then made arrangements for the comic to first receive a small role as a newspaper reporter in the gangster film *Crooks Can't Win* (1928). Brown acquitted himself well in this limited part, which was literally grafted onto the picture after he came on board at FBO, with *Variety* observing, "Joe E. Brown, from musical comedy and on a police assignment [reporting beat], packs an infectious grin. He should do well under intelligent direction. Held down here through lack of comedy business."[3]

Though Brown had been intimidated by Ince's *Hit of the Show*, there were three factors which obviously made the dramatic property more palatable for the former acrobat, once the production began shooting. First, his film character (Twisty), like the real-life Brown, was a comedian whose lifelong goal was to play Broadway. Second, Ince played to Joe's comfort zone by making Twisty's specialty a comic Apache dance, something for which Brown was already famous on

Broadway.* Third, since Joe was known for the exuberance he brought to his performances, this played into Ince's staging of the comedian's death scene finale, which was to
immediately follow a strenuous rendition of the Apache dance. That is, while Twisty
was supposed to have a bad heart, Brown's predisposition for giving 110 percent would
make such an over-exertion seem natural. Coupled with two additional plot points —
that this particular Apache dance was both Twisty's Broadway debut and a breakthrough
for his protégé (Gertrude Olmstead)— Brown's death scene made perfect story sense.

Ironically, while this *Hit of the Show* plot complication was considered melodra-
matically old-fashioned even for 1928, three years later a comparable story twist was
responsible for Wallace Beery winning the Best Actor Academy Award for *The Champ*
(1931). Twenty-two years later, Red Skelton would also find critical acclaim with a loose
remake of the Beery picture called *The Clown* (1953).

Brown's *Hit of the Show* performance was called "good" by *The New York Times*,
"as he imbues his part with some of the wistfulness of the also-ran."[4] The review itself
merited the title "A Tragic Comedian." *Variety*'s critique was also positive, but the publication still felt that both the public and this promising new screen performer would
be better served in a pure comedy:

> He had a homely but attractive face. As his business is making fun, that might be
> the main line of his next story, including permission for him to mug all over the
> lot if it's laughs that are wanted.[5]

This was not advice which Hollywood immediately heeded. Brown's next part was
in a Bebe Daniels comedy for Paramount, *Take Me Home* (1928), but Joe was largely
missing in action (one critic described it as "the burying of Joe Brown in a minor role"[6]).
The Broadway comedian soon found himself cast in a series of low-budget melodramas for economy studios FBO and Tiffany. Though this was a waste of Brown's gifts,
two of these features, *The Circus Kid* (1928) and *Painted Faces* (1929), are nevertheless
of interest.

The former film returned the comedian to one of his first loves — the big top.
Brown's long career was frequently peppered with ties to the circus, from Joe's turn-of-
the-century days as a boy acrobat, to his television series *The Buick Circus Hour*
(1952–53). As late as a 1961 interview in the *Los Angeles Mirror*, in conjunction with a
small screen appearance as the guest ringmaster for England's Mills Circus, he would
observe, "[T]he circus is still a great show — the greatest on earth. It puts the 'show'
back in show business."[7]

In *The Circus Kid*, Brown is the second lead to a youngster named Frankie Darro,
whose screen persona is reminiscent of silent cinema's greatest child star, Jackie Coogan,

---

*Eccentric dance numbers would be part of the comedian's standard schtick throughout his long
career; this probably served as the catalyst for the comic tango between Brown and an in-drag Jack
Lemmon during* Some Like It Hot *(1959).*

forever synonymous with his title role in Charlie Chaplin's *The Kid* (1921). While FBO's *The Circus Kid* had much in common with the studio's earlier melodramatic *Hit of the Show* (with Brown again dying in the finale), Darro's title character, Buddy Barnes, could have been patterned upon a young Brown. For instance, the viewer is informed, via a title card, that Buddy felt "a circus tent was heaven, and a circus performer was a pink-toed angel." Naturally, the boy runs off to the big top. Once there, he is lectured in perseverance by mentoring friend King Kruger (Brown), a former lion tamer trying to get his courage back. Again, there are direct links to the comedian's real biography, from young Joe's initial fascination with the circus being the allure of lion tamers, to his first big-top mentor, Billy Ashe, being a stickler for perseverance (see Chapter One). And throughout Brown's life he spouted "hard work" axioms, not unlike his Kruger comment that opens this chapter — "Never let your audience walk out on you — show ... your stuff."

Indeed, this quote further reminds one of Brown, by way of an occupational hazard he encountered when moving his circus acrobatics to vaudeville. Garnering less respect on the stage, gymnastic acts were often considered "closers" for the vaudeville bill, meaning audiences would frequently start to leave during a performance. Not surprisingly, Brown and other acrobats would constantly attempt to embellish their routines (a catalyst for Joe's comedy beginnings) in order to "Never let your audience walk out on you...." Lastly, the Buddy Barnes figure even replicated the young Brown's fascination with other exotic big-top animals. One of the most poignant scenes in *The Circus Kid* is when Kruger finds the boy innocently sleeping in the gorilla cage and first thinks he is in harm's way, though the viewer knows the truth all along.

One decidedly non–Brown plot point in *The Circus Kid* is that his Kruger character had had a drinking problem. The alcoholism resulted in a nearly fatal run-in with the circus lion "Muloch, the Killer," an animal, according to a title card, "so savage that no one had been able to master him since King Kruger's downfall." Only later in the picture, through a brief flashback, does the audience actually see the attack. With the encouragement of both the boy and a fellow circus performer (Helene Costello), Brown's character seems on the road to a professional comeback. However, an upbeat finish is an anomaly for a melodrama. Kruger has misread his relationship with Costello's character. When it becomes apparent she loves another, he returns to the bottle. In a redemptive finale, Kruger dies rescuing Costello's lover from the killer lion.

Though tear-jerking melodrama is not for everyone, Brown's *Circus Kid* performance scored well with the critics. *The New York Times* said, "Joseph E. Brown is quite good as the tragic Kruger," while *Variety* actually waxed poetic, calling the comedian "the twisted-mouth tragedian."[8] More important then even good notices, though, are fans in the industry. Brown's melodramatic work for FBO had impressed a future signature auteur of the genre, John Stahl (1886–1950). Stahl is most famous today for directing such stylish 1930s weepies as *Back Street* (1932) and *Magnificent Obsession* (1935, both with Irene Dunne), and *Imitation of Life* (1934, with Claudette Colbert).

In the late 1920s, the one-time stage actor Stahl was the major producer for Poverty Row Tiffany, sometimes billed as Tiffany-Stahl. After using Brown in such earlier Tiffany films as *Molly and Me* and *My Lady's Past* (with both of these 1929 movies starring melodramatic actress Belle Bennett), Stahl felt he had the perfect picture for Joe. The property was *Painted Faces*, which would be the best of the comedian's Tiffany films.

Like most of Brown's melodramas, this was another backstage story. Joe plays a Dutch-American circus clown on jury duty for a murder case. At first the picture seems to anticipate the later classic courtroom drama *12 Angry Men* (1957), in which Henry Fonda's character is the single jury member holding out for an acquittal in a murder trial. Along similar lines, in *Painted Faces* Brown is the only member of the jury pushing for an innocent verdict. But then this pioneering sound film assumes a new tactic. Through an extended circus flashback, the audience learns about the lives of Brown, a clown, and the murder victim (Lester Cole), another performer. The clown had adopted Nancy (Helen Foster), the daughter of his late partner, paying to have her reared in a convent school. At nearly 18 she cannot resist the allure of the big top. After joining her father-figure clown, she is seduced and abandoned by the man, who is later murdered. Ultimately, Brown plays yet another tragic clown, as he confesses to the jury members that the death of the cad came at his hands, just after Nancy's character had committed suicide.

On a technical level, *Painted Faces* now qualifies as a primitive, quasi–canned theater early "talkie." Yet Brown's largely straight role (his first starring movie part), with his German or "Dutch comic" accent, was not without a certain charm, especially his crack to the initially disrespectful jury after the bombshell revelation that he was the killer — "Now you all know the story about the funny clown [*he chuckles to himself*], why don't you laugh...."

There are several additional entertainment perks in this forgotten film. First, Brown is allowed to incorporate brief bits of his acrobatic and comic schtick into the movie, including an affectionate admonishment of the Helen Foster heroine in which Joe assumes the high-pitched voice used in his celebrated "Little Mousie" routine. Second, Brown's circus clown also has a sketch with a donkey that brings to mind a Charlie Chaplin donkey bit from *The Circus* (1928), released the year prior to *Painted Faces*. Third, because Brown's picture predates the censorship code (1934) by five years, his sympathetic vigilantism manages to go unpunished. The point is underlined at the close by the jury foreman's final instructions to his charges — reminding them they are not to discuss anything they have seen or heard during their deliberation.

Fourth, coming full circle back to Stahl, it is fascinating to see an early example of his work which has, until now, gone under the radar. To demonstrate the attention to melodramatic detail which become synonymous with his *oeuvre*, *Painted Faces* also includes a provocative wrinkle which further explains the clown's violent response to the suicide of Nancy. Brown's tragic figure was fighting romantic feelings towards the affectionate, beautiful Nancy. Consequently, the revenge is partly that of a surrogate father, as well as a platonic lover. Interestingly enough, while Brown greatly respected Stahl's artistry and felt *Painted Faces* was his (Joe's) strongest Tiffany movie, the comedian revealed in his 1956 autobiography that the most melodramatic performance associated with this property came courtesy of the producer himself. Through a pre-production private audience in Stahl's office, the melodrama guru read the whole script to Brown — expressionistically acting out every part. Five times during this marathon session, Stahl "had to stop and dry his tears. He was crying so he couldn't go on. My insides were hurting from restrained laughter, and when he reached the fade-out we were both as limp as rags, though from different causes."[9]

Brown was a burlesque veteran, which is another way of saying he was a genre parody artist. And spoofing melodramatic excess was a 1920s burlesque staple. It would have been hard for the comic to respond in any other way to Stahl's melodramatic bravado. But one might add, for all of the producer's entertaining excess, Brown's politely minimalist response was the greater acting job. Moreover, despite the "restrained laughter,"

Brown as the circus clown of the melodrama *Painted Faces* (1929).

Joe was still impressed by Stahl's passion for this genre, because the comedian's personal entertainment tastes also favored melodrama. In an early 1930s article documenting movie star's screening tastes, Brown was credited with enjoying "sentimental stories, the more Pollyanna-ish the better."[10] He even penned a later *Saturday Evening Post* piece that credited a melodramatic sequence from *Love Affair* (1939) as being "my favorite movie scene." Confessing that it nearly brought him to tears, Brown added, "It sounds silly, doesn't it? But comedians are not immune to deeper emotions, and any man can put himself in [a melodramatic scene] and imagine how he would feel..."[11]

A final footnote to *Painted Faces* which showcases real-life melodrama involves actor Lester Cole, who played the caddish murder victim. When his on-camera career proved less than successful, he turned to screenwriting in the early 1930s. Impressively, he was later one of the Screen Writers Guild founders (1933). But his creative life all but ended in 1947 at the hands of the inquisition-like Communist witch-hunting of the House Un-American Activities Committee (HUAC). In that year, Cole was a member of the now famous "Hollywood Ten," a group of filmmakers who challenged HUAC's right to badger citizens about their political affiliations. His contempt of Congressional citation

Irene Dunne and Charles Boyer in *Love Affair* (1939), the movie which so moved Brown.

resulted in both prison time and Hollywood blacklisting. Though now championed for his Thoreau-like "civil disobedience," his was one of many ruined lives.

Brown was now on the verge of stardom. After paying his dues at budget studios like FBO and Tiffany, the comedian's Hollywood climb was facilitated both by his 1929 signing with Warner Brothers, and an increased movie accent on laughter. Of course, though Warners was a promotion for Joe, this studio was in the midst of its own upward struggle, too. Warners' way of playing catch-up with the Paramounts and the MGMs was through its pioneering use of sound, color and lavish productions—all of which doubled as selling points to get audiences into theaters during the Depression, which was descending upon the world in late 1929.

Brown's comedy quotient would quickly go up at Warners, but the overriding melodramatic tone of his early pictures did not immediately disappear. For example, in the groundbreaking *On With the Show* (1929), which *The New York Times* called "the first dialogue motion picture in natural colors," Brown plays comic relief in a road

show spectacle that *Variety* labeled a "mostly melodramatic tale."[12] In *Song of the West* (1930), a Technicolor operetta, supporting character Brown is given more comedy schtick, but once again he dies at the picture's close. Fittingly, it is a Western shoot-out with Joe's cowboy managing to gun down two heavies. Sandwiched between *On With the Show* and *Song of the West* was the more promising musical comedy *Sally* (1929), but third-billed Brown gets lost in yet another Warner Technicolor spectacle. *Variety* even threw the comedy kudos to a former Mack Sennett star: "Joe E. Brown isn't exactly the type, and Ford Sterling is the outstanding comic individual."[13]

Cowboy Brown in *Song of the West* (1930).

Brown receives some hair styling tips from Marilyn Miller in *Sally* (1929).

With *Hold Everything* (1930), however, baseball fan Brown finally hit his cinematic home run. The top-billed comedian plays simpleton boxer Gink Shiner in a production the *New York American* called "A NEW high in hilarity," topped off with a comic boxing scene near the close, with Brown bouncing about the canvas via the ring ropes.[14] The *New York Herald Tribune* added that Joe and his romantic co-star, Winnie Lightner, "[held] the spotlight most of the time, [with] the two comics managing to keep, by their lively wisecracks and harum scarum antics, the audience's laughter with them continuously."[15] But *Variety* proved to be the most impressed: "Probably the best comedy picture Warners has turned out since talkers [sound films] came in ... there's something doing all the time, and it's mostly Brown."[16]

What made these critical hosannas all the more impressive was that the hoopla connected with *Everything*'s New York premiere threatened to usurp the movie itself. Warners chose this Technicolor extravaganza to open their new 1600-seat Hollywood Theatre on Broadway, the first facility specifically designed for sound films. Several critics keyed more on the pre-movie festivities than the film itself. The *New York Sun*'s review began by noting the "big names" in attendance, such as the mayors of New York (Jimmy Walker) and Philadelphia (Harry A. Mackey), each of whom spoke briefly.[17] The *New York American* even accompanied its critique with a second article, "Notable Audience Views Picture of *Hold Everything*," just to tally all the celebrities on hand.[18] Other prominent people in attendance included former New York governor Alfred E. Smith (the Democratic presidential candidate of 1928), Hollywood film censorship czar Will H. Hays, and various East Coast politicians, including a representative from New York governor Franklin D. Roosevelt's office — two years prior to FDR's winning of the presidency.

For today's student of Brown, *Hold Everything* now represents a prototype for one of his most distinctive character types in future Warner films — the simple-minded athlete. *Hold Everything* even includes a plot point which sometimes surfaces in the comedian's later non-baseball sports movies: being mistaken for a champion athlete. For example, in *You Said a Mouthful* (1932) Brown is thought to be a master swimmer, while in *Polo Joe* (1936) he is incorrectly seen as a great polo player. But given that these are all feel-good personality comedies, he invariably finds a way to succeed.

Hold Everything was the first of several Brown vehicles to feature a real champion athlete. With the comedian playing a boxer in *Hold Everything*, the film also features famous French prizefighter Georges Carpentier. Other Brown films to follow this precedent are *Local Boy Makes Good* (1931) with 100-yard dash champion Frank Wykoff, and Joe's baseball classic *Elmer the Great* (1933), which features footage of Brown's friend and New York Yankee hero Lou Gehrig. Though this could be explained away as simply good marketing, it goes beyond this.

Hold Everything opened at the end of the decade which had suddenly given birth to high-profile sporting events. Americans had both more leisure time and more spending money for a broad spectrum of entertainment activities, from college football to

'Hold Everything' Holds Everything

A *New York Sun* caricature of Boxer Brown in *Hold Everything* (1930).

major league baseball. Moreover, two new developments during the 1920s helped fuel the fascination with sports: radio and movie newsreels. And with the country becoming a car culture, more and more sporting events became accessible to the public. But this new fan base was further stoked by a level of athletic excellence which made the 1920s the "Golden Age of Sports."[19] A litany of legends dating from this decade would include baseball's Babe Ruth and Lou Gehrig; college football's Knute Rockne (Notre Dame coach), Red Grange (Illinois) and Bronko Nagurski (Minnesota); boxing's Jack Dempsey and Gene Tunney; and tennis' Bill Tilden. Though the 1930s Depression eventually cut into this new mass audience, spectacle sports, like the movies, for a time seemed to be "Depression-proof." Americans were reluctant to relinquish their love affair with athletics.

Fittingly, Brown's early 1930 movie popularity was based in part on his playing an assortment of sports figures at a time when America's interest in athletics had never been greater. And though his baseball role (*Fireman, Save My Child*, 1932, *Elmer the Great*,

1933, and *Alibi Ike*, 1935) are most synonymous with his small-town smart aleck persona, Brown also applied his anti-heroic milquetoast character to sports, too, such as his bookworm track star of *Local Boy Makes Good*. (There was heightened interest in track and field at this time, with the Olympics coming to Los Angeles in 1932.) Consequently, it made perfect sense for Brown's sports pictures to be peppered with real-life star players. In fact, given the comedian's well-known association with athletics, both as a baseball player and a collector of sports memorabilia, one could contend that the comedian's movie success was also boosted by his own authentic athleticism. To illustrate, *The New York Times'* rave review of *Elmer the Great* noted, "Mr. Brown is no greenhorn when it comes to baseball, for he was a professional player in his younger days, and this fact helps to make *Elmer the Great* all the more interesting."[20] And the *New York Daily Mirror* said of *Alibi Ike*, "Joe E. Brown, whose immoderate passion for baseball is quite as well-known as his spectacular mouth, plays the title role with vast enthusiasm."[21]

Besides the fact that sports roles allowed Brown to showcase his athletic gifts and capitalize on a popular period phenomenon (the aforementioned "Golden Age"), film comedies revolving around sports "provided a natural excuse for physical comedy."[22]

Harold Lloyd (glasses) and Babe Ruth on the set of *Speedy* (1928).

Silent film had already created some memorable models for Brown, from Charlie Chaplin's misadventures on a golf course in *The Idle Class* (1921), to Buster Keaton's inspired visit to Yankee Stadium in *The Cameraman* (1928), where he gives a masterful demonstration of batting and base running. The same year as the Keaton film, Harold Lloyd made his underrated *Speedy*, a tribute to baseball which also featured Yankee great Babe Ruth. The Lloyd connection is especially pertinent to Brown, since Harold's screen persona was often that of a hard-working small-town figure trying to make good — a scenario frequently applicable to Joe's movies, too. Along related lines, Brown's college football comedy *The Gladiator* (1938) has a great deal in common with Lloyd's college football comedy *The Freshman* (1925), from amusingly tough practices to the poignancy of trying to fit in on campus.

Interestingly enough, Brown's *Hold Everything* has another, more direct tie with the "Golden Age of Sports." The comedian's co-star, French boxer Georges Carpentier, was part of a celebrated 1921 bout with heavyweight champion Jack Dempsey which is now seen as the pivotal opening event in this uniquely athletic decade. Noted sports historian Roger Kahn observed:

> If you want to select an exact date when it was proven publicly that American sports had become big business, July 2, 1921, certainly makes sense. If you want to select a date when high-society America, Broadway and Hollywood America, Algonquin [literary] America ... [and so on] first came to embrace sports with a passionate hug, again you come to July 2, 1921.[23]

The bout between Dempsey and French champion Carpentier was boxing's first million dollar gate, an amazing figure for 1921. Over 90,000 fans turned out for the match, easily the largest fight crowd ever. No less a writer than the acclaimed Irish dramatist George Bernard Shaw claimed Carpentier would win, while an army of American sportswriters predicted just the opposite. Though it is safe to say most stateside males were confident of the Dempsey triumph that occurred, American women remained taken with the handsome Frenchman and his masculine legs. Thus, it seems ever so appropriate that a participant in this signature athletic event should later co-star in the picture which launched the career of that era's most sports-related entertainer — Joe E. Brown.

Hold Everything was so obviously earmarked to be a hit that the comedian signed a long-term contract with Warners even before the picture's release. During this productive studio era heyday, Brown would star in approximately three pictures a year. Still, the veteran performer waited until well after *Hold Everything* was a critical and commercial smash before permanently relocating his family to the West Coast. But for all the kudos one might accord this groundbreaking-for-Brown film, *Hold Everything* did create a controversial addendum — that Joe had stolen the comedy schtick which Bert Lahr (forever identified today as the Cowardly Lion in *The Wizard of Oz*, 1939) had used as the simple-minded boxer when *Hold Everything* was a stage hit on Broadway. Many publications running reviews of the screen adaptation, such as *The New York Times*, *New York Daily News* et al. made no mention of any performing parallels between Brown and Lahr.[24] Several other newspapers minimized the connection, from *New York Sun* critic John S. Cohen, Jr., simply stating, "if the charge be true — Mr. Brown doesn't copy him very well," to *New York American* reviewer Regina Crewe limiting it to a "Lahr influence."[25] But *Variety*, the entertainment bible for performers, was clearly of another opinion, addressing the subject at length with observations like, "Warners has got a sweet picture, Brown is plenty funny and the public will think Lahr is doing a Brown when they see him [in the *Hold Everything* stage production tour]."[26] Ironically, as both the opening of this quote and an earlier cited excerpt from the same review document, *Variety* still gave Brown and the picture a most laudatory endorsement. How does one reconcile this contradiction? Reading between the lines, *Variety* seems to suggest that any parallels between the two performances will be largely limited to insiders, the relatively few people who will see Lahr in the stage production, as opposed to a major studio distribution of a movie. *Variety*'s ultimate capsulization of the controversy ("But it can also be said, who cares?") would seem to endorse this position.[27]

Lahr's response was a letter to *Variety* published a week after its review of Brown's *Hold Everything*. Appearing under the headline, "Bert Lahr Labels Joe Brown 'Lifter,'" it said, in part:

> I am writing this in self-protection to let the *profession*, the exhibitors and executives of the picture world understand that I am the originator of all business methods, mannerisms, and unique phrases used by Joe E. Brown in the talking picture version of *Hold Everything*.[28]

Paradoxically for Lahr, his correspondence would result in a *Variety* rebuttal letter which did *not* come from Brown. Instead, veteran Dutch comedian Sam Sidman wrote that Lahr's simple-minded *Hold Everything* boxer, performed in the Dutch comic tradition, was consistent with his own (Sidman's) stage persona.[29] And Sidman went on to say he had stolen it from an earlier Dutch comic named Sam Bernard. In a nutshell, it was the suggestion noted earlier in this text that very little is original. Brown did not publicly respond to the copycat claim until his 1956 autobiography, in which he refers to the Sidman letter and flatly states, "I was in no way the least bit like the character [Lahr] portrayed in the stage version of the play."[30] Brown might also have added that he had previously played the Dutch comic type both on stage and in the aforementioned *Painted Faces*. Had this 1929 picture opened in more markets (distribution was limited for low-budget Tiffany), maybe *Variety* would not have raised the issue. Even so, its review of Brown's *Hold Everything* had briefly noted, as if in anticipation of Sam Sidman's letter, that Lahr had first done Dutch comic material years before, after watching a master of this schtick — Solly Ward. But the *Variety* bombshell here was that Ward, like Sidman, had based his Dutch comic mannerisms on the work of Sam Bernard!

In the exemplary biography of Lahr written by his son, noted theater critic John

Lahr, is the revelation that his father was supposed to star in the Warner screen adaptation of *Hold Everything*, but that Broadway producer Vinton Freedley (to whom the comedian was under contract) would not release him.[31] Freedley did not want to jeopardize his lucrative box office potential for the *Hold Everything* stage production tour. Consequently, part of Bert Lahr's sensitivity about the screen adaptation might have been pure frustration over a missed opportunity.

While Brown's book suggests the two comedians worked through the issue and later resumed their friendship, the tone of John Lahr's biography insinuates that his father nursed a lingering bitterness. However, a second accusation in the Lahr text would seem to underline again that documenting originality is the most slippery of subjects. John Lahr, by way of his father, posits that Brown stole the "Little Mousie" routine from comic Bert Wheeler (of Wheeler and Woolsey fame).[32] Unfortunately, the Lahr biography implies that Brown latched onto "Little Mousie" shortly before Joe's late 1920s exit to Hollywood. But as has already been noted in this text, Brown had been using "Little Mousie" on stage since the early 1910s. Moreover, the circular justification for Wheeler allegedly owning the routine was that it had been somehow ceded to him by an old vaudevillian! This is hardly a strong case for ownership. In writing about countless comedians over several decades, I have found very little "signature material" actually originated with the credited comic. For example, Charlie Chaplin's beloved "Oceana Roll" (or the "Dance of the Rolls") in *The Gold Rush* (1925) had been performed earlier by Fatty Arbuckle in *The Cook* (1918). The Marx Brothers' equally inspired "mirror sequence" from *Duck Soup* (1933) had its birth in a similar scene from the Charley Chase film *Mum's the Word* (1926); both were directed by Leo McCarey.[33] Laying unofficial claim to a routine is often more about performance quality, rather than who went first, or as film historian David Robinson compared the two "Oceana Roll" routines, "With Arbuckle it is an ingenious gag; with Chaplin it is touched with genius...."[34] One could also just quote Ecclesiastes in the *Bible*: "[T]here is nothing new under the sun."

Concerning the Brown-Lahr controversy, there can never be a definitive answer, since Lahr's interpretation of the role was never committed to film. But as *Variety* was the only major publication to make an issue of the subject, not to mention the publication's tendency to back pedal in the same piece (by noting Lahr's Dutch comic influences), it suggests this was an overreaction. Consistent with this perspective was Brown's claim that he could never get Lahr to see the screen version of *Hold Everything*, and that his friend's letter to *Variety* was entirely based upon that publication's inflammatory review.[35]

All in all, if there was any lingering bitterness on Lahr's part, it might also have been fueled by the fact that *Hold Everything* made Brown a film star, something the multi-talented Lahr never quite achieved. Oh, there would be numerous movies over the years, and his Broadway status would reach legendary proportions, but Hollywood stardom would somehow elude him. Like Ethel Merman, another Broadway giant with whom he was so memorably teamed in the 1939 stage production of *Du Barry Was a Lady*, Lahr's persona seemed too big for the screen. Only rarely, such as in the oversized fantasy world of *Oz*, did he find a movie comfort zone. In contrast, Brown was about to star in a series of pictures which would make him a major box office star of the 1930s.

FIVE

Top Speed—More Than a Film Title

After Joe E. Brown and his *Top Speed* (1930) sidekick give up their second story hotel room to two lovely young ladies, the girls toss blankets out the window so the boys can camp out. When one girl asks Brown if there is anything else he would like, the comedian responds, "Nothing you can throw out the window."

After the huge success of *Hold Everything* (1930), Brown's film stardom at Warners was headed forward at "top speed," also the title of his next picture. Though neglected today, Brown was a major box office star for much of the 1930s. In 1932, 1935 and 1936, he even made the Quigley Publication's annual elite "Top Ten Box Office Stars" poll.[1] Indeed, during his banner year (1935) he logged in at number five, just behind matinee idol Robert Taylor, and ahead of such still memorable stars as Dick Powell, Joan Crawford, Claudette Colbert, Jeanette MacDonald and Gary Cooper. Moreover, though Brown is now perceived as strictly having been an attraction in small towns, what *Variety* referred to as the "sticks," for much of the 1930s his films also played well in large metropolitan markets. They often opened at Warners' flagship theater in New York, the Hollywood. And occasionally Brown pictures, such as *Elmer the Great* (1933) and *When's Your Birthday?* (1937), were even showcased at America's premier movie palace, New York's Radio City Music Hall. Of course, this is perfectly consistent with a performer who was a Broadway star for much of the 1920s, and successfully brought his live act to the London Palladium in 1936.[2]

Despite Brown's long association with squeaky-clean comedy, however, one might posit that some of his pre–censorship code (1934) screen popularity at Warners was assisted by entertainingly provocative material, such as the *Top Speed* scene description which opens this chapter. Or, there is the film's minor car accident sequence in which Brown carries a beautiful young lady into the hotel. When the attractive victim is asked if she feels okay, the comedian answers, "She feels good to me." The follow-up question about any broken bones then elicits his reply, "Nope, [and] I've been over every one of them." Once again, this *Top Speed* title could be said to provide another metaphorical "reading," such as "fast" being equated with sexy. Certainly the reviews, which were uniformly good, did include warnings, from the *Harrison's Reports* comment, "There is some suggestive talk—with double meaning...," to the *Variety* statement, "Possibility of running up against censors in some states through the presence of some of the warmest [most provocative] gags ever attempted in pictures may stand in the way of its appeal."[3] Still, Brown's notices were superlative and often included critical asides that documented positive demonstrative responses from audiences, such as *The New York Times*' observation, "Mr. Brown, as the becheckered and beleaguered liar [posing as a millionaire], is a delight in his facile comedy scenes and kept those in the Strand [Theatre] yesterday afternoon in continuous laughter."[4]

Brown and cigar, looking a bit like a young George Burns, in *Top Speed* (1930).

Comedy historian Henry Jenkins suggests that when Brown plays parts like manipulative Ossie Simpson in *Broad Minded* (1931, a second cousin to his *Top Speed* character), one should label such personae the "fast-talking young playboys."[5] While I have no complaint with the description, it is misleading to establish this as yet another persona for Brown. As noted in previous chapters, the comedian's work basically fluctuates between two types, the milquetoast anti-hero and the breezy, egotistical athlete, full of personal tall tales. The "fast-talking young playboys" of the Brown trilogy *Top Speed*, *Broad Minded* and the similar *Going Wild* (1931) are merely early variations of the smart-aleck baseball player he would play so effectively in *Elmer the Great* (1933) and *Alibi Ike* (1935). In fact, during *Top Speed*, Brown's "millionaire" also claims to have been a runner-up at golf's British Open, played polo with the Prince of Wales, and been a college fullback at *both* Harvard and Yale. (His letterman sweater has a "Y" on the front and an "H" on the back.) Along related lines, Brown's character in *Broad Minded* claims to have interacted with big game, and been a champion swimmer, and later poses as a track star.

Historian Jenkins is on firmer footing when he suggests the smart-aleck Brown anticipates the later egotistical persona of Bob Hope.[6] For example, during *Going Wild* Joe pretends to be a famous aviator-author at a book signing. When a lovely young woman fawns, "You are the sweetest thing," he replies, "I think so, too." And when "author" Brown autographs book after book for a long line of pretty admirers, he poses an affected request to his assistant, after each signature, "Another pen, boy. Quickly."

Another comedian who merits mentioning here is Groucho Marx. Though his major con artist character would never be confused with Brown, the mustached one's earthy take on screen life was proving so popular with period viewers that it was impacting the face of American film comedy.[7] Groucho and the brothers Marx had scored a huge movie success with *The Cocoanuts* (1929), the screen adaptation of their hit Broadway play. Couple this with the lax pre–Code standards and many comedies from this era had an edgy, "going wild" quality to them, to paraphrase the title of Brown's later picture.

Appropriately, the New York opening of Brown's titillating *Top Speed* coincided with the premieres of the Marx Brothers' *Animal Crackers* (1930) and the Marx Brothers–like *Let's Go Native* (1930), a Jack Oakie film directed by comedy auteur Leo McCarey. All three pictures have that aforementioned bravado we associate with the early Marx movies. In fact, I posit in my McCarey biography that the celebrated team's first awareness of the director probably dated from the parallels in comedy tone between the Marx's *oeuvre* and *Let's Go Native*.[8] (McCarey would later direct, at the Marxes' request, the team's greatest picture —*Duck Soup*, 1933.) But returning to the joint opening of the similar *Top Speed*, *Animal Crackers* and *Let's Go Native*, period reviews would sometimes even note the parallels, such as the *New York Sun*'s *Native* critique connecting the comedy to *Animal Crackers*.[9]

Another common thread between these early Brown pictures and the Marxes might simply come down to the gifted writing team of Bert Kalmar and Harry Ruby. They did the music and lyrics for the Marxes' *Animal Crackers* (including Groucho's theme song, "Hooray for Captain Spaulding"), *Horse Feathers* (1932) and the all-important *Duck Soup*, as well as *Soup*'s screenplay. Brown's *Top Speed* was based upon Kalmar and Ruby's original musical comedy (co-authored by Guy Bolton), while the comedian's *Broad Minded* was drawn from a Kalmar and Ruby story. The writing duo also provided the screenplays for two excellent later Brown films, *The Circus Clown* (1934) and *Bright Lights* (1935). Though Kalmar and Ruby's comedy collaborations remain most synonymous with the Marxes, the two also provided music and scripts for signature films by other important early 1930s comedians, Eddie Cantor (*The Kid from Spain*, 1932) and Wheeler & Woolsey (*Kentucky Kernels*, 1934). The irony of Kalmar and Ruby's ongoing association with the Marxes is that they brought this same brand of satirical, sexy zaniness to nearly all their personality comedian projects; it is just that Brown, Cantor and Wheeler & Woolsey are simply not as well-known to contemporary audiences.

This pivotal early–1930s Brown trilogy of *Top Speed*, *Going Wild* and *Broad Minded* mixes its sometimes provocative dialogue and/or situations with a litany of standard components long associated with the comedian, from a propensity for the anti-heroic, to a recycling of his previous stage material. With regard to the latter, he is greatly assisted by being teamed with comic romantic interest Laura Lee in both *Top Speed* and *Going Wild*. This now sadly neglected talent looks and sounds a great deal like Gracie Allen, the scatterbrained half of Burns and Allen, the popular comedy team of stage, screen and television. Brown and Lee's most winsome joint scene occurs in *Top Speed*, when they reprise one of his eccentric Broadway dance numbers, which also features his off-camera trampoline. In this movie rendition of his eccentric dance, the trampoline is hidden behind Brown and Lee, necessitating that he casually step off the back of their dancing surface (a long bench) so that he can magically "bounce up" again. On Broadway the trampoline was concealed in the orchestra pit, requiring that Joe nonchalantly step forward off the stage, before mysteriously springing back. Regardless, Brown and Lee are so effective both here and throughout the picture that the sixth-billed actress was granted star treatment in the *New York Times*' title for their review, "Joe E. Brown in Comedy: Laura Lee Also Amuses in *Top Speed* at the Strand."[10]

Brown's most entertaining solo bit of familiar material in this early screen trilogy involves the opening of *Broad Minded*. Joe's character (Ossie Simpson) is at a Prohibition party which flirts with the surreal, both from excessive drinking and a costume theme that has everyone dressed as babies. But Ossie steals the show by first appearing in an oversized baby buggy, which makes him and his elaborate toddler get-up all the more effective. "Baby" Ossie tops this off with his face-splitting grin and a lengthy monologue in his high-pitched "Little Mousie" voice. *Variety*'s review, which called *Broad Minded* "an exceptionally good comedy program talker," added, "In infant's hat and gown [and] drinking hooch in the carriage, Brown here hits his fastest comedy pace."[11]

With the casting of Bela Lugosi in a supporting role, *Broad Minded* also plays with a parody component, too. Five months earlier, Lugosi had scored a personal triumph in the title role of *Dracula* (1931), and he retained both the accented voice and some of the mannerisms from his "prince of darkness" character for the Brown picture. The catalyst within *Broad Minded* for the spoof of Lugosi's horror persona involves a series of accidents he suffers at the hands of the anti-heroic Ossie, starting with a minor traffic fender bender. The escalating comic anger of Lugosi's character works on three levels. First, there is the shock humor of seeing a horror icon in a broad comedy. Second, Ossie's comic fear factor is out of proportion to the danger. This delightfully funny overreaction is entirely predicated upon Brown responding as if he had upset Dracula, instead of simply the South American businessman Lugosi is playing. Besides heightening the humor, it further cements our relating to Brown, since no one else in the cast seems aware of what is patently obvious to the viewer—Dracula got loose in a comedy! Third, the escalating of Lugosi's temper is set up like the comic "slow burns" associated with various Laurel & Hardy foes such as Edgar Kennedy or James Finlayson. The persistent comic incompetence of Stan and Ollie would eventually drive these long-suffering slapstick victims into a comic rage of revenge, just as the innocently anti-heroic Brown is pushing Lugosi towards *violent* distraction. While this horror icon is not in a slow-burn class with Kennedy and Finlayson, *Broad Minded* demonstrates that had Lugosi been so inclined, he might have found more time for the occasional comedy. Interestingly, Brown's last screen appearance was a cameo in the all-star horror parody film *The Comedy of Terrors* (1963), where his cemetery night watchman is shocked into one final classic big-mouthed howl.

Of course, in the early 1930s, the comic novelty of Brown's signature "crater mouth" and yell were an ongoing highlight for critics and fans alike in the *Top Speed-Going Wild-Broad Minded* trilogy. His autobiography reveals that "probably the most amusing (to me) time it was ever used was in the picture *Top Speed*."[12] This focus example occurs at the film's happy ending, when his "cavernous" mouth opens wide to yell "*Babs!*"—the name of his girlfriend (Lee). But there are other "monster-mouthed" moments peppered throughout *Top Speed*, such as when Lee all but romantically attacks him, and shocks a comic scream from the comedian. Equally entertaining illustrations occur in the other pictures, too. The *New York American* critic was especially taken with the *Going Wild* physical scene, where "Joe Brown saying 'ah' to the medicos [medical staff]—in close-up—is worth the price of admission all by itself."[13] *The New York Times* compared his *Going Wild* mouth to the Grand Canyon and noted that spectators "actually shrieked with laughter and really rocked in their seats."[14] *Variety*'s rave review of *Broad Minded* even opens with a most unusual claim for Brown's mouth—"The first story written directly into and around an actor's face. Exposure of Brown's tonsils is all that is necessary to get laughs, but FN [First National–Warners] surrounds the Joie [sic] map [face] with some pretty girls and customary comedy dressing."[15] All in all, *Variety*'s *Top Speed* take on the comedian's natural gift could serve as a summary of his most

Brown (center)with Bela "Dracula" Lugosi in *Broad Minded* (1931).

effective schtick in the early 1930s: "Big-mouth Brown and what he has done with his part makes up a large percentage of the entertainment. The bovine-like yawn he lets out every now and then as things go wrong gets the laughs through a lot of repetition."[16]

Through the years, studios have always tried to boost the box office by adding and/or keying upon topical events. Warner Brothers followed the pattern on this early Brown trilogy. *Broad Minded* capitalized on the aforementioned *Dracula* fame of Lugosi, while *Top Speed* mixed period interest in speedboats with new technological developments that allowed first-run theaters to widen the screen with a magnifying process during the race sequence finale. But *Going Wild* was the picture most immersed in an early 1930s phenomenon — the public's fascination with flying. Drawing heavily from the *Top Speed* storyline, *Going Wild* simply substitutes an aerial race for the motorboat variety. Plus, it ups the ante by making the flyer a popular but reclusive author, to better enable Brown to impersonate him.

At the time of the film's release (early 1931), America was wildly enthusiastic about aviation, thanks largely to two people — Charles Lindbergh and Amelia Earhart, who was known as "Lady Lindy." Lindbergh was the first person to fly solo across the Atlantic (1927), while Earhart was the first woman (in the company of two male pilots) to make the same flight (1928). Both had penned best-sellers about their adventures, and Earhart eventually married her financial backer and publisher (George Palmer Putnam), who specialized in producing books about flying which further fueled the public's interest. His list of titles would include a second aviation text from Earhart, the aptly named *The Fun of It* (1932). Putnam was tireless in his promotion of Earhart and her airplane exploits, from the numerous speed and distance records she established in the early 1930s, to the countless articles and public talks she produced about flying.[17]

Other prominent period players in America's love affair with aviation would include humorist Will Rogers and industrialist, producer and flyer Howard Hughes. "Flying Cowboy" Rogers, arguably the most popular and influential entertainer of the era, was persistent in his radio and newspaper praise of aviation. This was reinforced by the huge critical and commercial success of the World War I flying picture *Hell's Angels* (1930), produced and directed by the brash young playboy Hughes, years before he succumbed to reclusive eccentricity. Later in the 1930s, Hughes' own aviation accomplishments would rival those of Lindbergh and Earhart. Consequently, the flying theme which Warners plugged into on Brown's *Going Wild* was the proverbial "no-brainer." In fact, despite the decade's occasional air-related tragedy, such as the plane crash death of Will Rogers (1935) and the mysterious disappearance of Earhart (1937, on an attempted around-the-world flight), public absorption in aviation remained high. Consistent with that enthusiasm, two later Brown films would also make use of flying-related story-lines—*Son of a Sailor* (1933) and *Riding on Air* (1937). The latter picture especially underlines the country's ongoing interest in the airways, since Brown plays Richard Macaulay's popular *Saturday Evening Post* character Elmer Lane, a small-town journalist and pilot. (The *Post* was a mirror of America during the 1930s.)

Brown's busy screen career during 1930–31 was not limited to the very popular and provocative trilogy of *Top Speed, Going Wild* and *Broad Minded*—all of which even sport titles that suggest spicy subjects. But the four other movies he made during this two-year span—*Make It Love, The Lottery Bride* (both 1930), *Sit Tight* and *Local Boy Makes Good* (both 1931)—have much less in common. The first is a college football story with Brown in support of top-billed Joan Bennett. The second picture is an operetta set in Norway and done as a loanout to United Artists; Joe's orchestra leader is just one of several supporting players. The third film returns him to Warners but in support of Winnie Lightner, whom he was billed above in *Hold Everything. Local Boy* is finally a star turn for Brown, as he plays a timid botany student who also works in the college bookstore.

Make It Love was a popular success and, like Brown's *Hold Everything*, it was another sports film which drew from reality. But instead of *Hold Everything*'s single famous athlete (French boxer Georges Carpentier), *Love* features the entire 1929 All-American football team as well as University of Southern California football coach Howard Jones.

The movie's best gag is its opening, where each player does his specialty, one at a time —
passing, kicking and so on. Brown is the final man — a shifty half back who manages
to avoid all would-be tacklers, until Notre Dame center Tim Monahan flattens him.
Being that it is both football and a slapstick-oriented personality comedy, everyone
piles on the downed Brown, and he naturally produces his patented yell — possibly having it squeezed out. *Variety* even credited this vocalization with being "a new yell, featuring the large Brownesque mouth, and after the picture was over at the Strand
[Theatre] some of the audience picked it up."[18]

Of special interest today for film fans is that *Love* was directed by Hollywood legend William "Wild Bill" Wellman (1896–1975). I might have attached his name to the
earlier aviation section, since his World War I flying picture *Wings* (1927) won Hollywood's first Best Picture Academy Award. The impressive air sequences were drawn from
personal experience, since Wellman was a decorated ace with the celebrated Lafayette
Escadrille. His long career produced many other classics, in an assortment of genres:
The Public Enemy (1931), *Wild Boys of the Road* (1933), *A Star Is Born* (1937), *Beau Geste*
(1939), *The Ox-Bow Incident* (1943), *The Story of G.I. Joe* (1945) and *Battleground* (1949).
His strongest memory of the Brown picture was the aforementioned pile-up and the
direction he had requested of the comedian — to act groggy. Laughing out loud when
he talked to me, over 40 years later, he revealed that Brown's perfect playing of the
scene was the result of Joe *really* being groggy — that the comic had almost walked into
the camera![19]

In contrast to *Love*, *The Lottery Bride* was a misfire. Critics could not even decide
if the film had spoofing overtones. For instance, the *New York Evening Journal* reviewer
confessed, "It is somewhat difficult to figure out whether ... [*Bride*] is meant to be taken
straight or, as one would prefer to believe for the sake of everyone involved, as a satire
on screen operettas."[20] And while *The New York Times* felt supporting player Brown
"looks after the comedy ... extraordinarily well," the normally more forgiving *Variety*
declared, "there isn't a worthwhile performance in the entire cast, even Joey [sic] Brown
flattening into the general jumble of pitched and lazily artificial hoke."[21] If *The Lottery
Bride* is noted at all today, it is as part of the cult status attached to any Jeanette Mac-
Donald starring vehicle.

Like *The Lottery Bride*, critics had reservations about *Sit Tight*, with *Variety* sug-
gesting it was "best suited to neighborhood [theater] playing, where its weaknesses and
lapses will be overlooked."[22] Brown plays Winnie Lightner's assistant at a health institute, and while his comedy was considered the best thing about the picture, *The New
York Times* still entitled their review, "*Sit Tight* A Sad Film."[23]

Local Boy Makes Good, the last film of this second grouping from 1930–31, is of
such importance, however, as to rival anything else Brown had done in Hollywood up
until this point. But a thumbnail sketch of the story would hardly suggest anything
unique from the picture — an anti-heroic bookworm becomes a college track star and
gets the girl. Granted, this third screen adaptation of the stage play *The Poor Nut* did

Brown and Winnie Lightner in *Sit Tight* (1931).

slip by some critics, such as the unintentionally comic *New York Post* critique comment, "It's the usual collegiate stuff; swift moving, sometimes quite funny and generally harmless."[24] Nevertheless, an inordinately large number of reviewers were aware of a new wrinkle in Brown's comedy arsenal. *New York World Telegram* critic William Boehnel summarized it best: "Joe E. Brown hangs up his finest performance in *Local Boy* ... for here he departs from his usual broad-grinning, yelping role and attempts a real characterization."[25] Numerous other reviewers had similar things to say as well, from the *New York Herald Tribune*'s "Joe E. Brown attempts a characterization this time ... and as a result, it is the best thing that he has yet managed upon the screen," to the *New York American*'s "fast farce frequently reaching new highs in hilarity ... enables Joe Brown to contribute generously to the gaiety of nations. Not until the last reel is Joe his usual flamboyant self."[26]

While Brown had played the anti-hero before, he had never done it with such disarming sensitivity—a quality the performance still exudes. I was so charmed by the picture upon first seeing it in 2000 that it proved to be a major catalyst for my deciding to write the book in hand. But this breakthrough characterization was entirely predicated upon its contrast with Brown's breezy, entertainingly confident figure from the trilogy addressed earlier in this chapter—*Top Speed*, *Going Wild* and *Broad Minded*. Moreover, what is doubly impressive is that the comedian's smart-aleck type had not diminished in popularity. For example, Rose Pelswick's glowing *New York Evening Journal* review of *Local Boy* opens with a simple but impressive documentation of the comedian's broad appeal: "The moment Joe E. Brown appears on the screen there's a delighted howl from the audience. So, with the customers his from the start, Brown needs do little more than yawn, blink or shuffle his feet to ensure undivided attention."[27] Thus, Joe's milquetoast success in *Local Boy* was an admirable display of the comedian's willingness to experiment, rather than some desperate attempt to leave an overworked character.

If one pushes a loose comedy etymology of Brown's *Local Boy* figure a bit further, there are links to two earlier notable funnymen. First, by Brown giving his small-town bookworm glasses, one is reminded of Harold Lloyd's everyman, small-town, glasses-wearing screen persona. Spectacles were so synonymous with Lloyd that his figure was often referred to as the "glasses character." In Lloyd's 1928 autobiography *An American Comedy*, he equated those spectacles with the following character traits: "quiet, normal, boyish, clean, sympathetic, not impossible to romance ... an average recognizable American youth...."[28] While Brown did not otherwise attempt to mimic Lloyd, he successfully tapped into that timid bookishness mindset by wearing those glasses. Eventually, Hollywood simply made Lloyd's name shorthand for this type of character. To illustrate, Howard Hawks' remarkable *Bringing Up Baby* (1938) features an absent-minded professor (Cary Grant), with Hawks' direction to Grant having been, "You've seen Harold Lloyd in pictures, haven't you...?"[29]

Brown's athleticism in *Local Boy*, even when he is supposed to be awkward (such as his tryout for the track squad), is also reminiscent of silent comedy's superbly conditioned Buster Keaton, especially as showcased in his film *College* (1927). Keaton's various tryouts in that picture, in an assortment of sports, also go poorly. But when one sees the muscular bodies of both comics as they work out in each movie's track sequence, the "worm turns" storylines do not seem far-fetched. Brown's eventual realization of

Brown often comically focused on food in his films. Here he "co-stars" with some pie in ***Local Boy Makes Good*** **(1931).**

athletic skill in *Local Boy* does, however, occur earlier, and with more comic punch, than a comparable scene in *College*. Whereas Keaton must wait until the finale to pull all his sports finesse together and rescue the heroine, Brown comically realizes his track speed early — Joe's wayward javelin throw nearly shish-kebobs a celebrated sprinter and the comic realizes that fear can make those track feet fly. And when that angry, nearly speared star sprinter cannot keep up with Brown, our hero's track fortunes are made.

This pivotal early *Local Boy* running sequence is also sandwiched between two excellent comic bits. The set-up for the scene has the nearly victimized runner ask Brown, "Did you throw that javelin?" Joe, happy to get his spear back, responds in the most naively innocent manner, "Yes, I thought I lost it." That pleasantly vacuous line lifts this low comedy to high art, as well as giving the revengeful sprinter another reason to chase Joe. The second inspired gag immediately follows the fadeout of the chase. The viewer sees the text *Famous Suicides of History*, and the film cuts to bookish Brown reading this weighty volume. Poor Joe has been in hiding for two days, unaware that the near–shish kebob incident is all forgiven, due to his blinding speed.

Local Boy artfully maintains this balance of verbal and visual comedy throughout its 69-minute playing time. Period audiences were especially taken with the climactic track meet, when Brown not only defeats his arrogant archrival — he briefly toys with him by matching him stride for stride ... while running backwards! Equally entertaining to this viewer was Joe's comically succinct response to his coach's stereotypical pep talk. That is, just before the final race the coach movingly observes, "If you don't win ... if you ever have any children or grandchildren, how will they feel when the [track championship] Gold Cup is mentioned?" Joe answers, "They might not mention it." Or, as his essentially pacifist character noted earlier in the picture, "I'm not a fighter; I'm a botanist."

For all Brown's pre–*Local Boy* popularity, based upon critics describing responsive audiences, there were a few reviewers who found it refreshing that the comedian dropped, in the amusing words of the *New York Sun*'s John S. Cohen, Jr., "his nationwide grin and his coyote mating call, and endeavors to play it straight...."[30] For Cohen, this brought Brown more into the richer, pathos-oriented tradition of a Chaplin. This vantage point also found favor with *Chicago Tribune* critic Mae Tinée, though she had been a fan of Brown since his early "Little Mousie" days. Still, Tinée was tired of "his seal cries, [and] wide mouth grimaces."[31]

All in all, *Local Boy* seemed to meet with nearly universal critical acclaim. Not surprisingly, as film historian Leonard Maltin later noted, "This worm-turning story became the prototype for many Joe E. Brown vehicles...."[32] He would fluctuate between this timid underdog type and the more extroverted smart-aleck athlete who evolved from the previously examined trilogy of *Top Speed*, *Going Wild* and *Broad Minded*. Interestingly enough, as if to be consistent with Brown's evolving comedy formula that an athlete equals being entertainingly egotistical, *Local Boy* has an epilogue-like conclusion tacked on. It is some time after the track meet and a dapperly dressed Brown, *sans* spectacles, returns to the bookstore. There is a breezy confidence about him (*à la* the earlier trilogy) as he orchestrates his engagement to the beautiful clerk (Ruth Hall). When Joe's old boss starts to interrupt them as is his bullying tradition, a now far-from-mild Brown gives him what for. Then, as a final accent on the banishment of timid times, the picture closes with a kiss. Joe was on the verge of his first top ten box office year.

As the title *Top Speed* has doubled as a description for the rapidly rising trajectory of Brown's early 1930s career, it also characterizes changes taking place at this time in his personal life. In 1930, Joe and wife Kathryn settled permanently in filmland by buying a Beverly Hills home and, following a miscarriage, deciding to expand their family with an adopted daughter. That year their teenage sons (Don and Joe, Jr.) had a new baby sister, Mary Elizabeth Ann. The boys also received an older "brother" when UCLA freshman athlete Mike Frankovich needed some stability in his private life and joined the Brown family for the duration of his college career. (Don and Joe, Jr., would later be UCLA athletes, too, while Joe, Sr., was a tireless supporter of the Bruins.) In 1934, the Browns adopted a second baby daughter, Kathryn Frances. The comedian's parenting philosophy was lovingly direct:

> The secret of bringing up kids is very simple. Just let them know you're interested in them, and take an active part in their lives. When I was a boy [entertainer], I used to wish I had someone to talk to, someone who wouldn't laugh at what I said, who would care what I was doing. I've never forgotten that, and from the day the first boy was born, I've tried to be friend as well as father.[33]

An early 1930s *Los Angeles Times* article on comedians as dads also suggested that it helped to be a kid at heart, revealing that Brown "put a soda fountain in his home for his children not long ago! No greater love hath a dad! ... after the first week, the children did not make themselves sick on ice-cream sodas."[34] The same piece added, "Joe's children usually love his pictures, but he seldom clowns for them. He's just a devoted dad, not a comedian to them."[35] In 1934, Brown authored an article on marriage and family in which he confessed, "Children, I think, are the strongest bond, and the greatest blessing married people can have. I couldn't be happy, it seems to me, without a family ... children would be the greatest cure-all, in my opinion, for Hollywood's divorce habit."[36]

Good parenting was also like casting the proverbial bread upon the water, in that it came to be reflective of his screen work. The provocative dialogue and/or situations found in some of his pre–Code pictures notwithstanding, by the late 1930s he was defining himself through his popularity with youngsters, which included a children-oriented radio program, *The Joe E. Brown—Post Toasties Show.* In a 1938 article, the comedian wrote, "[W]hatever drawing power I have has been largely built up through appealing to children. Stage and screen are familiar with Joe E. Brown antics, the Brown yell and the timid, love-sick 'G-o-o-s-h.'"[37] Though this unfortunately neglects the sizeable *adult* audience he attracted for much of the decade, his later pictures were increasingly aimed at the juvenile market. But maybe Brown was just studying his fan mail. He was famous for monitoring this feedback more closely than most stars, and a 1937 press release noted his pride "that so many of the letters are from parents who write that they have come to count on his pictures as a safe bet for their children's entertainment. At least ten letters a day state that Brown is the only comedian they permit their youngsters to see without first seeing the attraction themselves."[38]

Fittingly, Brown's first picture after the watershed *Local Boy Makes Good* would return him to a subject close to "youngsters" of all ages — baseball. This defining sport of Joe's own youth would become his cinema talisman, inspiring three of his greatest pictures. The boy who almost gave up show business to play second base would be blessed, for a time, by having it both ways.

❖ Six ❖

Lardner & Brown
and the National Game

When Joe E. Brown's title character in *Elmer the Great* (1933) overhears Sterling Holloway's wish that he could bat like him, Joe responds, "Yes, so does Babe Ruth."

To this Holloway replies, "Oh, if you were only as good as you think you are."

"Say, I'm better than I think I am," answers Brown.

Given that Joe E. Brown was both a veteran baseball player (whose Warner Brothers team was often matched against Buster Keaton's MGM squad) and a fanatical memorabilia collecting fan, it was only a matter of time before he made a baseball film. National game or not, however, there was then a knock against baseball pictures — the belief that the sport could not score at the all-important box office.[1] But in late 1930, Brown had made a baseball believer out of Warners producer Darryl F. Zanuck when the comedian's limited-run holiday stage appearance in a Los Angeles production of Ring Lardner and George M. Cohan's *Elmer the Great* was a smash success.[2] (Impressively, Brown's version was a greater hit with audiences than the Broadway original, which starred Walter Huston in the title role.)

Lardner (1885–1933) is no longer a household name. But in 1914 he had both elevated baseball stories to comic literature and affectionately derailed the notion of the noble bloodless sports hero. The initial catalyst was a series of Lardner *Saturday Evening Post* short stories later collected in book form as *You Know Me Al: A Busher's Letters*.[3] The pieces, a fictional correspondence from a rookie Chicago White Sox pitcher (Jack Keefe) to a hometown friend, chronicled the comic misadventures of an entertainingly self-centered rube in the Major Leagues. Keefe is barely literate, and part of the humor comes from the misspellings and hyperbole, a comic form of writing especially popular with a late nineteenth century collection of American writers known as the "Literary Comedians."[4] But Lardner peppered his prose with inspired dialogue and American slang, especially as it applied to baseball. He did not so much take the air out of the national pastime as just remind us it was part of the human comedy, too. Lardner's later diamond tales, such as the short story "Alibi Ike" (1915) and the play *Elmer the Great* (1928), continued in the tradition of those original Jack Keefe comic letters.

67

During the 1930s, Brown would star in a baseball trilogy which one might subtitle a "Lardner Salute": *Fireman, Save My Child* (1932), *Elmer the Great* (1933) and *Alibi Ike* (1935). While the opening picture was technically not from a Lardner source, the original story was so similar (including a hick pitcher and a Lardner-like title — "The Bush Leaguer") that many film reviewers noted the obvious connection.[5] Ironically, there are even some basic Lardner-Keefe components showcased in *Fireman* which do not surface in the two later Brown adaptations of Lardner's work. The most obvious example involves the easy vulnerability to baseball groupies of the standard Lardner player. Indeed, a goodly portion of *You Know Me Al* documents Keefe being taken for the proverbial ride by two different women. In *Fireman*, Lillian Bond's diamond groupie (with the appropriate summer name of June) is what another generation would call a "Baseball Annie," only carried to the most manipulative extreme. Because this is a pre–censorship code (1934) picture, the movie matter-of-factly introduces June as the expensive companion for two of Brown's teammates. Thus, an immediate plot point has them unloading her on the gullible Joe.

Brown's character, Smokey Joe Grant, is a fireman from the small Kansas town of Rosedale. He is also a gifted pitcher, with the most entertaining corkscrew wind-up, where Joe's arms briefly twist around his head before unloading the ball. Add to this Brown the inventor, obsessed with marketing his fire extinguisher bomb. Fittingly, the device is designed in the shape of a baseball — all the better to "pitch" into a fire. Since the invention takes precedence over everything else, baseball often gets short shrift. Of course, for the boy-man Smokey Joe, everything is a distraction, especially fire engines and loud sirens. In fact, this character has more than a little in common with pioneering Major League zany Rube Waddell (1876–1914), a pitcher whose fascination with fire engines even delayed games, as he pondered their path from the mound. Baseball historian Lowell Reidenbaugh's description of Waddell, as someone "who pitched like a superman but whose child-like nature required infinite managerial patience and tact," could also be applied to Brown's Smokey Joe Grant.[6] (A decade later, Brown was in negotiations to star in a biography film of Waddell, but nothing came of the project.[7]) As if to accent a connection between Waddell and the Joe of *Fireman*, the movie's early Rosedale scenes seem to mirror the turn-of-the-century heyday of the original "Rube." That is, the Rosedale fire engine is pulled by horses, and the bucolic main street looks like a place where Tom Sawyer and Huck Finn might appear at any time. Only later, when Joe is pitching for the St. Louis Cardinals, does one realize this is *not* a period piece.

Though Joe is most focused on his invention, he has the healthy ego of a Lardner athletic anti-hero. For instance, when his Cardinal teammates set him up for June by saying, "She thinks you're the greatest ball player in the world," Joe responds, "She ain't far wrong." Or, in the ninth inning of the deciding World Series game against the New York Yankees, Joe prefaces his stroll to the plate with the breezy statement, "Well, I guess I might as well go up there and win it." Joe also has the comically cocky habit of

Brown's small town baseball hero in *Fireman, Save My Child* (1932, with Evalyn Knapp).

seemingly reaching to catch a thrown ball with his pitching hand, only to let it go by and have it surprisingly land in his gloved hand. But whereas a Buster Keaton would accent the comic sorcery of such a trick with his patented "Great Stone Face," Joe takes what might be called the "Red Skelton Position" of smiling broadly, as if to say, "Why should I be the only one who doesn't get the joke?"[8]

Despite the brash comic conceit of this Lardner-esque character, there is the pathetic (or is that poignant?) side to Smoke Joe, just as there was to Jack Keefe. Consequently, when Brown's pitcher plays at being modest for June, he blindly misses the gold-digger's obvious intent. The humble-for-him pontification begins, "When a fellow knows he's a big shot, he don't have to tell nobody. Take me for instance —" But with a hustler's timing, June interrupts his "Take me for instance" line with an under-her-breath, "Just give me time." And even when June has her hooks into Joe deeply, he remains oblivious to the ongoing scam. This is underlined in a letter (another footnote to Lardner) he writes home to his girlfriend Sally (Evalyn Knapp). With June having tricked him into an engagement, the only honorable thing to do is break it off with Sally. But Joe's simpleton slant on the triangle blames his animal magnetism. He writes, "I'm sorry I made you fall in love with me, but I couldn't help it. That's the kind of personality I got."

Naturally, everything works out in the end. Joe finds a backer for his invention, he returns to Sally, and, oh yes, this rube beats the New York Yankees in the World Series. As an addendum to the Yankees' famous "Murderers' Row" of hitters, an added *Fireman* bonus is the inclusion of newsreel footage of legendary slugger Lou Gehrig. Brown and Gehrig had been friends since the comedian's days on Broadway. This is a good thing because, through the movie magic of editing, Smokey Joe proceeds to strike out Gehrig on three pitches — killing a Yankee rally. Besides the entertainment value of a beloved but goofy clown striking out "The Iron Horse," there is the pure student of baseball enchantment of watching a Gehrig swing. Even Gehrig's misses are mesmerizing.

Defeating the Yankees almost closes the story, but the movie has a hometown epilogue where fire chief Joe is speeding through the streets in a fast car, siren blaring. Instead of a fire, however, he is late to his own wedding. The cause of Joe's tardiness was an emergency work session where he expanded the size of his fire extinguisher bomb. He had been concerned that a baby could swallow the baseball-like original. When his bride Sally says, "A baby couldn't," Joe responds with a patented big-mouth rebuttal, "*Our* baby could." While this is still an inspired gag today, it garnered special critical attention at the time, such as *Film Daily*'s comment, "The finish is more than you expect. It's a wow."[9]

As this praise for the *Fireman* finale suggests, the comedian's notices for the picture were strong, with *Variety* calling it "Surefire comedy material providing Joe E. Brown with the best part he's had since [getting] in pictures."[10] The *New York World Telegram* seconded this verdict, as well as insightfully recognizing the Smokey Joe-Rube

Waddell connection.[11] Under the title "*Fireman* Corking Comedy," *The Hollywood Reporter* pushed the positive meter further by stating, "[T]he Burbank boys [Warner Brothers] have a piece that will easily take rank as one of the best comedies of this season ... with more good hearty laughs than a case of Scotch."[12] *International Photographer* critic Sol Polito's *Fireman* review gave all these kudos box office validation when it noted that the picture was held over for a second week at Warners' Hollywood theater — "the first time in nine months" this had occurred.[13] The film was such an attraction at this studio showcase that Brown was asked to

Brown's friend and Yankee slugger Lou Gehrig (1939).

make a personal appearance during the second week. But even this was not enough. After taking two bows and speaking briefly, "the house [audience] would not let him go without giving [his celebrated routine 'Little] Mousie,' which ... is so identified with him that he probably never will shake it in this life."[14]

Variety's aforementioned rave review had suggested that *Fireman*'s appeal was so broad that it "can't help but win new admirers for Brown."[15] Interestingly enough, this sentiment surfaced among critics, too. For instance, the *New York Herald Tribune* reviewer wrote, "Mr. Brown, who has always seemed to me something less than a major comic, is ... in much better form than usual in his latest assignment."[16] The *New York World Telegram* critic added, "Never an enthusiastic admirer of Mr. Brown's peculiar

71

brand of screen comedy, I must, nevertheless, confess that I found his latest effusion ... entirely to my liking."[17] An unnamed reviewer for the *New York Sun* was even in the doubly odd situation of panning the picture but still upgrading his critical take on the comedian: "Mr. Brown grows on one. I never considered him really amusing in his early pictures, but he [now] seems to know a great deal more about screen acting than he did before."[18]

Of course, it was rare to dislike Brown in 1932, the release date of *Fireman*. The picture's popularity help put him, for the first time, on filmland's most coveted list — the annual top ten box office stars.[19] It was no wonder that *Film Daily* opened a superlative review of *Fireman* with everything in capital letters — ROLLICKING LAUGH-FEST WITH JOE E. BROWN PUTTING OVER FAT PART IN A BIG WAY."[20] Often coupled with this praise for his first baseball picture was the acknowledgment that the comedian's proven talent in this sport made the subject a natural for Brown's movies. For example, *The Hollywood Reporter* made just this declaration, and spiced it up with comparisons to two radically different period personalities:

> [P]utting Joe E. Brown in a baseball picture was as sound a piece of casting as showing [Jascha] Heifetz as a violinist. It's [Brown's] meat and he shows that he's as much at home on a baseball diamond as [Al] Capone with a bodyguard.[21]

Appropriately, a month after the Los Angeles opening of *Fireman*, *The Hollywood Reporter* announced, "One of the biggest crowds in baseball history is expected to attend the game between Joe E. Brown's team and Buster Keaton's outfit at [Los Angeles'] Wrigley Field tomorrow."[22] The two baseball-obsessed comedians had also arranged playing time for such other Hollywood students of the national game as Clark Gable, the Marx Brothers, Laurel & Hardy, Jimmy Durante and Wheeler & Woolsey. After the stars started the game, players from the Chicago Cubs and the New York Giants would complete the action. The two Major League clubs were on the West Coast for spring training, 26 years before the Giants would relocate to San Francisco. (Early the previous year, 1931, Joe's Warners team had played the Chicago Cubs at their standard spring training site on Catalina Island, just off the coast of Southern California.)

After the early 1932 critical and commercial success of *Fireman*, both Brown and Warner Brothers were anxious to make another baseball picture. By September of that year, the studio had acquired the rights to the Lardner-Cohan play *Elmer the Great* from Paramount, which had adopted the stage vehicle to the screen as *Fast Company* (1929, with Jack Oakie). But as previously noted, West Coast fans of Brown and/or baseball already identified the character with the comedian after his popular late–1930 Los Angles stage production of *Elmer*.

The cinematically prolific Brown appeared in two pictures, *The Tenderfoot* and *You Said a Mouthful* (both 1932, which will be addressed in the next chapter), before making the 1933 *Elmer the Great*. Though *Elmer* is largely a faithful adaptation, the film makes the title character a great home run hitter instead of a masterful pitcher (*á la* Lardner's Jack Keefe). Brown's movie Elmer remains, however, the same talented, entertainingly unlettered, small-town egotist of the play. Indeed, these are traits which apply to all three of Lardner's signature baseball characters — Keefe, Alibi Ike and Elmer. And since their baseball skills are only rivaled by a propensity to brag, all three figures have a tendency to comically alibi, too, when their tall tale-like hype does not produce. For instance, when one of Brown's spring training clouts as Elmer does not quite go for a homer, he alibis, "Shucks, that one hit the fence. I'll put the next one over. I'm always afraid of breaking windows."

Looking at this Lardner trio chronologically, Keefe and Alibi Ike appeared within a year of each other (1914–15). In contrast, Elmer did not surface on Broadway until 1928. Thus, while they are all similar smart-aleck rubes, Elmer is arguably the most fleshed-out composite of the bunch. Given this background, moreover, one could contend that Warners was perfectly in keeping with Lardner by making Elmer a power hitter, since Alibi Ike had been a slugger, too. Be this as it may, Lardner's original model for Elmer was drawn, in part, from the pioneering Major Leaguer "Big Ed" Walsh (1881–1959), whose Hall of Fame glory days were for the early twentieth century Chicago White Sox — a team that Lardner both knew and traveled with as a sports writer for first the *Chicago Examiner*, and then the *Chicago Tribune*.[23] The best pocket definition of Walsh's tendency for swaggering bluff and bluster comes from another prominent Chicago sports writer of that era, Charles Dryden: Walsh was the "only man in the world who can strut sitting down."[24] In Brown's autobiography, he also likened the Big Ed–Elmer ego to the later "sold on himself" nature of St. Louis Cardinal star Dizzy Dean — another comic braggart who delivered.[25] The comedian added his own personal embellishment by way of an earlier big leaguer — Philadelphia Phillies pitcher Harry Frank "The Giant Killer" Coveleski (1886–1950), who was especially effective against the New York Giants.[26] During Brown's vaudeville days, he closely followed Coveleski's career and was fascinated by the player's goofy lumbering walk, a sort of lazy swagger, with prominent arm swinging. The comedian adopted the gait and deliberate mannerisms for his take on Elmer.

Brown's screen version of *Elmer the Great* opens in the small Indiana town of Gentryville. Periodically during the picture, an instrumental rendition of the song "Back Home Again in Indiana" will be used as sort of a movie mantra for simpler small-town life. As with the beginning of *Fireman, Save My Child*, the visible in-town means of transportation suggests an earlier time period — a Chicago Cubs representative, in a horse-drawn sleigh, has come to sign Elmer. Also, as in *Fireman*, our comic anti-hero is less than excited about this opportunity. But whereas he was distracted by the inventing bug in that picture, this time around he cannot bear the thought of leaving Nellie (Patricia Ellis), who also doubles as his boss at the local general store. Sterling Holloway, in an early example of his country bumpkin persona, plays Elmer's brother. Holloway's character is the more enthusiastic baseball fan — sort of a non-stop comic Greek

Brown's title character in the film adaptation of *Elmer the Great* (1933) becomes a great hitter, instead of a pitcher.

chorus on why Elmer should accept the Cubs' offer. Holloway's observations also set up Brown's best lines, like the "better than Babe Ruth" quote which opens the chapter. On another occasion, Holloway's character says, "If you go with the Chicago Cubs, you're liable to turn out to be the greatest batter in the world!" To this an exasperated Elmer replies, "Liable to turn out to be...?!"

Only Ellis' Nellie has the power to make Brown's character act. Nellie does the sacrificial thing: She both breaks it off with Elmer, and also fires him from his store delivery position. With this, he signs the Cubs contract and is next seen at spring training, where he puts on an impressive display of hitting. His demeanor in and around the batter's box is especially entertaining. Before setting himself up to hit, he flips his bat in the air one-half revolution, catching the fat end of the stick. He then quickly reverses the process, and grabs the slender portion of the bat — all with one rapid hand movement. In the batter's box he displays a pronounced lean towards the pitcher, topped off with a conspicuous leer, like his eyes are assuming a special batter's focus. Whether this is a further comic tribute to Coveleski is unclear, but the characterization is inspiringly unique, something new for the modern fan. As a footnote to the fun, one should credit Brown with a novel scheme. A more typical approach to this situation, as demonstrated by a comedy genius like Buster Keaton or Red Skelton, is to nail in wonderful detail every *typical* batting nuance, from stooping for some dirt with which to dry the hands, to that hitter's wiggle as he digs in at the plate.

With all Elmer's comic distinctions, he is an easy target for kidding and/or pranks from his teammates — something he does not have the best sense of humor about. For example, like the eternally hungry little Joe Evan Brown of the early circus and vaudeville days, Elmer eats everything in sight. In fact, Brown's first extended comedy scene in the picture is predicated upon his Elmer eating the largest breakfast on record — stacks of pancakes and ham, apple pie, gingerbread, donuts and jam, assorted fruit (especially a comic's favorite — the banana), coffee and a large glass of milk. But unlike a more typical comic eating scene, such as when the Marx Brothers focus on pigging out in *Room Service* (1938), Brown's breakfast in *Elmer* has him talking away, too. He later confessed that this was no easy task "even with my mouth."[27] Ironically, when Brown first performed *Elmer* on stage, he had some minor health problems from eating too much ham during the breakfast scenes! This negative take on "method acting" (or is that "method eating"), years before this approach to performing was officially christened, was further exacerbated by weekends, when Joe did two shows each day. Of course, it might have been worse. Later in the 1930s, Red Skelton performed his first classic vaudeville sketch, a donut-eating routine, which necessitated his downing nine "sinkers" per show, and he was doing *five shows a day*. After this led to Skelton's first feature, *Having Wonderful Time* (1938), his studio had to first put him on a diet.[28]

When a picture's title, such as *Elmer the Great*, is really a satirical put-down of how "great" the central character thinks he is, it is only a matter of time before the supporting figures play a major prank on him. This occurs in *Elmer* when his teammates invite the rookie to speak over the radio. While the "broadcast" is totally staged, Brown's rube innocently wins the scene by turning his "air time" into an opportunity to communicate with his mother, instead of being his inflated self. Paradoxically, the teammates' attempt at ridicule has merely made them feel small. Plus, when this plot point comes out later in the story, it will briefly demoralize Elmer and contribute to an unfortunate decision on his part. Before this occurs, a montage of headlines encapsulates how Elmer Kane's home run record season has put the Cubs in the World Series:

"Kane's Homers Cinch Cubs!"
"Cubs Favored to Win with Kane's Batting"
"Cubs Depend on Kane!"
"Kane Scores 67 Home Runs"

The World Series scenes in *Elmer* feature real footage from the previous year's (1932) "Fall Classic" between the New York Yankees and Chicago Cubs. Brown and a Warners crew had gone east in late September (1932) to shoot Series filler material, with the comedian's friend Lou Gehrig being the star player most prominently showcased in the finished picture. Today the 1932 "Fall Classic" is most famous for Babe Ruth's "called shot," when he allegedly pointed to Wrigley Field's centerfield bleachers and then smashed the next pitched ball out there. Consequently, Brown's Series-winning home run as Elmer is in good company, just as his 67 homers would have passed Ruth's then-record of 60, set during the 1927 season.

In light of today's ongoing controversy about Pete Rose's gambling past, *Elmer* adds a modern twist when Brown's rube became innocently involved with a betting ring. His best friend on the Cubs, High Hips Healy (frequent Brown co-star Frank McHugh), takes Elmer to a gambling house where the food and drinks are free, courtesy of all the suckers that management fleeces. Healy figures his slugger friend, with that gargantuan appetite, will enjoy all the gratis items. Innocent Elmer, whose idea of a "drink" order is a "raspberry soda pop *à la* mode," initially limits himself to matters of the stomach. But eventually, like a curious child, he wants to play some of the gambling games. Unfortunately, Healy is not much brighter than Elmer and neglects to inform his friend that he is running up a large gambling debt.

The shifty owner of this gentleman's club is played by a performer on the verge of a memorable career as a villain — Douglass Dumbrille, whose future crooked characters would grace such comedy classics as *Mr. Deeds Goes to Town* (1936), *A Day at the Races* (1937) and *Road to Utopia* (1946). Dumbrille's club owner tells Elmer he will both forget the $5,000 debt and even pay the athlete handsomely if Kane helps out on a World Series wager. At first a pleased Elmer thinks the owner is betting on the Cubs. But when Brown's rube discovers they want him to throw the Series, he starts a fight that ends with both him and teammate Healy in jail.

During this time, Elmer is further humiliated to discover the team had staged the alleged radio broadcast. So when arrangements are later made to get him out of jail, he refuses. Meanwhile, Elmer's small-town girlfriend pays off the gambling debt. But when Dumbrille's character brings the I.O.U. to jail and explains that Nellie paid it off, Elmer accepts the bribe in order to pay her back, while bitterly observing, "I might as well be getting paid for being a fool."

Not surprisingly, once Elmer's girl visits him in jail, and the soundtrack offers yet another instrumental orchestration of "Back Home Again in Indiana," he decides to play in the "World Serious" [sic, how all of Lardner's rubes refer to the Series]. Naturally, when Chicago prepares to start Elmer, the gambling ring operator shows the Cubs owner documents which Brown's slugger has signed implicating him in a "fix." In the cold reality of today, or even the early 1930s (after all, "Shoeless Joe" Jackson had been banned for just such a "fix" ten years before), these gambling papers would have put the kibosh to Elmer's playing. But in the Hollywood world of clown comedies, the Cubs manager decides to let him play, though he will watch Elmer for any suspicious actions.

During the ensuing game, Brown's character is twice involved in questionable plays. First, he gets beaned by a pitched ball, and his follow-up loopy behavior on the base paths results in an out. Then, during the late innings, the game is being played in the rain and Elmer comically loses a hit ball in a puddle, which stretches the Yankee lead to 3–0. But when his manager decides to take him out, Elmer reveals that he has bet the $5,000 bribe on the Cubs to win, at 3–1 odds. Such chutzpah makes everything all right, as even the impressed owner observes, "So you double-crossed the gamblers!"

Still, this, the deciding game of the World Series, has yet to be won. What follows is the daydream of little boys and grown men everywhere. Elmer comes to bat in the bottom of the ninth with the bases loaded. This is Walter Mitty time years before James Thurber wrote "The Secret Life of Walter Mitty." After some shenanigans by the Yankees, which include pretending to throw the ball on this gray, overcast day and have two non-pitches count as strikes, Elmer hits the grand slam homer required for a happy ending. But unlike the majestic Ruthian blasts he smacks in spring training, filmed in single takes to reveal Brown's real hitting prowess, this finale dinger is of the inside-the-park variety. Thus, the viewer is treated to a comic mad dash around the base paths, topped off with a muddy homeplate slide that could be called the quintessential Mack Sennett moment. And in a brief epilogue, which completes the righting of one last wrong, Elmer is accorded a real radio spot, in which he predicts more baseball success, says hello to Ma, warns them to start cooking at home, and ends by kissing Nellie.

Elmer proved to be a huge critical and commercial success. While the *New York Herald Tribune* described the picture as "bordering on entertainment perfection," the title for the *New York American* review said, "*Elmer the Great* Is Hilarious Film of Lardner-Cohan Play."[29] *The Hollywood Reporter*'s opening praise was in baseball terms, which then segued into affectionate humor:

Chalk up a home run for Director Mervyn LeRoy and Joe E. Brown ... *Elmer the Great* is excellent entertainment from Brown's first yawn, which is nearly a black-out, to his last slide to a muddy home base, another near black-out.[30]

The admiring *New York Times* critique even documented how an enthusiastic Radio City Music Hall crowd was caught in "rapt attention during a closing stage [at bat] of the proceedings, most of the spectators were fearful lest Elmer might strike out, like [actor] De Wolf Hopper's [famous rendition of] Mighty Carey."[31] And besides periodic review references to Brown's very real baseball skills, *New York Evening Journal* critic Rose Pelswick also noted that the comedian had recently (early 1933) become "part owner of the Kansas City Blues" baseball team.[32] This was yet another way that Brown was synonymous with the national game for Depression audiences.

Despite all the urban kudos for Brown's small town *Elmer*, the *New York Sun* reviewer suggested the film would register even stronger "in the rural districts."[33] The best 1930s gauge of the small town–rural market can be found in the "What the Picture Did for Me" section of the period publication *Motion Picture Herald*. This portion of the *Herald* reprinted paragraph-length blurbs about then-current pictures from hinterland theater owners across the country. A sampling of the glowing *Elmer* notices found in this *Herald* section would suggest the *Sun* critic was correct. From Shenandoah, Pennsylvania, came this passionate praise:

> A sparkling and hilariously funny baseball yarn with that sensitive, wide open mouth of Joe E. Brown amidst the battery delivering home run entertainment and handing out laughs that literally knocked the audience in the aisles with his funny antics. Some observers laughed so hard that most of the gags were blotted out ... Play it and see Joe E. Brown's mouth swallow the grinning face of old man depression from view....[34]

A small-theater owner in Malta, Montana, mixed high compliments with low comedy of his own: "A knockout for laughs ... that will earn you more good will than free storage for homeless mother-in-laws."[35] From Ellinwood, Kansas, came, "Will please all of Joe E. Brown's fans, and that means extra business, as Joe is plenty well liked in the small towns," while a Greenville, Illinois, theater owner said, "Here's a picture you will do extra business with or I am greatly mistaken. I consider it Brown's best picture ... Held up exceedingly well the second night, which is very unusual for any picture at the present [Depression] time."[36] In tracking more than a dozen of these *Elmer* small market mini-reviews over several months (today's simultaneous saturation theater booking was many years away), I found *all* the critiques to be equally laudatory.

Comically, the only real *Elmer* complaint had nothing to do with artistic values. During Brown's previously cited gargantuan breakfast scene, part of his comedy schtick involved trying to drink coffee with a spoon in his cup. Instead of merely removing the utensil, Brown's simple-minded Elmer bent the spoon in half over the side of the cup — a comically drastic, yet effective action. This funny sequence produced hundreds of complaining letters from adult fans: Their copycat children had all but eliminated straight spoons from the silverware drawer![37] Consequently, after *Elmer* Brown attempted to be especially cognizant of his role-model image to young fans.

When Brown was later (1946) asked to guest-author *The Saturday Evening Post*'s regular feature "The Role I Liked Best...," he picked his screen Elmer. At that time he noted three reasons why the role was so special to him. First, the picture's director, Mervyn LeRey, "knew and loved baseballs, and therefore understood the situations completely."[38] Second, Brown felt Elmer was a touchingly real character from which natural comedy could be drawn. Third, "the best thing about the part was that during the days when I played ball on small town teams in Ohio, Indiana and Michigan I had come to know and admire many Elmers."[39]

Before moving on to another classic Lardner baseball figure played by Brown, Alibi Ike, I should note that the comedian never completely left his beloved Elmer behind. Indeed, even before his screen version of *Elmer* was released, he had starred in another highly successful Los Angeles stage production of the property. Limited to only 20 performances in late 1932, the El Capitan Theater was "faced with a mathematical problem ... how to accommodate the theatergoers who have been requesting to see Joe E. Brown in *Elmer the Great*."[40] On October 5, 1936, paralleling World Series time, the comedian did scenes from *Elmer* on radio's then–highly rated prestige program *Lux Radio Theater*. During the summer of 1940 he revived *Elmer* for a limited run at the Cape Playhouse in Dennis, Massachusetts. And in 1947 the comedian recorded a two-disc album entitled *How to Play Baseball*. Described as diamond lessons "lightened with humor," the album features Brown "[explaining the] refinements of the national pastime to a boy named Elmer...."[41] Having a surrogate disc audience answer to Elmer is fitting, given that some of his biggest foreign fans often thought of his baseball trilogy as synonymous with Elmer. For example, as noted in Chapter One, during World War II "Japanese prisoners who could speak English said they had seen his *Elmer the Great* movies. They wanted to talk baseball."[42]

In the roughly two years between Brown's movie version of *Elmer the Great* and his third baseball picture, *Alibi Ike* (1935), the comedian would appear in four other films — *Son of a Sailor* (1933), *Very Honorable Guy*, *The Circus Clown* and *6-Day Biker Rider* (all 1934). The three best movies in this grouping had Brown doubling as an athlete: a boxing sailor, a gymnastic clown and a champion cyclist. But, for three reasons, his most entertaining sports-related picture, baseball or otherwise, is *Alibi Ike*. First, unlike his previous two cinematic baseball stars, who were both initially reluctant players (distracted by fires and love), Ike is totally focused on the game. In fact, his first appearance in the picture — smashing through the center field fence in an out-of-control automobile — is a perfect metaphor for the explosive enthusiasm he brings to the sport. Second, Brown has an impressive supporting cast, starting with a future two-time Academy Award winner as his leading lady, Olivia de Havilland. The previous year (1934), famed German stage producer-director Max Reinhardt had chosen her to appear as Hermia in a Hollywood Bowl production of *A Midsummer Night's Dream* and in Warners' 1935 screen adaptation (which would include Brown and an all-star cast). This Reinhardt attention had gotten de Havilland a Warners contract, with her first screen appearance being *Alibi Ike*, though the *Midsummer* screen adaptation was actually shot prior to Brown's baseball film. *Alibi Ike*'s cast also featured the gruff but lovable William Frawley as the Cubs' manager. Best-remembered today as Fred Mertz in the classic TV sitcom *I Love Lucy* (1951–57), Frawley also had many memorable movie roles in support of comedy kingpins — *Professor Beware* (1938, Harold Lloyd), *Monsieur Verdoux* (1947, Charlie Chaplin) and *The Lemon Drop Kid* (1951, Bob Hope). Besides Frawley, *Alibi Ike* had two other high-profile character actors — Roscoe Karns and Ruth Donnelly, both of whom specialized in playing fast-talking insiders.

A third justification for calling *Alibi Ike* Brown's best sports picture is tied to the strong writing. For example, when Frawley's character asks Ike how many games he won in the minors the previous year, Brown's pitcher unloads the movie's best comic alibi, "Only 28, had malaria most of the season." But the humor does not stop there. Frawley's manager gets a comic comeback, "Where can I send the rest of our pitchers to get it [malaria]?" Or, when Frawley wants to see his rookie at the plate, Brown alibis, "Of course, I don't bat my best on Wednesday." The manager's snappy reply even tops the busher: "Don't you worry about that, I'll cancel all the Wednesday games." Writing credit must go to Lardner (with a variation of the malaria line in the original short story, too[43]) and screenwriter William Wister Haines.

Paradoxically, while Hollywood changed Lardner's Elmer from a pitcher to a hitter, they reversed the process with Ike — the slugger became a great hurler. The catalyst for this transformation was probably twofold. First, the previous year St. Louis pitching star Dizzy Dean had emerged as the living embodiment of a Ring Lardner egotistical, alibi-spouting country boy (see Chapter Two). Moreover, when Brown interacted with Dean, both during and after the celebrated 1934 World Series, the public undoubtedly further connected these two entertainers as similar free spirits. Plus, the zany antics of Dizzy were not limited to the sports page. On April 15, 1935, he made the cover of *Time* magazine, with the accompanying article noting:

> [I]t was clear that with Shirley Temple, Father Coughlin, the Dionne Quintuplets and Mrs. Roosevelt, Jerome Herman Dean was definitely one of that small company of super-celebrities whose names, faces and occupations are familiar to every U. S. citizen and whose antics, gracious or absurd, become the legend of their time.[44]

Thus, it was only natural that Warners' *Alibi Ike* would attempt to trade upon the Lardner-Dean-Brown connections, such as this bit of dialogue from William Frawley's manager after Brown's egotistical Ike vainly states that he must not realize who he is. Frawley retorts, "Sure I do. You're Dizzy Dean. But you've had your face lifted to fool the batters." Therefore, the Lardner-Dean-Brown link is often addressed in period reviews, from the *New York American*'s opening, "A Dizzy, Daffy (Dean) comedy of the baseball diamond, starring Joe Brown in a character as only Ring Lardner could conceive...," to the *Hollywood Reporter* observation, "Joe E. is cast as [a] screwball, more than slightly resembling the great Dizzy Dean."[45] The *New York Herald Tribune* even gave their review opening a soothsayer's slant, "Back in the days when Ring Lardner, with an artist's foresight was predicting the career of Dizzy Dean, he created an epic character called Alibi Ike."[46]

A second possible reason to turn Ike into a pitcher is to capitalize on all his comic parallels with Lardner's hurler Jack Keefe, created just a year before Ike (1914). For instance, when one reads the Keefe stories collected as *You Know Me Al: A Busher's Letters*, one immediately thinks he should also have been called Alibi. For instance, here is Keefe's take on how the great Ty Cobb got on base: "I pitched a spitter and Cobb bunts it right at me. I would of threw him out a block but I stubbed my toe in a rough place and fell down. This is the roughest ground I ever seen Al."[47] Or get a load of why Keefe's single could have been a double: "I took my healthy [cut] at the next one [pitch] and slapped it over first base. I guess I could of made two bases on it but I didn't want to tire myself out."[48]

There are enough parallels between all three of Brown's small-town simple-minded braggart ballplayers that sometimes even the comedian got confused. To illustrate, it was noted earlier that Brown drew part of his Elmer characterization from Phillies player Harry Frank "The Giant Killer" Coveleski. In the comedian's autobiography, he reveals that there is even a comic Coveleski incident recycled in his *Elmer* movie, where the title character's full wind-up with a man on first allowed the baserunner to steal second.[49] When the manager complained, the pitcher, with his brain in neutral, alibied that he had somehow been unaware of the runner, which provoked an inspired touch of managerial sarcasm that went over the player's head. *However*, in Brown's screen version of *Elmer* his title character is *not* a pitcher. The comedian is remembering a scene from *Alibi Ike*. The sequence unwinds just as described, with William Frawley's manager then calling the team together, and with tongue firmly in cheek, observing:

> From now on there ain't going to be no more secrets. I mean, not telling each other what's going on. Here's a guy [Ike] that wound up with a runner on first just because nobody told him the man was there. Now, after this when a man gets to first base, I don't want anyone to keep it secret from the pitcher!

Like Coveleski, Ike thinks the manager is criticizing the team, and compliments their leader, "That a boy, Cap [Frawley]...." To add to the confusion (or is that just character consistency), Lardner describes a scene reminiscent of the Coveleski-Ike example in one of his Jack Keefe stories from *You Know Me Al: A Busher's Letters*: "Cobb was on first base. First thing I knowed he had stole second while I held the ball. [Manager]

Brown demonstrates his trademark corckscrew windup in *Alibi Ike* (1935, with manager William Frawley).

Callahan yells Wake up out there and I says Why don't your catcher tell me when they are going to steal."[50]

Regardless, Brown's *Alibi Ike* chronicles the success of Lardner's title character during his rookie season with the Chicago Cubs. As in the author's original short story, this is a figure who alibis about everything, including the game of pool. After making a difficult shot against a teammate (impressively staged with an overhead camera placement), Alibi echoes his name by observing, "I ain't so good at this game, we don't play much pool back home." Ike's perennial excuses also lead to a pivotal scene in both Lardner's story and the adaptation — the temporary derailing of the character's romance. After Brown's Ike is kidded about being engaged, he says, "Sometimes a fella don't know exactly what he's getting into. Take a good-lookin' girl and a fella does just about what she wants him to do. When a fella gets to feeling sorry for a girl, it's all off [he's hooked]."

Unfortunately, this banter with his buddies is overheard by Dolly (Olivia de Havilland) and she calls off the engagement. (Ironically, though the statement might be

82

inflammatory for a lover, there is more comic wisdom here than in the usual dialogue from a Lardner ballplayer — sense in the nonsense.) Not surprisingly, the loss of Dolly impacts Elmer's pitching and the Cubs' chances for a pennant.

At this point, the screen adaptation interjects a new wrinkle — gamblers put pressure upon Ike to lose his last two starts for the Cubs. With the Chicago team heavily favored when Alibi pitches, this would be a huge windfall for the betting racket. And after Brown's character drops the first game through grief at losing Dolly, the gamblers mistakenly feel Ike is playing along. When they realize otherwise, the pitcher is kidnapped. (The 1932 abduction of Charles Lindbergh's baby helped fuel both the fear of kidnapping in real life, and its depiction in the popular arts of this era.)

The abduction of Ike allows the picture to replicate a finale factor of Brown's two previous baseball films — the comedian's ballplayer reaches the pivotal game at the eleventh hour. This time Ike escapes his kidnappers by way of using the very ambulance in which he had been abducted. When he ultimately crashes said vehicle through the outfield wall at the pennant-deciding game, the picture has come full circle from his similar stadium wall-shattering introduction.

The plate umpire will not delay this night game for Brown's Ike to get in uniform. But a forgiving Dolly is at the park and she manages to briefly shut down the stadium power and the resulting blackout enables Ike to change. But the uniform we suddenly see him in is many sizes too big. Consequently, Brown's subsequent comic schtick is amplified by what is literally a clown costume. (This anticipates the comic oversized uniform later worn by diamond funnyman Max Patkin, "Clown Prince of Baseball," who was featured in *Bull Durham*, 1988.) Brown's outfit soon proves to be an amusing liability, too, when Ike loses an in-play ball within this maze of clothing and the Giants tie the score. But when the Cubs come to bat in the bottom of the ninth, Ike hits a game-winning, inside-the-park home run. His amusingly speedy circling of the bases, encased in the oversized outfit, is then inspiringly topped by his eluding of the catcher's tag with a gymnastic somersault (ever the acrobat!) *over* said player and a safe slide home. The Cubs win the pennant and, in a brief epilogue, Ike marries Dolly.

This extremely entertaining baseball saga is further assisted by several additional ties to the national game, both from the sport's past history, and mid–1930s developments. First, besides using footage of real Major Leaguers, there are pertinent references to legendary ballplayers. Besides the aforementioned Frawley reference to Dizzy Dean, this manager also draws a parallel between Ike and Rube Waddell, the fire engine–obsessed pitcher who was an unofficial model for Brown's character in *Fireman, Save My Child*. Frawley himself plays a figure named Cap, which goes back to Lardner's original story. This is an obvious reference to pioneering ballplayer Cap Anson, the Hall of Famer sometimes considered the game's first superstar. More to point for the Chicago Cubs–focused *Alibi Ike*, Anson was also the very successful manager of Chicago's first National League team.

Brown's title character antics in *Alibi Ike* also play upon famous incidents associated with celebrated baseball stars. At one point, Ike attempts to show off his pitching by calling his teammates to the mound and throwing with no defensive support behind him. This tall tale–like example of ego has been attributed to a plethora of pitchers, from Waddell and Dean to Satchel Paige. When Ike drives his car onto the field, one is reminded of legendary pitcher Christy Mathewson. While "Matty" did not crash his automobile through walls, he did use the presence of an expensive car as an intimidation factor. Mathewson could also be a free spirit, such as his weakness for coasting with a big lead. In one such situation, he loaded the bases and immediately had a manager reading him the riot act. His response, "Take it easy, it's more fun this way."[51] He then struck out the side.

Late in *Alibi Ike*, a newsboy asks Brown's character a variation of the famous line allegedly requested by a boy of Shoeless Joe Jackson when he was first accused of helping "fix" the 1919 World Series — "Say it ain't so, Joe." The connection with Ike is that he, too, is thought to be in on a gambling fix, though that is not the case. In fact, *Alibi Ike* reverses the process by ultimately having the newsboy be an informant for the betting ring. Brown's picture even has a Major League footnote that involves the comedian himself. During the previous year's (1934) World Series, Detroit pitcher Schoolboy Rowe claimed that a strong handshake from Brown had injured his hand, a ludicrous claim which produced comic headlines across the country (see Chapter Two). Flash forward to 1935's *Alibi Ike*: Brown's character declines to shake hands with his manager before pitching in the finale, feeling it would be safer to wait until after the game! (Earlier in the picture, Ike had blamed a homer he gave up on having received too many congratulatory handshakes after one of his wins.) As the *Los Angeles Times'* review observed, "A sports reporter really should cover *Alibi Ike* at Warner's downtown theater. It's that technical so far as its baseball is concerned."[52]

Brown's picture was also up on the latest developments in Major League Baseball. Its crucial concluding contest is a night game. Though this phenomenon can be first traced to two obscure late nineteenth century games, the Major League's groundbreaking regularly scheduled night games began with seven Cincinnati Reds contests during the 1935 season.[53] The initial game (May 24) was played just two months before the East Coast opening of *Alibi Ike*.

For all the attention to baseball detail showered upon *Alibi Ike*, the picture does commit one error: While Brown's Cubs are said to be playing the New York Giants, the uniforms of their rivals showcase the logo of the St. Louis Cardinals. There is no obvious explanation but two theories come to mind. First, since Brown's characterization was influenced by Harry Frank "The Giant Killer" Coveleski, whose long-ago pitching exploits once derailed a New York Giants pennant drive, maybe Warners and/or Brown decided to honor this connection. Second, *Alibi Ike* generated a lot of connections being made between Lardner's character and St. Louis' Dizzy Dean. Maybe the powers that be felt having Brown's movie team then play the Cardinals would be overkill.

This small-potatoes discrepancy notwithstanding, *Alibi Ike* was yet another critical and commercial hit for Brown. As the *Hollywood Reporter* reviewer said, "With Joe E. Brown in a baseball story its happiness ahead for everybody, producer, audience and critics."[54] The *New York Post* called it "a one hundred and ten per cent American comedy-drama ... and if it fails to move you either to mirth or excitement then you better go back to Union Square or wait until the next Russian film comes to the Cameo [Theatre]."[55] The *New York Times'* high praise started by calling Brown a studio icon — "Joe E. Brown, who is to Warners what Garbo is to Metro [MGM] and Shirley Temple is to Fox, returns to Times Square (via the Cameo) in a genuinely amusing little comedy patterned after one of Ring Lardner's most famous baseball stories...."[56] The title of *New York Evening Journal* critic Rose Pelswick's July 17, 1935, review might have best summed up all these kudos: "Joe E. Brown Amusingly Plays Goofy Pitcher in Baseball Classic."

As was the norm by this time, Brown's direct links with the national game were grist for reviews. This recognition could be purely informational, such as the *New York Sun* critic Eileen Creelman stating his "knowledge of baseball includes some professional playing as well as a current part ownership in a team ..."[57] But reviewers could also wax poetic on the subject, as *New York Daily News* critic Wanda Hale does in her *Alibi Ike* critique:

> It is said of [Brown] that had he never learned his funny face was his fortune he should have followed the game of hit and run for a livelihood. Thus when Joseph dons a monkey suit and performs a feat of magic with what our sports writers call "the old apple," he does so with more than cinematic proficiency.[58]

Mixing Brown's lifelong love of baseball with critical hosannas such as these, and having 1935 find him back on the box office top ten list, is it any wonder that he would later write, "I think my best motion pictures were baseball stories. But pictures are only fantasies. My real-life [baseball] interests were stronger than that. I even mixed baseball with business [from a studio team to part-owner of the Kansas City Blues]."[59] For such a quintessential American comedian, what would make more sense than a defining trilogy based upon the national game. While one could bemoan the fact that he never returned to baseball in a screen role, at least the legacy of *Fireman, Save My Child, Elmer the Great* and *Alibi Ike* remain to savor.

❖ SEVEN ❖

Between the Baseball Pictures: 1932–34

In the tradition of his entertainingly egotistical ballplayers, Joe E. Brown's title character in *Son of a Sailor* (1933) brags at a party, "So I says to the admiral, no use landing a flock of Marines. Just land me and I'll put down that uprising in a hurry."

Charles Dickens' classic opening to *A Tale of Two Cities* (1859), "It was the best of times, it was the worst of times…," is a universal axiom that might be applied to any era. But the saying seems especially applicable to the early 1930s. America was struggling through its worst-ever Depression, yet Hollywood was in the beginning stages of what has come to be called its Golden Age — producing an escapist elixir for a troubled nation and world. At the beginning of the Great Depression, America's 123 million population attended nearly a movie *every week* — numbers we are still nowhere near today. President Franklin D. Roosevelt would observe, "During the Depression, when the spirit of the people is lower than at any time, it is a splendid thing that for just 15 cents an American can go to a movie and look at the smiling face of a baby and forget his troubles."[1] And though sports' own "Golden Age" of the 1920s was past, the American public still had a litany of athletic champions to follow, from life imitating art with the breezy Ring Lardner–Joe E. Brown–like baseball pitcher Dizzy Dean, to the blue-collar sluggers Lou Gehrig and Hank Greenberg. Moreover, given the Depression times, 1930s sports were often about underdog heroes, such as James Braddock's amazing 1935 upset of heavyweight boxing champion Max Baer. The win was so unlikely, Braddock became known as the "Cinderella Man." This was a perfect underdog backdrop for Brown's non-baseball sports figures, who often struggled to victory. Appropriately, this "Cinderella" reference was applied to Brown's characters even before Braddock. *Variety* described Joe's anti-heroic swimmer in *You Said a Mouthful* (1932) as having "a certain distorted Cinderella quality," and the *New York Sun* called the eventual success of his wannabe circus gymnast–high wire artist in *The Circus Clown* (1934) a classic "Cinderella Story."[2]

For Brown, the 1930s were the "best of times"; the comedian later wrote of this period, "If I never got anything else besides those years between 1930 and 1940, I would have had it [all]."[3] Happily married to Kathryn, he doted on his burgeoning family — two teenage sons, two adopted baby daughters and several other youngsters who were unofficially adopted by the Browns. Like Miriam Marx's (Groucho's oldest daughter) funhouse description of her Uncle Harpo's home at the same time, Joe and Kathryn's place was also a magnet for neighborhood children.[4] Adding to this "playhouse" environment was an abundance of food, including that dispensed at its real ice cream parlor. Brown never forgot what it was like to always be hungry as a child, with comic eating scenes surfacing in many of his 1930s films, too. The comedian's studio biography from this period wryly states, "He dislikes early morning [studio shooting] calls. If he is awakened, however, by the younger Browns, he will play with them and overlook the fact that it is time to get to the studio. His favorite pet is a wirehaired terrier."[5]

The comedian enjoyed describing his "joiner" nature as belonging "to more clubs than a retired Iowan." (California was an especially popular retirement home for Iowans during the 1920s and '30s.) Plus, Brown's "people person" nature (a trait he inherited from his club-joining mother) had him accepting every invitation to make a public appearance. In fact, one could recycle an old vaudeville gag to describe the comedian's proclivity for accessibility: "He would go to the opening of an envelope." For instance, the following *Hollywood Reporter* news item was typical of his non-stop 1930s itinerary: "Joe E. Brown is to be crowned King of the Raisin Carnival here [Lodi, California] today. He arrived from Hollywood by plane last night. Tomorrow the Warner star goes to the Sacramento [California] State fair as a guest of honor for the day."[6] As he later confessed, "Home is swell, but I'm still a ham at heart. I always want to be out doing a show."[7] This hectic public appearance routine was, of course, sandwiched between the time spent making two or more films each year.

Despite this fast-paced existence, Brown's screen appearance for much of the 1930s remained surprisingly youthful, given that he turned 40 in 1932. Like most film clowns, his persona had direct ties to being young. For example, many of his movies during this decade might be described as coming-of-age stories, where a small-town boy, or college undergraduate, pulls his life together. Brown would not have been credible had he looked his age. Moreover, the youthful slant often goes beyond the mere needs of plotlines. Since so many of our favorite funnymen are mischievous metaphorical variations upon Greek mythology's Pan (the god of field, forests and wild animals), there is a certain incongruity in their aging. This phenomenon helps explain why getting old was more of a problem for Harpo Marx's very Pan-like persona, while brother Groucho's proverbial dirty old man (which he began playing as a teen) allowed him to have the much longer career. During the 1930s, Brown's case had much more in common with the youthful needs of a Harpo. Paradoxically, when Brown later played a dirty old man himself in *Some Like It Hot* (1959), he had not simply grown into the part, *à la* Groucho. His Osgood character, the millionaire smitten with Jack Lemmon in drag, works precisely because it is an incongruity with what the Brown

Brown and daughters Mary Elizabeth (right) and Kathryn Frances.

persona stands for — youthful innocence. *Some Like It Hot* writer-director Billy Wilder cast Brown for this reason — to make an inherently provocative part palatable. Brown's Osgood defuses any chance of controversy and somehow even imbues this old womanizer with a sense of poignancy. (Pictures of Brown's mother through the years consistently showcase a woman who looks younger than her age. Anna lived to be 94, dying in 1961.)

For all Brown's 1930s youthfulness, this was the decade in which his early rough-and-tumble years as an acrobat caught up with him. Beginning in 1932, the comedian would periodically be hospitalized for treatment and/or surgery related to an old spinal injury.[8] The slapstick nature of Brown's movie career had further exacerbated these back problems, as would a later (1939) automobile accident. But true to his good-natured image, on-screen and off-, he always treated these hospital visits with patented Brown humor. For instance, when the aforementioned car accident also necessitated a number of facial stitches, he riffed some self-deprecating humor at the expense of his oversized kisser: "Might have been a good idea to have sewed up part of my mouth while you were at it," he told the doctor through a painful grin.[9]

Just as the coming of sound had helped Brown's screen career, with that signature yell from his "cavernous mouth," the censorship code of 1934 was a further boon to his Warners work. While a comedienne like Mae West, whose métier was double entendres, was limited by this blue-nose development, Brown's small-town persona (whether the smart aleck or the milquetoast type) had no need to change. Ironically, as noted in Chapter Five, some of his early sound films included racy lines and/or situations. Yet, they were not intrinsic to his character. Indeed, one could call Brown "censorship proof."

Even when his movies had provocative (for the period) material, the general public just saw a clean comic. To illustrate, his pre–Code classic *Elmer the Great* (1933) was not without obscenities, such as when his baseball manager tells him to warm up before going to bat. Brown's title character responds, "Warm up? Hell, I ain't been cool since February!" Yet, when one reads the *Elmer* mini-reviews by small-town theater owners in the "What the Picture Did For Me section" of the *Motion Picture Herald*, the optimal word amidst all the praise is "clean." From Malta, Montana, came, "Good clean fun," while a Lebanon, Kansas, theater owner said, "The kind of show it is a pleasure to exhibit. Funny as they make 'em but clean."[10] The same superlatives and "clean" comments surface in the *Herald* mini-reviews for the pre–Code follow-up to *Elmer*, *Son of a Sailor*. This picture was not without its provocative scenes, such as the sexy near-seduction of Brown's title sailor by the attractively curvaceous Thelma Todd. But a Greenville, Michigan, theater owner wrote, "Clean and entertaining and very funny," a critique seconded by both a Montgomery City, Missouri, theater operator, "Swell comedy. Clean as a hound's tooth..." and an owner in Aron Park, Florida, "An excellent Joe Brown [film] and clean as a whistle."[11]

Though Brown's predisposition for family entertainment stretched back to his earliest days on stage, the nature of these mini-reviews and other pre–Code comments from heartland theater owners would have been hard to ignore, especially for someone who monitored his public as closely as Brown. Moreover, this small-town fan base sometimes coupled censorship-related *advice* and/or heart-to-heart *revelations* with their reinforcement of "clean" comedy. For example, a Montpelier, Idaho, theater operator noted of *You Said a Mouthful* (1932), "When Brown comes to town the people know they are going to get an evening's entertainment instead of one evening of [controversial] agony. Keep 'em clean, Joe, and you will have [Harold] Lloyd, Chaplin and all the rest backed off the map."[12] A similar perspective on *Son of a Sailor* came from Menard, Texas: "a dandy clean comedy, the best Brown has had yet and that's saying a good deal. Warners make so few pictures that can be used in the small town on Friday and Saturday that we always put Brown on those dates..."[13] But the most angst-ridden railing against provocative early 1930s entertainment to surface in a positive Brown mini-review came from a critique of *You Said a Mouthful.* The Napa, Idaho, theater owner stated, "Old but refreshing, as it had no connection with the depressing, disgusting best-sellers now being made into pictures, much to the pain of the folk hereabout who still venture to buy tickets...."[14] Comments such as these would have undoubtedly further cemented Brown's commitment to family entertainment.

Unlike so many entertainment celebrities who initially handle fame poorly, if at all, Brown managed to remain "common," to utilize a popular 1930s phrase. That is, he did not let all that success inflate his hat size. Of course, there were a few lapses. For a time he kept a stable of race horses, the luxury of a man whose salary eventually climbed to $100,000 a picture. (During the Depression, hired help on a Midwestern farm frequently worked for a dollar a day, plus room and board.) Paradoxically ... or maybe *appropriately*, given his comic background ... Brown's horses never did very well in competition. The comedian also once had Warners "recall thousands of movie posters because his name was not printed in big enough type."[15] But his strong marriage helped work as an effective brake on any egotistical lapses. For instance, in 1931 Kathryn felt Joe was "going Hollywood" and gifted him with a $16,500 Duesenberg, at a time when a new Chevy cost $600. "That's a pretty snazzy buggy, Mom," he said. "Who do we know who can afford it?" Kathryn replied, "Nobody. But *we* own it. I figured if we can afford race horses we can afford a Duesenberg."[16] Movie star Joe got the message. His studio biography for the following year noted, "He has two moderate-priced automobiles. He believes in living within his income and making sensible investments...."[17] And yes, the horses were gone, too.

Attempting to lead a practical private life was consistent with Brown's movie career — such as taking parts which enabled him to utilize his athletic skills, especially as it pertained to baseball. But he could not be a ballplayer in every picture. Interspersed among his diamond trilogy of *Fireman, Save My Child* (1932), *Elmer the Great* (1933), and *Alibi Ike* (1935), were five additional pictures: *The Tenderfoot, You Said a Mouthful* (both 1932), *Son of a Sailor* (1933), *The Circus Clown* and *6-Day Bike Rider* (both 1934). Fittingly, four of these films have their own sports subplots, too. *Mouthful* is about marathon swimming. *Sailor* has him as a boxing seaman. *Clown* has Joe putting his gymnastic skills to use in the circus. *Rider* keys on endurance cycling. While one can trace Brown's athletic movie connection back to his boxer in *Hold Everything* (1930), a better starting point is his track star picture *Local Boy Makes Good* (1931). This is implied in a 1933 *Motion Picture Herald* mini-review of *Elmer the Great*. Indeed, this capsule critique also suggests dating Brown's emergence as a star comic to the sports-related *Local Boy*: "Two seasons ago Brown was only an average bet. Since this series of athletic pictures [which started with *Local Boy*] he has grown rapidly and everyone likes him."[18] (A late 1932 *Variety* review of *You Said a Mouthful* had also referred back to *Local Boy* as "Brown's high water mark."[19])

The beauty of this development is that Brown's ongoing interest and involvement in sports during the 1930s further fueled these athletic plots and subplots. While the comedian's sports activities during the decade have already peppered this text, here are some additional high-profile examples. During 1932 the studio baseball teams of Brown and Buster Keaton helped raise money for the summer Olympics, held in Los Angeles that year. Always a fixture at the World Series, during the 1930s Joe haunted UCLA athletic events even more, partly because his sons were varsity football players. His many activities for the university resulted in his receiving a letterman's sweater (the first ever for a non-player), and having a UCLA baseball field named after him. Already part-owner of a minor league baseball team, in 1934 Brown acquired the controlling interest in former Golden Gloves boxing champion Lou Jallos,[20] who was from the comedian's home state of Ohio. Brown also found a small part for Jallos in *6-Day Bike Rider*. (Before Major League baseball came to the West Coast in the 1950s, following boxing was a much favored pastime for the movie colony.) In 1936 the comedian accompanied the American Olympic team to Berlin and "scandalized Nazi dignitaries by undiplomatic noises whenever, as frequently happened, he considered their rulings incorrect."[21] During April and May 1937, Brown spent four weeks in Chicago doing radio broadcasts for both the Cubs and the White Sox.[22] (In two of his three baseball pictures, he was a Cub player.) In early spring 1937, he brought his *Alibi Ike* to the airwaves' prestige program *Lux Radio Theater*. (The previous fall, *Lux* had showcased Brown in a radio version of *Elmer the Great*.) The comedian was a popular emcee at athletic dinners during the decade, with the crowning achievement for "Pacific Toastmaster Brown" being his hosting of Notre Dame's football banquet for 1938 — a national championship year for the Irish. The event received a great deal of national publicity, such as the *Indianapolis News* article with the punning title, "Notre Dame Grid Banquet Done Up Good and Brown."[23] Besides all the sports and comedy-related reasons to have Brown as host, his selection was also, no doubt, a product of the comedian's very popular football film *The Gladiator* (1938) having opened that same fall.

With all this athletic activity, the first of Brown's pictures interspersed in the baseball trilogy, *The Tenderfoot*, gives the comic a break from sports. Yet this screen adaptation of celebrated playwright George S. Kaufman's *The Butter and Egg Man* is not without ties to Brown's film athletics. A thumbnail sketch of the story has a small-town type coming to New York and being conned into investing his family nest egg in a turkey stage production, which he naturally nurses into a hit. Kaufman's original title character was a milquetoast, but Brown plays him as a confidently breezy Texas cowboy — very much in the tradition of his Ring Lardner ballplayers. While Brown's screen *Elmer* had not yet been made, the comedian had successfully played the part on stage. Consistent with this link, *The Tenderfoot* also has an overeating breakfast scene which seems straight out of *Elmer*. Egotistical or not, both of these entertaining simpletons are easily distracted by food.

The *Tenderfoot* huckster who hoodwinks Brown's character, Peter Jones, is effectively played by Lew Cody. But this con artist's trump card is utilizing a pretty girl (Ginger Rogers in an early role) as romantic bait. Rogers' character is a secretary to Cody's wheeler-dealer Broadway producer, but she soon feels remorse over her actions and aligns herself with Brown. Rogers' guilt is driven, in part, by another plot point from *Elmer*— Brown's character in each picture is amazingly close to his mother. Thus, when Jones dictates a loving letter home, secretary Rogers realizes she has taken advantage of a sappy but sweet small-town fellow. (Rogers is another Brown leading lady who would later go on to win a Best Actress Academy Award.)

Despite the Kaufman connection, the film is most effective today for its basic Brown schtick, such as his oven-sized mouth making with a Texas-sized "*Whoopee!*" every time something pleases him. In one scene, his cowboy character has just arrived in New York's theater district when he spots what appears to be several fellow Texans, in Western regalia, entering a Broadway café. Overjoyed at seeing some down-home types, he unleashes his patented window-rattling "*Whoopee!*" But when his cowpokes turn around in this pre–Code picture, they are very obviously gay actors in Western garb, with heavy makeup and thin penciled-in eyebrows. This is comic surprise number one. But these sagebrush sissies then double the comic quotient by serenading Brown's manly man with their own most effeminate chorus of "*Whoopee!*" Brown's inspired startled expression anticipates Judy Garland's later *Wizard of Oz* (1939) line, "Toto, I have a feeling we're not in Kansas any more."

This *Tenderfoot* adaptation is also interesting today for its time capsule reflection of that era's fascination with the modern gangster film. The genre had taken off with the release of two watershed works, *Little Caesar* (1930) and *The Public Enemy* (1931). In fact, the same issue of *Variety* (May 24, 1932) that reviewed *Tenderfoot* also had a critique of *Scarface* (1932), the third signature gangster picture from this era. Consequently, Brown's film adds kidnapping hoods in the final reel, a new twist to the Kaufman story. And while period reviews occasionally implied opportunism, such as the *New York World-Telegram*'s aside, "as a sop to audiences who like gangster pictures," the comic confrontations between Brown's cowboy and the New York hoods play very effectively.[24] With the comedian on horseback using his trusty lariat, these scenes anticipate a comic *Coogan's Bluff* (1968) or the more humor-laced television series spawned

Cowboy Brown visits New York City in *The Tenderfoot* (1932, with a young Ginger Rogers).

by that film, *McCloud* (1970–77). Regardless, mixing clown comedy and gangster parody during the early 1930s was a popular phenomenon, and probably most entertainingly showcased in the Marx Brothers' *Monkey Business* (1931). Brown himself would later return to this combination on several occasions, including *Wide Open Faces* (1938), the underrated *So You Won't Talk* (1940) and, of course, *Some Like It Hot*.

Though *Variety* felt *The Tenderfoot* was not up to the comic standards of Brown's previous picture *Fireman, Save My Child*, the reviews for the Kaufman adaptation were uniformly good.[25] For example, under the headline "Delightful Picture," the *New York Evening Journal* described *Tenderfoot* as "an amusing farce that drew appreciative howls yesterday afternoon from Joe E. Brown admirers."[26] The *New York Times* appreciated the comedian's "opportunity to call attention to his capacious mouth" and said "Mr. Brown gives quite a humorous showing...."[27] His *Tenderfoot* performance even converted some critics, such as the *New York Sun*'s Stephen Rathbun:

> Mr. Brown is much funnier than I had expected him to be. Indeed, he is very funny. From the time when he arrives at the Grand Central Station up to the end of the

picture his comedy seldom misses fire. That is a lot to say for any comedian ... But it was the star himself who surprised me. He can act when occasion requires it and his comic antics made me laugh.[28]

With *Variety* measuring *The Tenderfoot* against Brown's previous baseball picture, and the *New York Times*' *Tenderfoot* opening notice featuring an athletic-oriented mini-biography of the comedian, it is hardly surprising that the Kaufman adaptation was followed with another sports-related film, *You Said a Mouthful*.[29] Brown plays an Iowa inventor who creates a sink-proof swimsuit — perfect for people afraid of the water, like himself. Taking a cue from earlier mistaken-identity plotlines in Brown's *Top Speed* (1930) and *Going Wild* (1931), *You Said a Mouthful* has the comedian innocently mistaken for a marathon swimmer. This coincides with Joe's visit to California shortly before the $25,000 race from Catalina Island to the mainland. But unlike the breezy extroverts he played in the earlier mistaken-identity stories, *You Said a Mouthful* has Brown reverting to his milquetoast persona — last seen in the botanist-turned-sprinter tale *Local Boy Makes Good* (1931). Throughout the comedian's tenure at Warner Brothers, the studio did a good job of alternating Brown between his two small-town types — the mild-mannered anti-hero and the self-centered smart aleck.

Despite this quasi-return to athleticism (Brown comically struggles as a swimmer), the film's most entertaining device is actually some art house parody at the expense of playwright Eugene O'Neill's 1928 *Strange Interlude*. The angst-ridden production had been adapted to the screen just a few months prior to Brown's *You Said a Mouthful*. A signature device in the original tragedy was periodic monologues in which characters express their inner thoughts, as the present is haunted by the past. With that in mind, *You Said a Mouthful* has an occasionally mournful Brown go deep-dish with his own special "strange interludes." For instance, shortly after he has both met the girl of his dreams and been mistaken for the "greatest long-distance swimmer of all time," his insecure character looks into the camera and one hears Brown in voice-over: "What is he driving at [a fellow swimming rival at a pre-race party]? I must watch this man. He suspects me. I saw the jealous, angry desire in his eyes for Alice [Ginger Rogers]. Alice — she likes me. It burns him up." The comedy here works on several levels. First, there is the simple element of surprise. One does not expect "strange interludes" in the normally non-cerebral world of Joe E. Brown. Second, there is the in-joke recognition factor — "Oh, they are spoofing such and such" — which drives all parody.[30] Third, this O'Neill device seems comically ludicrous when applied to subject matter far removed from tragedy.

Another example of this eccentric introspective technique has Joe (also his screen name here) comically carrying his anti-heroic nature to the intellectual voice-over: "What shall I say — that horrible [long-distance swimming] race again. [I see] love and pride and hope in [Alice's] eyes for the man she thinks I am. Why am I not heath [sic, I mean] ... him...." The mistake is funny because one is not supposed to get it wrong in your head. This is analogous to one of Charlie Chaplin's romantic fantasies in *The Idle Class* (1921), where he actually fails! To mess up in one's own daydreams, or a thinking-out-loud "strange interlude," is to be the ultimate anti-hero. These entertaining spoofs of O'Neill only suffer by comparison to Groucho Marx's earlier *Animal Crackers* (1930) take on this phenomenon. The mustached one's lines seem wittier, but more than that, we actually see Groucho deliver his "strange interlude" monologue, as opposed to Brown's voice-over. Any time a self-conscious device, like giving a voice to an internal monologue, is parodied, it becomes funnier the more obtrusive the break with a traditional narrative. Consequently, Brown's direct-address look at the camera, followed by his serious-toned voice-over ponderings, comically derail the *You Said a Mouthful* storyline. But it is still more amusingly disruptive to actually see Groucho speaking comparably otherworldly lines, like a possessed zombie clown. However, Brown might not have taken the Marx approach to avoid any copycat criticism.

Besides the period connection of spoofing O'Neill's play, having *You Said a Mouthful* key on an inventor (Brown) of a sink-proof bathing suit works on two additional Depression-era levels. First, there is the escapist dream of getting rich with some pie-in-the-sky scheme. In 1934, W.C. Fields would follow a similar path with his *You're Telling Me* (even his title is reminiscent of Brown's), where Fields finds wealth inventing a puncture-proof tire. Second, Joe's sink-proof trunks also represent an equalizer in a difficult time, especially when the central character is attempting to win a long-distance race ... despite being afraid of the water! Of course, as often happens in a clown comedy, the quasi-magic item gets switched, and our hero–anti-hero manages to succeed, as long as he is misinformed. Had Joe been given one more "strange interlude," he might have then spoofed through some Horatio Alger-Harold Lloyd axiom about always having had that inner strength. Yet, enough other factors play into his winning marathon swim, such as briefly thinking he has a shark on his tail, that his victory feels as random as the Depression itself. Like the screen persona of his former Broadway colleague Harry Langdon, Brown prospers not so much by a Lloyd work ethic (though Joe has one, too) but rather by the "grace of God." This perspective would also explain why Lloyd's continued screen faith in old-fashioned values did not play as effectively during the chaotic Depression, while Brown's equally vulnerable yet haphazardly lucky figure spoke more to an unstable decade looking for its own change of luck. (In reality, Brown was an excellent swimmer, with his mother later often bragging about her son's fancy diving — more acrobatics — as a boy in Toledo's Swank Creek.)

Like a throwback to the great silent comedians, Brown's *You Said a Mouthful* has several memorable sight gags. A personal favorite for this biographer would be the one when the comedian emerges from the ocean, after a stroll on the bottom, looking like a seaweed mummy. This surrealistic bit might have come from Buster Keaton's earlier *The Navigator* (1924), with its own inventive underwater scenes. But *You Said* has an even larger number of winning verbal lines, maybe inspired by the picture's "strange interlude" segments. To illustrate: When Joe goes to a doctor for a physical, the physician finds a litany of complex-sounding ailments from which the comedian is suffering. Brown responds, "I wouldn't be a bit surprised to find that I'm dead." Earlier, after the doctor had noted a particularly long-winded disease, Joe observed with knowing under-statement, "My Elmer died of that in Dubuque." Later, when the comedian fights the giggles during the pre-race grease-down (for warmth and added buoyancy), girlfriend Ginger Rogers tells him, "Swim as you've never swum before." Brown, who is afraid of the water and *cannot* swim, answers with complete honesty, "That's the only way I can swim!"

As was becoming the norm for Brown, his *You Said a Mouthful* notices were espe-cially strong. Indeed, they do not get any better than the opening of Marguerite Taze-laar's *New York Herald Tribune* review: "Joe E. Brown's new picture at the Winter Garden [Theatre] will make you forget the depression and that a hard winter lies ahead. It is that kind of comedy ... spontaneously funny, without ever being maudlin or offensive."[31] (While Brown's audience has often been linked to men and boys, Tazelaar is just one of the many women critics of the 1930s to consistently give the comedian high marks.) The *New York World Telegram*'s William Boehnel nearly matched Taze-laar's superlatives: "By some trick of timing, combined with an inexhaustible supply of fresh witticisms ... Mr. Brown has succeeded in propelling himself into the front ranks of amusing screen wags. Perhaps *You Said a Mouthful* is the funniest of his pictures. I think so."[32] Both the *New York Sun* and the *New York Post* seconded the critical notion that this was his best picture.[33] In fact, Brown's reviews were so good, Warners ran a *Hollywood Reporter* composite quoting several critiques and punningly entitled it, "That's Saying a Mouthful! About JOE E. BROWN in *You Said a Mouthful*."[34] And given Brown's cavernous kisser, both *The New York Times* and the *New York Daily News* opined on how appropriate the film title's was, with the latter publication comically adding, "If any ordinary individual says a mouthful, it's not news. But when Joe E. Brown does that big little thing, it's like the man biting the dog ... And it's really awfully funny."[35]

At this point in Brown's career, he was truly on a creative roll. The hit *You Said a Mouthful* was followed by the now celebrated *Elmer the Great* (see Chapter Six). Impres-sively, the next outing, *Son of a Sailor*, was the best of the Brown pictures interspersed among his legendary baseball trilogy. As the cocky quote that opens this chapter sug-gests, the comedian's title sailor character is in the swaggering, confident mold of his ballplayers. Once again, the comedian is posing as a champion athlete — a boxer. But unlike earlier pictures, we do not initially know this posture to be false. First, peren-nial cinema sidekick Frank McHugh, here a fellow sailor, talks up the fact that Joe's character's father and grandfather were great fighters. Then an egotistical Brown, with the fitting name Handsome Callahan, implies that he manhandled arguably the great-est heavyweight champion in history —"Did you ever notice that lump in Jack Dempsey's ear?"

Only when he first attempts to dodge a tough fight on his ship, followed by trounc-ing in the ring, do we get the true comic picture. But his underdog bout provokes some of the picture's best lines. When one of his cornermen (former All-American football player Johnny Mack Brown — no relation) tries to encourage him with the comment, "You're not half licked yet," Joe responds, "No? You go in and take the other half." And when the comedian's second cornerman (McHugh) begins combing Joe's hair, the disheveled boxer comically complains, "What are you doing that for? I'll only get messed up again." Brown further expresses this funny fear factor between rounds when his handlers start to exit the corner as the bell for more abuse rings — "Hey, don't you fellas leave me!"

So how does this cavernous-mouthed comic escape a nasty ring fate? The ship's bugler distracts Brown's opponent, and Joe delivers a gift punch which knocks him out. But there are greater metaphorical upsets to come for this goofy-looking comedian, because his Handsome Callahan is a lady's man, too! Not since the diminutive, cross-eyed comic Ben Turpin accidentally managed — thanks to those eyes — to successfully flirt with two women simultaneously in the silent short subject *The Pride of Pikeville* (1927) has a movie comedy had such an unlikely lover as Brown. However, Callahan's romantic abilities are largely assisted by a most inventive routine — a pick-up story involving a pair of baby shoes. Brown had first briefly used this sketch, called "The Gob," on Broadway in the 1923–24 revue *Greenwich Village Follies* (see Chapter Three). *Sailor* provides Joe with several inspired variations of the routine, such as telling a pretty girl that the baby shoes were his own, and his mother gave them back to him so that he would both respect women and forever remain a little boy at heart! Moreover, Callahan's unlikely success anticipates the following line from the parody fantasy *Play It Again, Sam* (1972), just after Humphrey Bogart (Jerry Lacy) has given Woody Allen's character his own unbelievable pick-up story which works — "She bought it!"

Brown's multiple variations of the baby shoe routine (his sister's child, his brother's boy, etc.) are all "bought" by an assortment of pretty girls. One young lady is so moved by the sailor's shoe pitch (this time they allegedly belonged to Callahan's late father, and his mother wanted him to remember dear old Dad) that the girl actually wants the baby shoes for herself. This unusual twist allows Brown to dovetail the scene into comic absurdity. That is, when his character denies the request, claiming he would never be able to look his father in the face again, his surprised pick-up date responds, "I thought you said he was dead." Without missing a romantic con artist's beat, Joe's Callahan answers, "Well, that's the funny part about it; we've never been sure."

Ultimately, Brown ends up going home with a girl who turns out to be the granddaughter of an admiral. But the attraction is not so much romance as the draw of a hifalutin party (or, as Joe comically described it to another Navy guest, "She said that [Benito] Mussolini, 11 admirals and Babe Ruth were going to be here"). Just as Callahan's boxing match offers the comic surprise that he is *not* a great fighter, this tony gathering offers evidence that he talks a better "love match" than he plays. Brown's character has stumbled onto a spy ring out to steal a Navy secret plan involving a remote-controlled plane. One of the enemy agents is played by sexy comedienne Thelma Todd, who had previously surfaced in Joe's *Broad Minded* (1931). This time her assignment is to distract him with what she does best — the flirtatiously provocative come-on. But instead of welcoming these advances like any good Lothario, Brown literally runs scared. When she kisses his ear, it elicits one of Joe's famous yells. Then, as she begins to wrap herself around him, one is reminded of the sexual innocence of a Harry Langdon, or Stan Laurel, both of whom played the bedroom victim so effectively. Luckily for Brown's character, at this point they are interrupted and he escapes. But his lover boy image has been tarnished.

The movie makes time for some flying sequences. Indeed, there is even an indirect recognition of Gen. Billy Mitchell (1879–1936), who had been court-martialed less than a decade before (1925) for his criticism of both the Navy and War Department's lack of imagination with regard to air power, not to mention mismanagement of the planes they did have. A central point in the Mitchell defense was the superiority of aerial bombing. Though he would not be totally exonerated until after the December 7, 1941, attack on Pearl Harbor (during his 1925 court-martial, Mitchell predicted just such an air strike

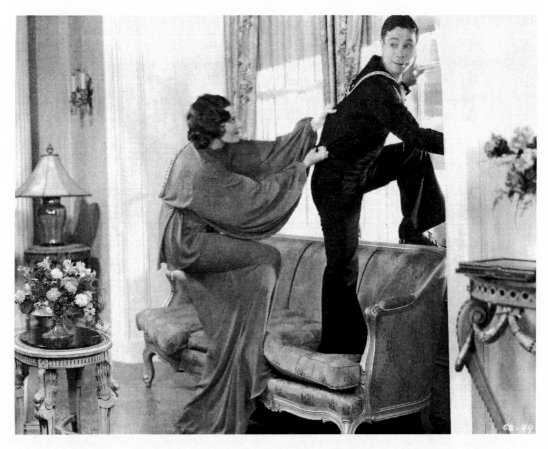

Brown and the always sexually provocative Thelma Todd in *Son of a Sailor* (1933).

by the Japanese), by the time of Brown's movie (1933) the significance of aerial bomb-ing was gaining general acceptance. So much so that *Sailor*'s near-finale trades upon the subject's then-notoriety and its inherent cinematic quality by placing Joe's anti-hero on a target battleship for American bombers. Before the planes arrive, Brown does not realize the danger he is in, and he plays at being an admiral on this deserted tub. His child-like innocence here is reminiscent of Buster Keaton's attitude toward his own nearly empty ocean liner in *The Navigator* (1924). Naturally, Joe survives the eventual Navy target practice (taking Harold Lloyd's patented "thrill comedy" in an entirely new direction), and the film closes with what Brown does best — working his romantic scam by way of the baby shoes. But the location is now an unnamed port in China, and the native woman responds affectionately to him in Chinese. Comically, Brown's closing seemingly nonsense lines have a distinctly Chinese sound to them. Though the propriety police might now do a Joe E. Brown yell and say this is politi-cally incorrect, it is both brief and underplayed and without any of the offensiveness one might connect with the extremes of Jerry Lewis' Asian schtick as late as *Hardly Working* (1981).

Sailor proved to be yet another critical hit, with the *New York World Telegram* reviewer William Boehnel being Brown's biggest large-city champion. Under the head-line, "Joe Brown Sets New Mark in Slapstick," Boehnel wrote, "it is one of the most continuously hilarious of all the pictures which this increasingly amusing comic has made ... Brown is rapidly developing himself to the point where he becoming one of the more important slapstick comics now appearing before the talking cameras."[36] Other promi-nent publication praise ranged from *The New York Times* stating, "The boisterous fun is continued from the moment Mr. Brown appears...," to *The Hollywood Reporter*'s opening paragraph, "Some new gags, a really bang-up ending, and a character into which the comedian slips with unusual ease will make this picture go big in those houses which go for rough and ready comedy...."[37]

While these notices proved that "those houses which go for [Brown's] rough and ready comedy" were often in large cities, a survey of *Motion Picture Herald* mini-reviews for *Sailor*, from small-town theater owners, chronicles an even greater drawing power in the "sticks." Though already hinted at in the earlier censorship-related portion of this chapter, the following comments are just a few of the amazing superlatives *Sailor* received from Brown's adoring "small market" public. A Montpelier, Idaho, exhibitor wrote, "What a picture. The best yet from Joe. It's just one long scream of laughter. A moneymaker for every exhibitor, large and small. Get it quick and tell the people you have the best comedy of the year."[38] From the Michigan hinterlands came, "This is a riot from start to finish. Not a dull moment. Entertaining all through. This guy has got the country people all for him. The picture gave 100 per cent satisfaction."[39] A Napoleanville, Louisiana, theater owner said, "I have a double reason for making a favorable report on this picture. It just about doubled my Friday night receipts and doubled my patrons."[40] And as these mini-reviews have sometimes already demonstrated, Brown did not have a corner on folksy humor. For example, from Flomation, Alabama, came these *Sailor* comments:

> A few weeks ago one of my country patrons remarked that he'd come and bring a truck load [of customers] if we'd have another picture with that big mouth fellow [Brown] ... And yes — the fellow came and brought a truck load and I gave him a free pass.[41]

Brown's box office successes often set the tone for other Warner pictures. For instance, the year after *Sailor* was released, no less a star than James Cagney made a comedy, *Here Comes the Navy* (1934), which had more than a little in common with Brown's film, including Frank McHugh as the best friend–sidekick. Of course, it should be noted that Joe's pictures were also assisted by great production values, something the comedian sorely missed later in the 1930s when he left Warners to work with independent producer Dave Loew. Thus, *Sailor* has an impressive major-picture look about it through the shooting of several scenes on and near the *U.S.S. Saratoga*.

Brown's own special warm feeling for the picture, however, brings one back to the most intimate of objects — those baby shoes used as a *Sailor* comic catalyst for romance. Joe included these tiny movie prop shoes in what he called "My Room of Love" — a den in his home where he showcased his pioneering collection of sports memorabilia and the rare non–athletic-related treasure. Consequently, this diminutive footwear must have meant a great deal to Brown to have qualified for his favorite room.

After Brown's breezy brash Handsome Callahan in *Sailor*, he returned to his milquetoast type in *The Circus Clown*. Actually, it is milquetoast times two, since he plays the dual roles of small-town youngster wanting to be a circus star as well as that young man's father. This was a natural progression for family man Brown, since his films often accent family values by showcasing the importance of pivotal relatives in his character's lives. To illustrate, he underlined mother love in both *Elmer the Great* and *Alibi Ike*. With the later *Gladiator*, he tries to live up to the athletic legacy of a famous father and grandfather at Webster College — with pictures of Brown in period costumes doubling as these relatives. In *Beware, Spooks* (1939), Joe's character attempts to emulate a legendary policeman father. And *The Daring Young Man* (1942) borrows a page from *Clown*— with Brown playing both his standard underdog and the character's zany grandmother.

The father figure in *Clown* had once been a circus star but now runs a small-town hotel. Something has soured him on big-top life but there is no immediate explanation. Later, a drinking problem is hinted at. Despite all this, the picture's introduction of young Brown, Happy Howard, finds him bouncing on a trampoline in the family barn, with an old circus poster of his father on the wall. Happy wants to follow in the gymnastic–high wire tradition of his dad. While this is Brown's third circus-related film, after *The Circus Kid* (1928) and *Painted Faces* (1929), *The Circus Clown* is his first comic look at the big top, as well as a story which draws more upon his own acrobatic circus past. Thus, part of the fun attached to the trampoline barn scene in *Clown*, as we watch Brown do elaborate flips and twists, is as a time capsule peek at the comedian's entertainment roots. When Happy's father finds him practicing, he feigns surprise, yet a glimmer of pride shines through. Soon he is demonstrating his own technique to his son. This extended scene is a good example of an observation by comedy historian-theorist Henry Jenkins on how Brown's funny films "depend less upon extended sequences of comic performance than upon small bits of character business."[42] Put another way, Brown's comic schtick seldom derails the narrative the way an inspired Chico piano solo stops a Marx Brothers film — just for the sheer entertainment factor.

Jenkins' insight about Brown's comedy business being better integrated into the story is a point well taken, and could be equally applied to the comedian's signature massive mouth and yell, which can be dovetailed into so many plots, such as Happy out-roaring a circus lion in *Clown*. But my only concern with the Jenkins position is that he then suggests this integration makes for a less distinctive personality comedian — that Brown is not playing the same character in movie after movie, *á la* the Marx Brothers. But when one recognizes Brown's two basic small town personae, milquetoast and smart aleck (with both frequently linked to sports), there is a great deal of comedy commonality to the screen world of Joe E. Brown. Moreover, many of comedy's distinctive personalities often have more than one comedy mode. This is best demonstrated by W. C. Fields, who fluctuated between playing the huckster, as in *The Old-Fashioned Way*, and the henpecked anti-hero, in such films as *It's a Gift* (both 1934).[43]

Brown's title character in *The Circus Clown* (1934).

Fields' *Old-Fashioned*

Way is a good segue back to Brown's *Circus Clown*. What are the odds that two such great comedians would simultaneously revisit their entertainment beginnings — these 1934 films were released within a month of each other. A broader irony linking the duo, as noted in Chapter One, is that while we now so associate Fields and Brown comedy with their voices, at the start they were totally visual — a comic juggler and an acrobat.

For today's viewer, *The Circus Clown* has one comic subplot that draws special attention — Brown's Happy falls for a beautiful bareback rider ... who turns out to be a man! This is 25 years before his *Some Like It Hot* millionaire becomes engaged to an in-drag Jack Lemmon. Paradoxically, this gender mistaken identity was perceived as more provocative in the 1950s than the 1930s. *Variety*'s strictly ho-hum take on this earlier plot twist was, "Old gag of the country lout falling for a female impersonator serves to induct Brown into the circus."[44] Granted, as will be addressed later in the text, the real controversial component to Joe's *Some Like It Hot* role is his character's final unfazed reaction to the revelation that Lemmon is a man — followed by that immortal tag line, "Well, nobody's perfect." But the simple short-term answer for these two different takes on cross-dressing comedy is that *The Circus Clown* works as a personality comedy, whereas Billy Wilder's *Some Like It Hot* is farce. The former genre is usually about a given comedian getting things wrong and/or being fooled. Thus, it is par for the course for Brown's circus clown to be hoodwinked by someone in drag. In contrast, farce is fueled by ridiculously improbable sexual situations. Consequently, Wilder's picture, true to form, is purposely embracing the provocative. (A contemporary pushing-the-envelope farce would be celebrated playwright Edward Albee's recent Tony award-winning *The Goat*, where a marriage is threatened by the husband's affair with a barnyard animal.)

While *Clown* is not a melodrama like the comedian's two earlier circus pictures, there are sometimes melodramatic moments. These, mixed with the broad comedy, give Brown a chance to register a wide range of emotions. There is the standard funny schtick, such as his bedtime rendition of the *Peter Pan* story to a friend's child — which Joe recites in the squeaky, high-pitched voice of his famous "Little Mousie" routine, about the drunken rodent and the upset cat. *The Circus Clown* also showcases Brown's affinity for pathos, such as the devastating impact of being fired from the circus. This is movingly described by historian Henry Jenkins, "The film lingers on a close-up of Brown's tear-streaked face as the circus train pulls away into the night, leaving him alone and dejected on the open road."[45] In addition, there is often a warmly whimsical tone to Brown's *oeuvre*, especially when applied to a sense of family. Comedy essayist Donald Phelps captures that mood in his description of a *Circus Clown* scene that features Brown as both father and son:

> One quietly delightful shot, like a comic daguerreotype, shows the two fishing together side by side. Brown invests the old man with a gentle, minimally campy gravity. In one magical moment, the father is perusing a happy communication about his son in the circus, and we see, like predawn light, the advance of a smile at the corners of his eyes and mouth.[46]

Though Brown as the father receives less screen time than the son, there is emotional variety here, too. My favorite example would be a "slow burn" scene Brown the elder plays with a young Ward Bond, the character actor later so synonymous with the Westerns of director John Ford. The story has the proud father and Bond as audience members watching young Brown perform as part of a high-wire act. But Bond is constantly critical, starting with the line, "That ain't so hot." This escalates over time, with Brown's father character getting progressively more steamed. (Periodic cutaways allow the viewer to see Brown the younger actually performing in this aerial act.) Ultimately, the comic pay-off has the father literally attacking Bond and driving him from the big-top tent. Yet, there is more. We next see the son do two and a half flips in the air — something for which vaudevillian Brown was once famous. The movie cuts back to the pleased papa, who is doing the comedian's classic cavernous-mouthed yell — which is both endearingly funny and provides a sort of lineal look (within this film) of the father-to-son evolution of the technique.

Given this ambitious, entertainingly complex *canvas*, *The Hollywood Reporter* probably coined the most appropriate *Circus Clown* kudo — "The comedian has seldom been seen in a role that carries more human, fundamental appeal. Real believable and amusing comedy takes the place of the slapstick gags that [have driven past] Brown vehicles...."[47] While other reviews were often equally positive, such as the *New York World Telegram*'s comment that, "Mr. Brown plays his dual role with undeterred good humor, which is something pleasant to report," the film was frequently described as more for the youngsters.[48] The *Motion Picture Herald* suggestion for theater owners was — "The young folk are the patrons to go after for this show ... [followed] by the grown-up circus fans."[49] *Variety* added, "Made to order for juvenile trade. Kids will like it better than a western but not much to say for its adult draw. Family trade is assured."[50] Now, Brown being an attraction for children was hardly news. But the youth-orientated nature of these notices anticipated a time in the late 1930s when the comedian's metropolitan reviews would largely relegate his movies to the bubblegum set.

The last and weakest of Brown's five pictures interspersed among the baseball trilogy was *6-Day Bike Rider*, with a title that largely summarized the movie. Like the 1930s Walkathons and Danceathons, the marathon indoor cycling competition gave Depression audiences cheap entertainment which also rewarded the period's key survivor instinct — persistence. But unlike Walkathons and Danceathons, the cycling phenomenon also traded in vicarious danger for the viewer. During the late summer (1938) production of Brown's cycling movie, journalist Robert Edgren's syndicated pictorial-facts column "Miracles of Sports" reported: "THE MOST DANGEROUS SPORT is Bicycle Racing ... according to Dr. Gately of Madison Square Garden ... 63 ACCIDENTS IN 60 MINUTES opened the 1933 Boston six-day race."[51] Ironically, the catalyst for this column might have been an accident on the comedian's film. The week before Edgren's "Miracle of Sports" piece ran, a 16-cyclist collision during production generated a front page banner headline in the *Los Angeles Examiner*: "9 HURT IN FILM

CRASH."[52] Among the injured was Lou Rush, a former American national cycling champion. (Brown's sports pictures tend to be peppered with real athletes from that activity.) The movie-related accident took place at Los Angeles' Winter Garden indoor, wooden, steeply banked track (velodrome), which, in another paradoxical connection to the "Miracle of Sports" column, was actually doubling for the Madison Square Garden cycling track.

Luckily for the production, Brown was not part of this crash. But shortly before the picture's West Coast premiere, the comedian's favorite hometown columnist (Mitchell Woodbury) revealed another cycling accident that included the star. In the movie, Brown's character, Wilfred Simpson, is part of a two-man racing team with his perennial picture pal Frank McHugh. But a plot twist has initially kept Wilfred from the track, with an overworked McHugh pulling successive cycling shifts. (A variation of this occurs in the 1979 cycling comedy *Breaking* Away, when Dennis Christopher's racing team must cover for their star's temporary absence.) When Brown finally arrives, he saves time by comically stripping down to his racing outfit while pedaling away. Though this plays very entertainingly in the finished film, the first take was a disaster. Woodbury chronicled "a sweater stuck over his [Brown's] head, blinding him. He wobbled into another rider causing a bad spill of several machines. Joe's old acrobatic training came in handy at this point. He instinctively turned a somersault as he started to fall and landed with only a few minor bruises."[53]

For the comedian, filmmaking was becoming a truly slapstick profession, because *Rider* was the second successive shoot in which he had been injured. During his previous picture, on *The Circus Clown*, he had suffered "deep lacerations on his right forearm" from a lion clawing.[54] But Brown was willing to put himself at risk for what film theorist André Bazin would later label "a comedy of space." While Bazin's example is taken from another comedian, it is equally applicable to Brown: "In *The Circus* Chaplin is truly in the lion's cage and both are enclosed within the framework of the screen."[55] That is, the thrill comedy is heightened because we see Chaplin/Brown is performing his schtick with the lion, as opposed to editing together separate clips of a comic and a lion to suggest they are in the same film space. Perversely, period commentators not only neglected the significance of such at-risk comedy, they often kidded the kidders. For instance, there had been an earlier near-clawing on the *Clown* set prior to the actual accident. But it was simply chronicled as a comic take on a scared lion; "At any rate Joe's mouth took second place in size for the first time in his life."[56]

The *6-Day Bike Rider* is yet another variation of the popular Brown formula, where the small-town boy makes good in the city. While there is much to admire here, particularly after the race portion of the picture begins, my reservations stem from the introductory moments with his Wilfred Simpson character. Instead of assuming one of Brown's standard two small-town personae (milquetoast vs. smart aleck), Simpson seems an odd mix of both, from his bookish glasses to his cocky attitude. Moreover, instead of the winsome "tall tale" quality of his breezy ballplayers (rather like Ring Lardner meets Dizzy Dean), Wilfred's confident nature merely registers as hickville smugness, a junior Babbitt from the pages of Sinclair Lewis. All this is not to deny the satirical side of Lardner. But it is very toned down in the Brown screen adaptations. Plus, the comedian plays these figures with such enthusiasm that one cannot help but be won over. Even his *Rider* character eventually pulls the viewer in. However, Wilfred ultimately works because Brown slowly moves his characterization more to the milquetoast mode. This point has been reached when a series of incidents tied to the loss of his girl has him leaving town as a failure. Picked up by a cyclist (McHugh) motoring to New York for the race, Wilfred asks the driver if he is wanted anywhere. When his soon-to-be partner inquires why, Brown's reply documents that his character's transformation to anti-hero is now complete: "The way my luck has been lately, it's just like me to tie up with somebody that's wanted from some nut hatchery."

The notices for this underdog cycling victory were uniformly good, and after the "kids only" accent of his previous circus picture, the *Rider* reviews were back to discussing things in adult terms. *The Hollywood Reporter* even mixed high praise with its own humor in strongly recommending the film, "The six-day bicycle race stuff has been

Celebrating Brown's (center) birthday on the set of *6-Day Bike Rider* (1934), with director Lloyd Bacon and co-star Maxine Doyle on the left, and the comedian's wife (Kathryn) and son Don on the right.

very well done and presents more laughs and thrills than anybody, while sober, has ever got from one of these events."[57] *New York Evening Journal* critic Rose Pelswick described *Rider* as "an entertaining piece, dotted with amusing gags and winding up with a bicycle race that provides laughs as well as excitement."[58] *New York American* reviewer Regina Crewe said Brown "is hilarious all over the place," while *The New York Times* chronicled a pleased *Rider* response at the Rialto —"the merry spasms of yesterday's audience."[59] And the comedian's favorite hometown paper (the *Toledo Times*) affectionately embraced hyperbole —"[*Rider*] gives you a six-day laugh supply in the miraculously short duration of 70 minutes."[60]

Though this clown for all ages was definitely back at the big people's table, *Rider* does merit two child-related footnotes. First, in conjunction with Iver Johnson bikes and Quaker Oats cereal, Warner's *Rider* was also promoted with a "Joe E. Brown Bike Club" giveaway of $50,000 worth of free bicycles.[61] Second, the *Rider* finale features a now-married Wilfred riding a special bicycle built for two with his wife (Phyllis Jenkins). But this bike has them seated side by side, with a baby carriage arrangement between them. The couple keep hearing a bell, like a cyclist is trying to pass them, but there is no one there. Then they realize their baby has a bike bell in its mouth. The surprised mother asks how this could have happened. Wilfred chuckles, and with Brown's patented pause and exercise-like broad opening of that oven-sized mouth before his line, the comedian matter-of-factly states, "I guess you forgot whose baby it is." Though this makes for a cute conclusion, the real heartwarming slant surfaces when one discovers that the 18-month-old youngster is played by Brown's youngest daughter Kathryn. "When two youngsters would do nothing but cry in the final scene," the comedian took Kathryn to the studio and "she behaved perfectly before the camera...."[62]

While 1934 closed with this burst of parental pride, the major professional accomplishments of 1935 would soon give Brown a case for being as boastful as one of his Ring Lardner ballplayers.

❖ EIGHT ❖

Brown's Memorable 1935

In *Bright Lights* (1935) Joe E. Brown is a burlesque comic whose signature bit is playing a drunken heckler in the balcony. He interrupts a girl singer's (Ann Dvorak) act with cracks like, "A cow makes the same noise and gives milk besides."

When an athlete is doing everything right, he or she is often described as "being in a zone." For the always athletic-orientated Joe E. Brown, 1935 was a "zone" *year*. The comedian was back on Hollywood's all-important top ten box office list, after a two-year hiatus.[1] This accomplishment was driven by three outstanding motion pictures, which also showcased Brown's amazing diversity. With *Alibi Ike* (1935, see Chapter Six) he returned to his beloved world of baseball and the diamond trilogy which best defines his screen comedy. *Bright Lights* is a brilliant revisiting of his musical comedy theater past, with inspired acrobatic and novelty dance footnotes, too. And stealing some of the best notices from an all-star cast in Warner Brothers' celebrated adaptation of *A Midsummer Night's Dream* (1935) could be called his greatest professional accomplishment. What is often forgotten today is the momentous reception accorded this groundbreaking picture. *New York Evening Journal* critic Rose Pelswick spoke for many viewers when she stated:

> Unquestionably the most important film event since the advent of sound, *A Midsummer Night's Dream*, arrived last evening at the Hollywood Theatre to make film history. Just as, some nine years ago, Warner Bros. launched Vitaphone and brought about a cinematic revolution from silent to talking pictures, so this same company's courage and vision in bringing Shakespeare to the screen opens a new field for the magic of the camera.[2]

The comedian's 1935 box office clout was also a reflection of carryover ticket sales from his popular pictures *The Circus Clown* and *6-Day Bike Rider* (both 1934). The film industry was still many years away from a movie opening simultaneously across the country. Regardless of when a 1930s picture premiered on the East or West Coast, it routinely took *months* to reach the hinterland small-town market. *Alibi Ike*'s New York opening was in mid–July of 1935, but note the holiday mentioned in this *Motion Picture Herald* mini-review of the movie from a theater owner in Mason, Michigan, "Played this three days at Thanksgiving to good business."[3]

In many ways for Brown, 1934 was just about surviving, too. He had suffered minor injuries on both of his film productions that year — stitches from a clawing lion, and assorted bumps and bruises courtesy of a cycling crash. More disturbing to the Brown family was the threat of kidnapping. In May of 1934 their millionaire neighbor, William Gettle, was abducted. Later that month, Mae West and director Leo McCarey were both targets of kidnappers. McCarey told the *Los Angeles Evening Herald*:

> At present I am in the midst of directing Miss West on her new picture [*Belle of the Nineties*, 1934] and they [organized crime] apparently believe that, if they cannot kidnap Miss West, it would cause the studio a great loss if they were to kidnap me.[4]

Even prior to the attempts on West and McCarey, kidnapping-related headlines peppered filmland newspapers that May, such as the *Los Angeles Examiner* article, "Cinema Stars' Homes Under Heavy Guard." After noting additional kidnapping threats against Marlene Dietrich and Bing Crosby's one-year-old son Gary, the article described Hollywood as an armed camp, where "High Fences, vicious dogs, armed guards, the latest electrical alarm devices and barred windows guard the homes of ... practically every star."[5] (As mentioned in Chapter Six, the 1932 abduction of Charles Lindbergh's baby helped fuel the escalation of this type of crime and/or threat during the Depression.)

Given Hollywood's heightened alert at this time, the often nomadic Brown (a frequent traveler since his circus performer youth) encouraged immediate filmland getaways for his whole family. On June 1, 1934, the comedian's clan left by ship for a Hawaiian vacation.[6] While Brown was obligated to start shooting *6-Day Bike Rider* later that summer, both of his teenage sons would be safely out of Hollywood for an extended period. Don, the oldest, was booked on the ship *President Coolidge* for a four-month cruise as a student cadet. Joe, Jr., was traveling with the Mission baseball team of the Pacific Coast League. *Toledo Times* journalist and Brown family friend Mitchell Woodbury would write at the time that Junior was "a bigger baseball 'bug' than his father, if that be possible."[7] (This is the son who later became general manager of the Pittsburgh Pirates.) Along related baseball–Brown lines, when the comedian made his annual World Series trip East that fall (1934), he left early in order to visit his mother in Toledo. Brown always maintained those hometown ties, and when a syndicated newspaper article from late 1934 championed the star's life as a Horatio Alger story, it was showcased prominently in the *Toledo Times*.[8]

The comedian had indeed made amazing strides since his road show company of *Twinkle Twinkle* had come to Hollywood in 1927. Granted, he was already an established Broadway star at that time. But the movies made his fame international, giving him a creative freedom that ranged from headlining at London's famed Palladium to eventually signing the most lucrative of independent film contracts (both 1936).[9] During Brown's Hollywood heyday at Warners, his box office numbers gave the comedian a great deal of clout at the studio. A naturally egalitarian nature and a similarly minded wife helped keep his ego in check. But at the same time he had no liberal guilt about being well off. Early in his film career, the star had gotten in an argument with a truck driver who had slurred Brown's success. The comic's comeback — "What's wrong with earning big money? I worked like a galley slave, seven days a week, since I was nine years old. I've been walloped around all my life. But I never gave up...."[10] If Brown threw his weight around at the studio, it was usually in the cause of a democratic prank. For instance, one of Warner's prestige performers of the 1930s was Paul Muni (1895–1967), who won a Best Actor Academy Award for the title role in *The Story of Louis Pasteur* (1936). But Muni could be self-consciously serious about his art, and had a strict no-visitors decree on his set. "When Brown heard this he invaded the Muni sound stage with a gaggle of Japanese girl swimmers. Muni rocketed into the [Warners] executive offices and demanded that Brown be reprimanded. Learning that this could not be done [given Joe's greater box office power], he [Muni] walked off the lot..."[11] This was all to no avail, and the *serious* actor came back to the studio with egg on his face.

Brown's popularity as one of the premier 1930s screen clowns might be compared, in part, to his beloved game of baseball. A pivotal argument for this sport's ongoing ascendancy over football as the country's national pastime is tied to baseball's everyday nature, as opposed to football's single game of the week. Diamond historian Michael Shapiro has observed, "Almost every day brings another [baseball] game for the home team, week after week, month after month, all with the power to approximate painlessly the sensation of life — anticipation, joy, sadness, uncertainty."[12] Along related lines, Brown's ability throughout his Warners years to make an unusually large number of entertaining pictures gave film fans an ongoing comedy catharsis they could use and/or relate to as they attempted to weather their own anti-heroic problems in that universal battle called the human comedy. While Brown was not in a class with Charlie Chaplin, no on else was, either. Moreover, while Chaplin only made two pictures during the 1930s (*City Lights*, 1931, and *Modern Times*, 1936), the cavernous-mouthed clown averaged three movies a year that decade.

Following Brown's first 1935 film, the *tour-de-silly* baseball film *Alibi Ike*, the comedian's career year continued with *Bright Lights*. This tale of a burlesque comic who makes it to Broadway might also have been called *Joe E. Brown's Greatest Hits*. The comedian had long been lobbying Warner Brothers for a chance to reprise the stage schtick which made him a Jazz Age star of the Great White Way. Indeed, influential syndicated filmland columnist Louella Parsons wrote in 1934:

> Joe E. Brown yearns to do a song, dance a few steps and take his place with the musical favorites of the screen world. And why not, when he used to be in musical comedies on the New York stage. Jack Warner has finally consented to let Joe E. be the bright and shining light in *What New York Wants* [which became *Bright Lights*].[13]

When the picture premiered, reviews sometimes made note of Brown's longtime goal. Thus, *New York Sun* critic Eileen Creelman opened her critique by stating, "Joe E. Brown has finally made that musical for which he has been pleading for so long."[14] One should hasten to add that Warners was not reluctant about his talents. After all, the comedian had sung and danced early in his screen career. But there had been such a glut of musicals with the coming of sound that the genre had been all but verboten for a time. Plus, a 1934 musical green light for Brown makes further sense, given that Warners had helped stake the genre to a comeback the previous year with *42nd Street*, *Gold Diggers of 1933* and *Footlight Parade*. Coincidently, the man who staged the inimitable, groundbreaking production numbers in this musical trilogy, Busby Berkeley, was the director of Brown's *Bright Lights*. Ironically, the *New York Times* review of the latter picture voiced surprise that there were no Berkeley "gigantic dance sequences."[15] But given that the Brown vehicle was only Berkeley's second picture as a solo director, it is logical that he would want to demonstrate he was more than just a choreographer of spectacle escapism.

The bluenose critic could also imply that maybe Brown's clean comedy nature had acted as a brake on Berkeley's extravaganza numbers, given their inventively erotic tendencies. But the more reasonable explanation is simply that this was an intimate story about the life and comic times of one Joe Wilson (Brown), which mirrored much of the real comedian's background. Besides, Berkeley's fluid camerawork is creatively showcased during *Bright Lights* in a number of other ways, from a comically drawn-out opening of Joe catching a train (twice), to the various elaborate stagings of Brown's balcony heckler — who ultimately exits said perch by swinging from a rope, followed by a seemingly impossible slide down the stage curtain.

So what kind of past material did Brown reprise and/or embellish in *Bright Lights*? First, the comedian finally committed to film his celebrated "Little Mousie" routine, an event of which critics invariably made note. Under the headline "New Brown Musical Is Field Day for Star," *New York Daily News* reviewer Wanda Hale focused her critique's opening on the sketch: "Joe E. Brown's renowned monologue concerning the 'itsy-bitsy mouse and the great bwig pussytat' makes its public [screen] debut at the Strand Theatre this week ... [and puts] his drunken rodent in competition with Mickey Mouse."[16]

Second, and equally winsome, is Brown's eccentric dancing, in both an abbreviated number with co-star Ann Dvorak, and later in an expanded solo version. The comedian's complex routine is so loosely changeable, he often resembles a dancing marionette. There is a child-like skipping gait which segues into a stationary position, where the legs (now straight and stiff) alternate in flying out from his body, side to side (like a one-legged jumping jack). Brown then returns to movement by appearing to throw his right leg forward while simultaneously sliding backwards on his left leg. Finally, there is a rolling gait (like a bow-legged cowboy) that is reminiscent of Groucho Marx's imitation of a Western figure in the party sequence of *Monkey Business*

Brown and his screen wife–stage partner (Ann Dvorak) in *Bright Lights* (1935).

(1931). While each of Brown's movements are comically entertaining, the real charm of the routine comes from his fluid ability to connect these eclectic exercises into a seamless dance number. There is also a historian's fascination with the fact that one element of Brown's zany dancing schtick, appearing to throw one leg forward while sliding back on the other leg, is actually used by Charlie Chaplin one year *later* in *Modern Times* (1936). In fact, that moment in repetition is largely the extent of Chaplin's eccentric dance in that picture. Whether the screen's greatest clown actually borrowed from Brown will probably never be known for sure. But *Bright Lights* was a high-profile critical and commercial hit long before the debut of *Modern Times*.

A third example of Brown's past repertoire to surface in *Bright Lights* involved his acrobatic beginnings. These gymnastic bits are liberally peppered throughout the script, such as the dressing room backflip his character does to relax. Or, there is the off-camera trampoline hidden in the orchestra pit during his dance number, with Joe casually stepping off stage and magically bouncing back — seemingly oblivious to any break in the action. (See Chapter Five for an earlier film recycling of the trampoline schtick in *Top Speed*, 1930.) Ironically, *Bright Lights'* most ambitious homage to acrobatics is an affectionate spoofing of a nightclub gymnastic act. Brown's character has become a Broadway star, and celebrity Joe is invited to interact with a floor show when he is out on the town. It is the kind of act where one sits upon the feet of a reclining figure and he manages to flip said person to a similarly positioned partner — a routine with parallels to Brown's early show business adventures with the Bell-Prevost Trio. That is, in both the Trio and this *Bright Lights* routine, Brown plays the flipping human projectile. But since the latter example is played for parody, Joe and the nightclub troupe rarely get it right. But this is narratively to be expected, since the celebrity has simply been selected to spice up the floor show for the in-film audience. That being said, however, this burlesque of an acrobatic act works on several levels. First, like the nightclub audience, the film viewer enjoys the anti-heroic attempts to nail a certain routine. Second, the misfires occur in so many creative variations, before that final, inevitable success, that even a Martian (somehow tuning in Brown for the first time) would intuitively recognize and enjoy the comedian's gymnastic skills. Lastly, the scene would also qualify as one of Brown's favorite comic situations — what he called "the downfall of dignity."[17] At this point in the movie, Joe is the proverbial "swell," out to be seen by his public. This spoof manages to derail that dignity, without being mean-spirited.

A final way in which *Bright Lights* revisits the comedian's entertainment past is to give the former musical comedy star a song to sing. The amusing ballad is entitled "She Was Only an Acrobat's Daughter," and is obviously patterned upon "The Man on the Flying Trapeze," which had been a hit the previous year in director Frank Capra's pioneering screwball comedy *It Happened One Night* (1934). As in the Capra picture, where the song is sung on a bus to demonstrate a populist fellowship among the passengers, Brown does his number on a train to showcase a similar *esprit de corps* among the burlesque troupe. But even with this Capra connection, Brown's rendition of the "Acrobat's Daughter" is both funny and serves the plot well. And by starting the chorus each time with a big-voiced, drawn-out "Ooooh," the comedian is able to plug his signature large mouth and yell into the number and milk it for added funny effect. Not surprisingly, the song was well received by period audiences. *Time* magazine felt the ballad was the picture's "outstanding innovation," while the *New York Evening Journal* called it "a gusty tune which should catch on."[18]

If *Bright Lights* were simply limited to this imaginative revisiting of Brown's bag of stage tricks, it would still qualify as a film deserving of rediscovery. But what pushes the picture into the realm of major revisionist criticism are a number of additional comedy components. For starters, it has a flat-out funny script, thanks to the gifted writing team of Bert Kalmar and Harry Ruby, who had a hand in several other inspired comedies of the 1930s, such as the Leo McCarey–directed Marx Brother classic *Duck Soup* (1933; see Chapter Five for more on this writing duo).

Kalmar and Ruby's writing for *Bright Lights'* show-stopping heckler scene alone would merit special kudos. Presented three times in the course of the picture, with variations, Brown's lines remain funny more than 70 years later. Sometimes the bits are simply biting, like Joe interrupting the singer to ask what is going on behind the curtain. When she answers, "Not a thing," he wisecracks, "Well, take it [the curtain] up; because there's nothing going on in front of it!" On other heckling occasions, the comebacks are a more predictable yet still entertaining reworking of the comments by the girl singer-"straight man" (Ann Dvorak). For example, when she says, "You ought to be ashamed, I'm trying to sing," he replies with the speed of a comic's snare drum for accent — "You're trying to sing? You ought to be ashamed!" Old or new, Brown sells every crack with an effective drunken slur, and the added comic distraction of someone forever on the verge of falling from the balcony.

These *Bright Light* variations upon the scene are a special treat for the student of comedy, since the drunken heckler and/or disruptive audience member is a bit of comic schtick as old as the theater itself, with filmed examples stretching from Charlie Chaplin's *A Night in the Show* (1915), to those cynical old men muppets who sabotage *The Muppet Show* from their balcony perch. Indeed, Brown's physical comedy embellishments to the Kalmar-Ruby lines merit a footnote to the aforementioned *A Night in the Show*, a short subject which Chaplin adapted from his old music hall skit *Mumming Birds* (also known as *A Night in an English Music Hall*).[19] Chaplin's film expands his disruptions to two characters, from a drunk in the auditorium (Mr. Pest), to a tipsy blue-collar type in the balcony (Mr. Rowdy). The latter figure is frequently in danger of tumbling to the main floor, something Brown's heckler is constantly flirting with, also. While their drunken acrobatic variations do not exactly mirror each other, it is safe to assume that Chaplin's physical take on the subject impacted Brown's comparable *Bright Lights* scene; the cavernous-mouthed comedian had long been a huge Chaplin fan.[20] But at that point in time, most of the known world had a friendly affliction called "Chaplinitis." Whether one was a fan or a funnyman, it was paramount to study his work. Brown would have known *A Night in the Show*. In point of fact, given Joe's many years in vaudeville, he would probably have seen some stage version of *Mumming Birds*, too, since Chaplin did two stage tours of the United States as part of the Fred Karno troupe during 1910–13. Thanks to Chaplin, the sketch was the company's most popular. But even after comedy film pioneer Mack Sennett discovered the English comedian in late 1913, another Karno troupe continued to crisscross America with *Mumming Birds* in its repertoire.

Whether precariously balancing from the balcony railing or simply ripping his target with repartee, Brown's disruptive drunk act is also effective because it seems a natural extension of his *Bright Lights* Joe Wilson character. That is, Wilson is yet another version of Brown's small-town smart aleck, though neither as dumb nor as egotistical as some of his athletics. Still, like his heckler, Wilson is fast with the cutting quip. For instance, when he questions the musical tastes of the one man on the train who does not like "She Was Only an Acrobat's Daughter," the critic claims never to have been so insulted. Joe's quick comeback — "Well, that's because you don't get around enough." Plus, the combination of athleticism and acrobatics that always keep him from falling out of the balcony also carry him through most of his *Bright Lights* scenes, from the quasi-sprinter catching the train to open the picture, to the nervous performer who relaxes by doing back flips.

Brown then manages to couple this less caricatured, more realistic character to a story with genuine pathos. His small-time burlesque comic is happily married to the girl singer-comic victim of his balcony heckler, the aforementioned Ann Dvorak. But when a beautiful runaway heiress (Patricia Ellis) joins the troupe and helps put him on the fast track to Broadway, he romantically loses his way for a time. It was a provocative triangle, since Ellis had been Brown's love interest in both *Elmer the Great* and *The Circus Clown*. But Dvorak was a name actress, with such showy dramatic parts as Paul Muni's kid sister in director Howard Hawks' classic *Scarface* (1932), and the heroine of James Cagney's memorable "G" *Men* (1935), which opened just a few months prior to *Bright Lights*. However, the casting works, with Dvorak managing to give some gradation to what could have been a one-note, long-suffering "loyal wife" part. But more impressively, Ellis is a revelation in this mildly bad girl role. She is given a chance to drop any previous small-town restraints and play sexy, as well as sing and double as Brown's "straight man" (as she replaces Dvorak in the balcony heckler routine.) And it results in a performance which holds its own with that of her more high-profile co-stars. Moreover, the first funny line in *Bright Lights* entertainingly kids the ripe sensuality Ellis brings to the part. The bit is voiced by comic character actor William Demarest, who has a brief cameo as a detective on the trail of Ellis' runaway as the movie opens. After a reference is made to the newspaper headline "Madcap Heiress Missing Again," Demarest matter-of-factly observes, "It may say missing, but that girl ain't missing a thing."

Not surprisingly, the almost uniform metropolitan critical raves for *Bright Lights* came in two basic varieties. First, there were the ones which took on a "Brown's greatest hits" perspective, such as the *New York Daily News* review which affectionately itemized much of what the comedian did, and then followed it with a glowing final score: "he's a pretty busy fellow — and a very funny one."[21] *Variety* said, "It's a one-man show by one of the screen's most versatile players...."[22] And *The Hollywood Reporter* followed suit with this review opening: "Chocked with Joe E. Brown antics as a tramp burlesque comedian who makes the prosperity grade from tank towns to Broadway helps *Bright Lights* to be one of the best Brown pictures."[23]

The second metro market take on the picture keyed on the comedian's newly found range as a funnyman. For example, *The New York Times* observed:

> [T]he best thing about his performance is his creation of an attractive, believable and well rounded character ... Mr. Brown plays the part with exuberance and understanding, never making the man a complete fool, and never slurring over the [in film] comedian's vanity and weaknesses.[24]

While the *Times* went on to insightfully add that this "study of the burlesque clown" was something "new," the *New York World Telegram* further praised the mature growth of Brown as a performer:

> A much more reserved and diversified clown ... Mr. Brown has now become a comic who depends upon characterization rather then tricks and as such is a welcome addition to the small but rather choice group of low comedians.[25]

Ironically, it took one of those small market mini-reviews from the *Motion Picture Herald* to more baldly state what the second wave of metro critics were getting at — "Entirely different than any of his [Brown's] other performances."[26]

Of course, maybe this was not so paradoxical, given that small-town stereotypes are all about not mincing words — which is equally applicable to the comedian's various village characters. Plus, when one peruses multiple 1935 issues of the *Motion Picture Herald* in order to track those *Bright Lights* mini-reviews by small-market theater owners, there is no mincing here either. But instead of finding that the critiques fall into two camps, as happened with the metro reviews, these small town mini-takes on the movie were all unabashed hosannas. From Preston, Idaho, came, "The best Joe E. Brown picture ever made. Did tremendous business and everyone went home laughing and trying to tumble."[27] A Robinson, Illinois, theater owner wrote, "[Brown] shows more real versatility in one reel than most so-called stars do in a whole picture. Played this against my toughest competition of the late summer to dandy business and may bring it back."[28] The report from Rugby, North Dakota, said, "It unquestionably establishes Brown as the screen's most able comedian," while a Pearl River, New York, theater manager stated, "The best Joe Brown picture in years. We said the same about *Alibi Ike*, but this was even better. The situations were hilarious and Joe showed his accomplishments at singing and dancing. Business was very good."[29] These are just a representative few of the many amazing endorsements of *Bright Lights* by small-market picture people. One might have thought Brown's real-life mother was filing reviews from every tank town in America. But as the metro critiques also suggested, 1935 found the comedian in that aforementioned "zone" in which he could do no wrong. Thus, what better time would there be to launch Brown into the most unlikely of territories — a Shakespearean screen adaptation. However, as the subject (Brown meets the Bard) is played out in the following pages, this combination will be seen as less and less of a stretch.

The road to Warner's 1935 film production of *A Midsummer Night's Dream* began at the Hollywood Bowl the previous year. Acclaimed German theater producer and director Max Reinhardt (1873–1943) staged an adaptation of *Dream* which bowled over the film capital. Calling him "a master showman," *The Hollywood Reporter* went on to say, "There is not a single false note in his presentation ... It is hard to believe that even the art of a Reinhardt [who was instrumental to the birth of German Expression] could have achieved such magnificent results in such a short time."[30]

Fittingly, the magic of Reinhardt's live production would foreshadow several things about his follow-up screen adaptation of *Dream*, which he co-directed with William Dieterle. First, the star of both presentations, beyond Shakespeare's timeless writing, was the mesmerizing spectacle. The headline for the aforementioned Hollywood Bowl review underlined this fact — "Reinhardt's Production of *Dream* Superbly Beautiful."[31] This glistening fantasy forest world is also wonderfully realized in the movie, thanks in part to Hal Mohr's Academy Award–winning cinematography (the only time this category was taken by a write-in candidate). Second, the Bowl actors most often singled out were Mickey Rooney as Puck, Walter Connolly as Bottom and Sterling Holloway as Flute. A similar pecking order was played out in the picture. But whereas Rooney reprised his Puck characterization to further acclaim, a new Bottom (James Cagney) and Flute (Brown) joined him for a lion's share of the best film notices. Third, like the surprising critical and commercial success of the live *Dream*, Reinhardt's screen version was an unlikely box office hit, as well as being the darling of the critics.[32]

If a Shakespearean play was to be adapted to the screen in the mid–1930s, there was a certain logic to it being *A Midsummer Night's Dream*. A new film genre had surfaced at this time called screwball comedy, though one might also refer to it as a revisionist take on American farce. Two pivotal examples of this battle of the sexes (though with the most attractive of combatants), *It Happened One Night* and *Twentieth Century* (both 1934), had already surfaced, with an army of zany couples about ready to follow. The Shakespearean connection comes from screwball comedy scholars like Stanley Cavell, who posit that a number of films in this genre log time in a country setting, particularly the later *Bringing Up Baby* (1938), which becomes a key movie for him.[33] Attempting to place these films in the "tradition of romance," he draws upon what theorist Northrop Frye calls "the greenworld," best exemplified by the pastoral settings in several Shakespearean comedies — the most important for Cavell being the forest of *A Midsummer Night's Dream*.[34] (A stronger case for the pastoral screwball setting would be the country sojourn of Clark Gable and Claudette Colbert in the watershed *It Happened One Night*.)

Using the phrase "the greenworld" in the most metaphorically universal manner — as a place of restful renewal — one might very generally link it to the use of the country in screwball comedy. Cavell seems to suggest this when he defines Frye's greenworld as "a place in which perspective and renewal are to be achieved."[35] While I charted certain pitfalls for this analogy in my first screwball text, such as the inherent innocence of the lost-in-the-wood *Dream* couples versus the manipulative nature of the screwball heroine (as when Katharine Hepburn leads Cary Grant into the Connecticut forests of *Baby*), it would still not be unfair to call Shakespeare's *Dream* a first cousin to the later American genre of screwball comedy.[36] Indeed, a richer vein of connection between the two, especially as it applies to Brown, would be the treatment accorded rustic characters in both *Dream* and screwball comedy. That is, while this Shakespearean play and the later screwball genre celebrate the inherent romanticism of the pastoral setting, the bucolic inhabitants of the region often qualify as full-blown fools. This certainly describes the company of laborers Brown belongs to in *Dream*. He plays Flute the bellows-mender, with James Cagney as the weaver Bottom. Other members of this artisan band include Brown's frequent cinema sidekick Frank McHugh as Quince the carpenter, and Hugh Herbert (with his trademark "woo-woo" sound) as the tinker Snout.

The plot purpose of these comic fools is to perform a play for a royal wedding party, with the focus on Bottom (the most dominating of the artisans) and Flute as the lovers Pyramus and Thisby—ultimately necessitating that Brown appear in drag as Thisby. This play-within-the-play is yet another way in which *Dream* anticipates a basic screwball component—the proclivity to parody a traditional love story to such an extreme that one yells farce. Moreover, the spoofing nature of the Pyramus and Thisby love story does not exist in a vacuum; it doubles as a comic commentary on all those mismatched couples in the forest, victims of the mischievous sprite Puck (Rooney) and Oberon, king of the fairies (Victor Jory).

Shakespeare scholar Harold C. Goddard calls Bottom symbolic of "the earthy, the ponderous, the slow, in contrast with Puck, who is all that is quick, light, and aerial."[37] Not surprisingly, Puck sees Bottom as an ass and, for a time, he even gives him the head of this creature. But in Bottom's favor, as well as that of his similar laborer companions, they are the foundation or ballast to life, *à la* the weaver's name—*Bottom*. The group's resiliency factor is at the heart of all clowns, that plodding ability to soldier one's way through all of life's travails.

So how did Brown get involved in this prestigious project? One might say he was roped in by the scope of the picture. With Warner Brothers investing more than a million dollars in the production (a large budget for the time), the studio attempted to maximize as much of its talent as possible in the adaptation. Still, Brown was reluctant to join the cast. Like the real life Ring Lardner, who enjoyed pretending he was not any brighter than those simpleton ballplayers he created (and Brown played on stage and screen), the comedian savored playing the rube, too. Consequently, when Jack Warner approached him about *Dream*, Joe claimed to not know the name Shakespeare, asking if the fellow would also be in the picture. Then, sounding even more like a Lardner sports figure, Brown added, "The only Shakespeare I knew played for Notre Dame, but I didn't know he could act."[38] The story became a popular anecdote around Warners for several days, though the comedian was still no closer to signing. Finally, after

Brown and James Cagney camp it up as Shakespearean lovers in *A Midsummer Night's Dream* **(1935).**

intense lobbying from a litany of Warners power brokers, including Reinhardt himself, Brown became part of the cast.

The comedian would later summarize his character, Flute, as "an addlepated fellow who is forced to play a female role in the amateur show ... [which made an insecure Brown feel] scared, and obviously wrong as a female impersonator."[39] Yet, he soon realized that Reinhardt had used the actor's real embarrassment over the aforementioned antics of Flute (as the girl Thisby) to better approximate the comic shame of the character. This anticipates the later "Method" approach to performing, where the actor does not so much "act" but rather live the part.

Before examining those scenes which feature Brown's character Flute and the other rustic laborers, it should be noted that each of the diverse personages which Shakespeare blends into the play has his own distinct speech pattern. These differences range from the Duke's high blank verse to the light rhyme of the fairies. But the commoner crew of Flute and company converse in the halting prose speech of the less than articulate, with a generous helping of malapropisms. In other words, though this might be Shakespeare, the laborers' language was merely an antecedent for the familiar (to Brown) lingo of his previous, often struggling buffoons, including the illiteracy of the Lardner characters. Of course, the educational supplement that Warner Brothers had prepared for the production (to encourage school-related screenings) was most direct about Flute being typecasting for Brown, since he was long known as "the inarticulate fool who triumphs with a flourish (as in *Six-Day Bike Race* and *The Circus Clown*)."[40] And *Screenland's* positive *Dream* review went so far as to entertainingly suggest the duo of Brown and Cagney were so perfect for their parts that "[w]ere it not for a slight anachronism involving some three and a half centuries, one might be tempted to think that Mr. Shakespeare of Stratford wrote at least one play with certain screen actors in mind."[41]

So what were the scenes which allowed Brown and his fellow laborers to critically shine? Though they surface four times in this lengthy adaptation (over two hours in its original release), the first two appearances are largely preliminary introductions. But even so, Brown manages to establish certain comedy components here. As in earlier pictures, the comedian has his character continually eating. In this case, the food of choice appears to be sunflower seeds. This comic culinary slant works on several levels. First, since he is the only artisan so involved, it amusingly helps draw attention to his figure. Second, this focus on eating further fuels the image of Flute as a fool — he is playing little attention to Quince's attempts to explain the play they are to perform. Third, the sunflowers are also directly related to several comedy bits which will soon follow in the group's inspired forest rehearsal. For instance, as Bottom and Flute later practice playing the lovers Pyramus and Thisby, Cagney has a line, "So doth thy breath, my dearest Thisby...." But he cannot finish it, because Brown as Flute/Thisby victimizes him with his bad breath. Later in this parody love scene, Thisby again destroys the romantic ambience with a comic coughing attack, presumably caused by the seeds. The proof of that assumption is soon proved once Pyramus and Thisby return to a semblance of their spoofing romantic revelry. Brown almost immediately breaks the mood by comically coughing up a seed, which goes flying by poor Bottom/Pyramus. Finally, this seed-popping character brings one full circle back to so many earlier food-obsessed Brown characters. His Flute might be Shakespeare, but this parallel with the comedian's past probably represented a comfort zone for period viewers not as well-versed in the Bard.

As these descriptions suggest, the forest run-through of the laborers' play, *The most lamentable comedy and most cruel death of Pyramus and Thisby*, is sort of an ongoing comedy communion for all fans of funny. Like the period teamings of Groucho and Harpo Marx, or Buster Keaton and Jimmy Durante, much of the rehearsal comedy is driven by the non-stop verbiage of Cagney juxtaposed with the visual-physical schtick of Brown. For example, if Bottom had his way, he would assume all the parts in this play within the play. In fact, commissioning a rewrite to further embellish his opportunity for glory would suit him just fine. In comic contrast to this entertainingly egotistical talking dynamo is Brown's seemingly single-celled bumpkin. For Flute, there is neither movement nor much being said. Top that off with his most vacuous of looks, especially those eyes narrowed to comic slits, and one is reminded of Stan Laurel's description of Laurel and Hardy: "Two minds without a single thought."

Interestingly, however, there is a second teaming during the rehearsal, besides that of Bottom and Flute, which produces more demonstrative comedy from Brown. This pairing involves Flute and Frank McHugh's Quince, who has evolved into the quasi-director for the laborers' play. An especially winsome interaction between the two has Flute woodenly droning through his dialogue while Quince physically adjusts *everything* about the pose to be assumed by Brown's lovesick character. This involves rearranging feet, arms, head and even the separating of Flute's fingers — which produces a comic shriek from Brown. Moreover, as one might assume, Quince's makeover of his friend also involved Brown's trademark mouth — which is manipulated into the broadest smile this side of a jack-o'-lantern, all while Flute keeps mumbling through his lines.

The Quince-Flute interactions reach a humor apex when Brown's character's inability to grasp the nuances of playing a woman (Thisby) nearly drives Quince into a comic fit. This is then topped by simpleton Flute mistaking verbal directions from Quince as additional Thisby lines and incorporating them into his rehearsal dialogue. As this growing body of errors builds, a frustrated Quince is reduced to both pounding the text with his hand and jumping up and down. Predictably, but very comically, Brown's Flute also adds these physical actions to his performance, thinking them to be yet more stage directions. Ultimately, Flute realizes he is at fault, and with humorous economy Brown ad-libs the line, "I won't play any more."

Frustrations notwithstanding, the forest run-through is soon broken up by the disruptive return of Bottom — who, thanks to the mischievous Puck, now has the head of an ass. The less than astute Flute is the last to note this transformation, and even then, Brown effectively milks the comic horror which slowly comes over his character's face. Finally, Flute utters, "Oh me," and joins the rest in running away. But the devilish Puck toys with Flute by transforming himself into fire and scaring the bellows-mender into a forest pond. Such a fright is excuse enough for Brown to uncork one of his signature big-mouthed yells before he hits the water. Upon surfacing, he comically recycles a variation of an earlier line that is now even more heartfelt, "I don't want to play any more."

One might say that this brilliantly amusing take on the laborers' forest rehearsal is a collaboration of sorts between the Bard and Brown, since much of the comedian's schtick here is not in the original text, particularly with regard to his interactions with both Bottom and Puck. Everything, I hasten to add, is consistent with the characters involved, and the general tone of the scene. But co-director Reinhardt encouraged Brown to embellish his role, since Flute's nominal partner in parody (Bottom) is a much more dominant figure in Shakespeare's original play. And given Brown's gift, like all great clowns, of being able to transform his countenance into countless comedy masks as fast as the magic of Puck, there was no need to fatten Flute's part with a multitude of new lines.

As a final footnote to the rehearsal scene, one should note that the charming interactions of the characters played by Brown, Cagney and McHugh were probably assisted by the fact that they were all close friends in real life. Indeed, they frequently lunched together in Brown's bungalow on the Warners lot, where the food was prepared by the comic's man Friday, Douglas Keaton. (Keaton had also been responsible for all those breakfast items Brown consumed in the celebrated opening act of the comedian's Los Angeles stage productions of *Elmer the Great*.) While *Dream* would be the last of several pictures in which Brown and McHugh co-starred, this was the only film in which Cagney and the funnyman appeared.

The final *Dream* sequence showcasing the laborers, with more of a focus upon Flute and Bottom, is their presentation of the play within the play at the court of the duke. But how does such a delightfully bad amateur troupe get to the "palace"? Puck, as if making amends for his forest shenanigans, briefly befuddles the evening's master of ceremonies and the group becomes the chief entertainment.

The opening love scene between Cagney's Pyramus and Brown's Thisby has them passionately talking to each other through a chink in the wall, with said brick obstacle being played by Hugh Herbert's forever giggling Snout. More to the comic point, that chink in the wall is represented by one of Herbert's hands. While one would normally be hard-pressed to beat the imaginatively funny forest run-through, just Brown's first appearance here — in a dress and milkmaid-styled braided wig — tops all that has preceded it. As with most personality comedians, the laughter simply begins with how funny Brown looks. Add to this a sappy male lover (Cagney) synonymous with tough guy gangsters (*á la The Public Enemy*, 1931), and a giggling wall, and one has an instant formula for funny. The scene's high point is the noisy kisses made through Herbert's hand ... or, rather, the hole in the wall.

The lover's next scene is a romantic rendezvous near Ninny's tomb. Brown's Thisby arrives first but ends up losing some clothing as he is frightened away by a lion. When Cagney's Pyramus appears, he thinks Thisby has been killed and decides to join "her" in death. After a comic suicide by Pyramus' own sword, with much kicking of the feet, Thisby makes another comic entrance. However, this time the laughter goes beyond Brown in drag. He is skipping and throwing flower petals and singing "La-la-la-la-la...." When Thisby sees Pyramus' body, "she" lets out a scream. But Brown's character is so impressed by his newfound thespian skills (the scream) that he cannot help but laugh.

Returning to the play's text, Thisby decides to end "her" life, too. With comic solemness, "she" states, "Come trusty sword." Unfortunately, Thisby has neglected to bring said sword, and now Brown's flighty figure totally panics as he repeats his line, "Come trusty sword." By the third repetition of this refrain, the unglued Thisby is reduced to comic crying. As his off-stage colleagues scramble for a weapon, Brown's fool has a rare epiphany and taps on Pyramus' armor — he will borrow his dead lover's sword. With a disgusted Bottom helping out, Thisby prepares to off "herself." But just at that nearly fatal moment, a cast member rushes out and places a second sword in Thisby's other hand. Now the slow-witted "maiden" is completely befuddled. First, "she" starts to scrape the two swords together in a sharpening movement. Next, "she" decides to simply give Pyramus his sword back. So with Thisby's child-like simplicity "she" again taps on "her" lover's armor. As Bottom's conscientiously comic character takes back his weapon, still prostrate on the ground, Pyramus decides to die one more time — in case the sword exchanges have confused the audience.

With the weapon issue resolved, Brown's Thisby now stabs "herself." But the thrusting movement tickles, and "she" laughs out loud. Returning to the challenging business of comic suicide, Thisby stabs "herself" again ... several times. The always sports-orientated Brown then pitches forward hard over Bottom's body, like a defensive back going for a fumble. The impact is enough to make Bottom's legs briefly rise off the ground. Thus ends *The most lamentable comedy and most cruel death of Pyramus and Thisby.*

Again, there has been much embellishing of the Bard by Brown, but always in keeping with the parody elements of Shakespeare's original. Though my synopsis does not do comic justice to it, there is hopefully enough demonstrative joy in the retelling to make it apparent why Brown and his fellow *Dream* comics stole the lion's share of the critical acclaim. Of this much-praised prestige picture, *The New York Times'* most insightful critic of the 1930s (the now neglected Andre Sennwald) observed, "Joe E. Brown as Flute the Bellows-mender gives the best performance in the show. It is a privilege to roar with laughter when he is rehearsing ... or playing the timid Thisby to James Cagney's Pyramus."[42] Along similar lines, *The New York Post* added, Brown's "comicalities as the coddling Flute are not only entertaining in themselves but are remarkably in the vein of the Elizabethan fool. Mr. Brown steals every scene he is in, and he does it without reminding you of his last baseball picture."[43] Several other critics agreed with this time-tripping appraisal of Brown's skills, from the aforementioned *Screenland* magazine reference, to the *New York Herald Tribune's* comment, "Mr. Brown ... is a Shakespearean clown born after his time. As Flute ... he is quite magnificently comic."[44] While one could also pencil *The Hollywood Reporter* into the same huddle that saw Brown in "the perfect spirit of Shakespearean burlesque," this publication should be credited with the most entertaining, insightful take on why this picture is still a crowd-pleaser:

> Aside from staggering production value and the class angle of the film, it captures the thistle down whimsy of Old Bill's faery fantasy and combines it with earthy bladder and slapstick comedy with which the Bard made his play to the gallery. The result is an exposure of picture patrons to culture which is not only painless but pleasureful to the masses.[45]

Even the rare critic who was not generally taken with this adaptation, such as *The New Republic's* always engaging Otis Ferguson, was a fan of *Dream's* comic laborers. Singling out Cagney, Brown and Hugh Herbert as "the best cast figures in the production,"

Ferguson added, "With their various interpolations and properties, they are made into something that can be laughed at because it is real and funny, rather than a classic thing to laugh at."[46]

One senses that Ferguson, a pioneering realist and the most fiercely egalitarian of liberals, was not so much bothered by the movie but rather the pushy marketing of *culture*. With a large budget and a long *art* film to sell, Warner Brothers was unrelenting in its public relations blitzkrieg about the picture, not to mention a road show opening ticket price of $11 in some markets (at a time when the average movie admission was 24 cents[47]). Ferguson's most telling take on *Dream* was a comically philistine crack which probably reflected what much of Brown's meat-and-potato public was thinking: "there is going to be a powerful minority of American husbands who will get one load of the elves and pixies, and feel betrayed away from their stocking feet and sports page, and say as much, violently."[48]

Along *Dream* marketing lines, Brown was one of several performers from the film to do a promotional short subject. But unlike his co-stars, who usually found themselves on stage before an audience plugging the picture, Brown was presumably at Warner Brothers' Studio Café having lunch with Pat O'Brien. This seems ever so fitting, given that Brown often managed to use eating scenes for comic effect in his movies, such as Flute's obsession with sunflower seeds. The gentle banter here between two real-life friends is played for humor, too (they joke about O'Brien taking Cagney's place at the table). While their comments on *Dream* are fairly generic, such as Brown's observation, "the things that Shakespeare wrote 300 years ago we comedians are still using," the seemingly casual restaurant setting and affectionate ribbing make it a much more palatable sales pitch, especially since O'Brien was not even in the movie. An added bonus, despite the staging, is the "window" it provides on Brown the raconteur. He was an absorbing storyteller in private life, and this bit of manufactured voyeurism would seem to document that fact.

Paradoxically, despite a plethora of positive reviews, *Dream*'s critical reputation would suffer in later years. While the movie was not without flaws, such as some of the romantic leads being a little overwhelmed (such as Dick Powell as Lysander), the dominant 1935 critical take on this Shakespearean experiment (beyond the kudos for the clowns) was resoundingly positive. *Variety*, the show business bible, had been the most methodically direct in addressing this issue: "Question of whether a Shakespearean play can be successfully produced on a lavish scale for the films is affirmatively answered by this commendable effort."[49] Moreover, besides the critical boost *Dream* gave to Cagney and Brown, the picture literally launched the career of pint-sized Mickey Rooney. Though he was no stranger to film, after having long starred in the "Mickey McGuire" short subject series, *Dream* made the movie colony take notice of the teenager. Indeed, even prior to the Hollywood Bowl staging of *Dream*, in which he also starred as Puck, influential film columnist Louella Parsons chronicled how "astounded" she was by the young talents of this Reinhardt discovery.[50]

As a brief addendum to Reinhardt's triumph at the Hollywood Bowl, history seems to have forgotten one fascinating bit of casting which sadly did not come to pass. A June 1934 piece in *The Hollywood Reporter* had Charlie Chaplin consenting to appear in Reinhardt's live production of *Dream*. Though the brief notice stated, "His role is not yet announced," it is absorbing to speculate on what part he might have chosen.[51] Given Chaplin's Puck-like pastoral scene in *Sunnyside* (1919), this is the character which first comes to mind. But Chaplin's mid-forties age by this time (1934) would probably have nixed the role. Regardless, if he had been part of the celebrated production, it is equally interesting to contemplate Chaplin as a carryover, like Rooney, to the film adaptation. Besides Brown being able to work with his comedy hero, Chaplin would have been pressed into speaking on screen prior to 1936's *Modern Times*. But pre-production work on *Times* had Chaplin bowing out of the Hollywood Bowl *Dream* by August 1934. Coincidentally, Louella Parsons broke the news in the same column which announced Brown was about to do a musical — what became *Bright Lights*.[52]

Even without Chaplin, *Dream* was both the capstone to Reinhardt's long and distinguished career, and a unique acting opportunity for Brown, Cagney and the others. Hollywood tough guy Cagney would observe:

> Only one thing could have made me happier than actually playing in *A Midsummer Night's Dream*. And that is the knowledge that Shakespeare might have been aware of how carefully Reinhardt adhered to the spirit of his imagery. I honestly believe that the great playwright would have gotten an enormous kick out of seeing the *Dream* in a new medium.[53]

Years later, in his autobiography, Brown struck a similar but more comical chord: "I really believe Shakespeare would have liked the way we handled his low comedy [by drawing from our burlesque background] ... The Bard's words have been spoken better, but never bigger or louder. It turned out to be one of the most successful things I ever did."[55] In fact, one could almost say he topped the Bard, since "Hollywood laugh clockers reported that the best [*Dream*] audience reaction followed his [Brown's ad-libbed] line, 'I won't play any more.'"[55] But at the time, the comedian could not rest on his Shakespearean laurels; his memorable 1935 was about to be followed by another monster year at the box office.

NINE

Before the Fall

In *Polo Joe* (1936), Joe E. Brown's title character once again pretends to be something he is not. When he is finally forced to play, his naïve girlfriend (Carol Hughes) says, "I want you to get out on that field and play polo like you never played before." Joe responds with the most honest of answers, "You can depend on that!"

The Joe E. Brown comic quote from above is the best line in the picture. But just as it borrows from an earlier scenario in *You Said a Mouthful* (1932), where non-swimmer Brown is told to "Swim as you've never swum before," and responds, "That's the only way I *can* swim," the comedian's 1936 film work often has a recycled tone. Paradoxically, these movies (*Sons o' Guns*, *Earthworm Tractors* and *Polo Joe* were critical and commercial successes. Indeed, in 1936 Brown would once again rate inclusion on Hollywood's prestigious top ten box office chart, even moving up to the fifth spot, after 1935's ninth place finish.[1] Thus, one could argue that this was yet another career year. Besides the box office numbers, Brown would play the London Palladium that August, squeezing this tony stage booking into a busy European schedule already committed to accompanying the American Olympic team to the summer games in Berlin. In addition, Warner payroll figures for 1936 reveal that Brown was the studio's highest-paid male actor for the year at $201,562, with Englishman Leslie Howard second at $185,000.[2] In fact, county tax records for the year even had the comedian's assessment for his jewelry collection value well beyond that of Mae "Diamond Lil" West's ($5,000 versus $3,500).[3] Mid–1930s life was very good for Brown and his family, and the financial picture looked to get rosier; in 1936, the comic signed a contract with independent producer Dave Loew that would substantially increase his per film salary.[4] Though Warner obligations would keep Brown tied to the studio through the remainder of that year, the new business arrangement would eventually make the comic's asking price $100,000 a picture.

The decision to go with Loew had been strongly encouraged by Brown's new agent at this time, Mike Levee. The comedian remained close to his previous playbroker, Ivan Kahn, but felt that Kahn's excessive drinking was getting in the way representing him. (Brown was a teetotaler.) Initially, the comic missed Kahn's sense of humor. For instance, when Warner Brothers first attempted to get Brown to accept a role in *A Midsummer*

Night's Dream (1935) for no extra payment beyond a token new car perk (since the studio was pitching the film as a joint "family" effort by studio personnel), Kahn brought the powerbrokers back to reality. His opening salvo, which ultimately translated into a healthy payday for Joe, was the comic comeback: What would be the commission on a car — a bicycle? Unfortunately, Brown would ultimately have another reason, beyond humor, for which to miss Kahn. New agent Levee's advice to go with Loew was "a disastrous move. None of the independent pictures were up to the standards set at Warners."[5]

In 1936, there was also a drop-off in the quality of his Warners pictures. Nineteen hundred and thirty five's trilogy of *Alibi Ike, Bright Lights* and *A Midsummer Night's Dream* had so raised the comedy bar that it was the proverbial hard act to follow. There was also the intangible fact of 1936 being Brown's lame duck year at Warners, never the most ideal setting for creativity. I am reminded, however, of a comment made by film critic Richard Schickel on the nature of the artistic gift:

> Inspiration is a rare and flighty bird most of us never catch a glimpse of. Very occasionally it settles down helpfully in the corner, cawing advice to artists as they pile up those bodies of [classic] work ... More usually ... it touches down briefly, then darts away. The artist may catch tantalizing sight of the creature as he walks on through the woods, but it never again perches long on his shoulder.[6]

While Schickel's metaphorical bird of creativity was basically a permanent lodger at Charlie Chaplin's house, it had rarely been more than an intermittent visitor to the world of Joe E. Brown. What is worse, after 1935 this feathered muse "never again [perched] long on his shoulder." Brown, a comedian whose earlier work sometimes flirted with greatness, was on the verge of becoming a journeyman performer. This decline began with Joe's aforementioned last three Warner pictures, what film comedy historians James Robert Parish and William T. Leonard have colloquially described as "hardly up to snuff."[7]

The best of this lesser Brown trio was the first to arrive in theaters — the World War I comedy *Sons o' Guns.* Though not in a comedy class with the "Great War"–related pictures of Chaplin (*Shoulder Arms*, 1918) and Harry Langdon (*Soldier Man* and *The Strong Man*, both 1926), Brown's picture is a minor but serviceable vehicle about a war bond–selling entertainer initially reluctant to serve in the military. His lack of patriotism anticipates Gene Kelly's later screen debut as the self-centered vaudevillian in the musical World War I–set *For Me and My Gal* (1942).

Sons o' Guns is slow-moving until Brown reaches France as a soldier, and his character's stage background is allowed to trickle through. The movie's one show-stopper scene is a singing-dancing duet he does with a French barmaid (Joan Blondell). Finding themselves alone in the pub, their charming joint refrain of "On a buck and a quarter a day" dovetails into one of Brown's patented eccentric dance numbers (*á la Bright Lights*), with Blondell soon joining in. The big finish has them both doing a total back flip over the bar.

Sons o' Guns' other signature scene has doughboy Brown pressed into entertainment services when the talent troupe for an Army show does not arrive. Just as the comedian had recycled the eccentric dance turn from his theater past, this second routine also revisits that period. In a pantomime playlet within the picture, Brown is a French thug in a bar, running through a litany of tough-guy antics, from lighting a match on a man's face, to a display of excessive drinking. But the comedy payoff has the action evolve into a parody of an Apache dance number (that popular cabaret act where a gangster-type mishandles his girl in a brutal yet masterful way). Brown's Apache dance partner is the funny female impersonator Frank Mitchell. Joe had previously spoofed this dance on Broadway in the *Greenwich Village Follies* (1921–22) and on the screen in *Hit of the Show* (1928), though cinema's most famous rendition occurs in Chaplin's *City Lights* (1931). In this latter example, a drunken Tramp mistakes a nightclub's featured entertainment as an abusive husband and attempts to defend the lady.

Had *Sons o' Guns* continued in this revue vein, peppering the story with these winning routines, as Brown's character became part of some sort of Army entertainment corps, the picture might have flirted with the inspired lunacy of *Bright Lights*. Instead, it overreaches by first having Brown serve Army stockade time, after being mistaken for a spy, followed by a Sergeant York–like success on the front lines, with seemingly the whole German army surrendering to Joe. Still, at some level, the powers-that-be intuitively knew that *Sons o' Guns* would be best served by a revue approach. That is, the best part of both his stockade silliness, and going to the front, involved the ethnic comedy schtick of masquerading as a British officer and a German commander. The bits are still funny today, and would undoubtedly have been all the more effective during the ethnic comedy–orientated 1930s. However, Brown's funny renditions of English and German accents are such obvious set pieces, artificially grafted onto the story, that once again, they would have been better served as components of an Army entertainment troupe, since "puttin' on a show" is a form of artificiality which doubles as a legitimate show business reality.

Given these high points, and closely following Brown's amazingly creative 1935, the reviews for *Sons o' Guns* were respectable. *The New York Times* said, "Throughout, Mr. Brown is his colossal self, and even a pair of handlebar apache mustaches [during the pantomime playlet] can't hide that telltale orifice [his trademark big mouth]."[8] *Variety* praised the comedian but had reservations about the overall picture: "Brown again clicks individually, with his versatility given full play, but the one-man Brown variety show isn't well supported for 79 minutes' duration."[9] Yet, despite the picture's faults, the latter criticism seems unduly harsh, given that Blondell and perennial movie servant Eric Blore both provide Brown with some diverting assistance in the comedy department. In addition, the scene-stealing comic character actor Mischa Auer turns up briefly in the stockade scene as an amusing spy. (Auer would receive an Academy Award nomination for Best Supporting Actor that same year for *My Man Godfrey*.)

Brown's second film of 1936, *Earthworm Tractors*, represents something of a poser for the conscientious biographer. Seen today, this is simply a one-joke movie; the comedian causes non-stop destruction every time he attempts to operate various large bulldozers which give the film its name. As the *Brooklyn Daily Eagle*'s review stated, "The director rather belabors a good idea, and one gets a little tired of Joe's wholesale destruction of the landscape."[10] But one should never underestimate the popularity of comic demolition, or what John Candy's 1970 *SCTV* mayhem-obsessed critic liked to describe as, "It blowed up reeeal good!" The *Brooklyn Daily Eagle* notwithstanding, most critics gave high praise to this low comedy. For example, the *New York Sun* opened its review by observing, "It has taken a tractor to prove that the art of slapstick comedy has not been entirely taken over by Walt Disney's cartoonists."[11] Along similar lines, the *New York Evening Journal* said, "Joe E. Brown can have a whopping time just by himself without any props but with a tractor — which he doesn't know how to run — Joe E. has one fine time."[12] The *New York American* added, "Check your troubles at the Roxy box office if you're a Joe Brown fan and an addict of the broad [destructive] hilarity provoked by the Grand Canyon [big mouth] of the Cinema at his hilarious best."[13] The rare critic not enamored of bulldozer slapstick still often felt the need to chronicle a wildly positive audience response. Thus, *The New York Post* reviewer confessed, "Personally, we didn't find the picture so funny. But the kids in front of us and those behind roared their heads off."[14]

While this *Post* perspective might make it easy to suggest that bulldozer Brown was now simply kiddie fare, that would not be entirely correct. Warner Brothers managed to stage a few of the mechanized scenes with a magnificent thrill comedy perspective that even Harold "Safety Last" Lloyd might have envied. This is best demonstrated by a finale in which Brown and his mechanical co-star must navigate an epic-sized but rickety wooden bridge. It is shot in mesmerizing long shot, and one is reminded of the locomotive–wooden bridge finale of Buster Keaton's *The General* (1927), a picture also named after a large moving machine.

Though forgotten today, *Earthworm Tractors* had another playing card which would have attracted adults to the theater: The movie was based upon a popular series of *Saturday Evening Post* short stories by William Hazlett Upson. The star of these comic tales, one Alexander Botts, was made to order for Brown. Upson's character is a "dumb-bell salesman with [a] super-ego who snatches victory from almost certain defeat as a drummer for Earthworm Tractors...."[15] It was as if Upson had patterned the figure after Brown's self-centered small-town persona. *Variety* projected "good returns at the box office ..." and *The Hollywood Reporter* felt that the film would translate to "Brown's best box office bet to date and that means money everywhere."[16] (Of the comedian's three 1936 pictures, the commercial returns of *Earthworm Tractors* were most responsible for him turning up on that year's top ten box office chart.)

Like Buster Keaton in *Cops* (1922), Brown's *Earthworm Tractor* character gets in comic hot water because of pressure from a girlfriend to succeed. But while Keaton's comedy heyday was a more youthfully innocent optimistic 1920s, Brown labored during the tough times of the 1930s, when comedians tended to be harder, older and more cynical, like Mae West, W. C. Fields and Groucho Marx. As previously noted, part of Brown's *oeuvre* is a throwback to the small-town go-getter innocence of the 1920s Harold Lloyd. But Joe's other screen persona, the breezy self-centered sort of *Earthworm Tractors*, is a first cousin to the Depression hucksters of West, Fields and Marx. Though devoid of their intelligence, he is just as apt to make it up as he goes along, forever confident he will succeed. Consequently, Brown manages to get an Earthworm Tractor sales position by lying through his teeth. In reality, he knows nothing about the vehicle, which soon becomes obvious when he destructively tries to demonstrate the machine. His ultimate success here is not unlike a Harry "by the grace of god" Langdon victory — the *deus ex machina* twist that has saved many a comic fool. One could argue, therefore, that Brown's popularity during the Depression was a product of comically double-dipping. He often showed the period moxie of a Fields huckster by bluffing his way through every situation. But since he lacked sufficient gray matter to orchestrate a con (such as Fields' outrageous selling of a "talking dog" in *Poppy*, also 1936), Brown fell back on the more sympathetic guise of a vulnerable Everyman character in need of a break.

Earthworm Tractors also benefited from a solid supporting cast which included gifted character actors Guy Kibbee and Gene Lockhart. Kibbee, the pudgy, put-upon anti-hero type best known as the puppet governor of Frank Capra's classic *Mr. Smith Goes to Washington* (1939), played the father of Brown's love interest and his hardest potential tractor customer. According to Brown's autobiography, the comic fear Kibbee registered every time he rode with the comedian on one of the giant tractors was very real.[17] But that was probably fueled, in part, by Brown's manic glee in operating this mechanized battering ram. In fact, he not only flattened every target in the script, but also a few other eyesores on the Warner backlot! Though Brown, unlike his screen character, became very adept at operating these bulldozers, his ready excuse for any excessive destruction was that the machine got away from him. Appropriately, the comic demolition that so attracted the public, particularly the youngsters, was also something that fascinated Brown.

Lockhart, perhaps best known today as the landlord figure in the celebrated Leo McCarey picture *Going My Way* (1944), appears as a rival salesman in *Earthworm Tractors*. And Brown's primary leading lady in the picture, after his brief dalliance with Carol Hughes' small-town girl, was the promising young actress June Travis. Though Travis' career never really took off, she merits a special note here by way of her connection with Brown. With the comedian then arguably Warner's biggest star, he had a great deal to say about casting in his pictures, such as close friend Frank McHugh often turning up as his cinema sidekick. Travis was the daughter of Harry Grabiner, vice-president of the Chicago White Sox, and often traveled the baseball circuit with her father.[18] Brown, the eternal baseball fanatic, had known the Grabiners for years. So one would assume that the comedian had had more than a little to do with getting then-budding

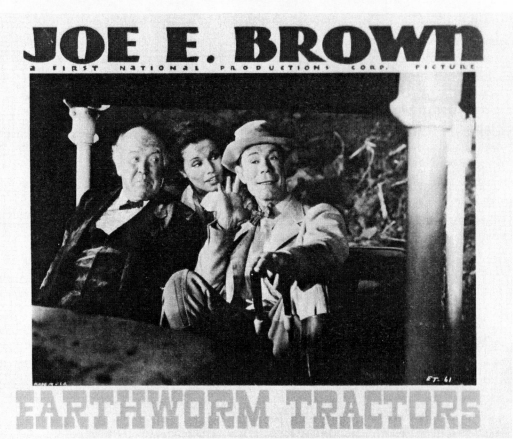

Brown and his most difficult customer Guy Kibbee, with Kibbee screen daughter June Travis in *Earthworm Tractors* (1936).

actress June a prominent part in his picture. Moreover, the fact that Brown did the radio play-by-play broadcasting of a number of White Sox and Cubs games the following year (1937) might have been facilitated by such a kindness.

Ironically, the most challenging part of the picture was *not* the grueling shoot but the summer heat wave premiere in Peoria, "the world's tractor center."[19] Besides a lengthy parade in an open car, Brown persevered his way through tours of a multitude of local charities and businesses, including the mammoth Caterpillar Tractor Company, the original catalyst for the picture. (The *Saturday Evening Post* author of the stories upon which *Earthworm Tractors* was based, William Hazlett Upson, had once been one of that company's salesmen.) As was typical for "people person" Brown, he completely charmed Peoria, the city which had also proclaimed the date of the premiere "Joe E. Brown Day." Everything the comedian did found favor with his Illinois film fans, starting with braving a 108-degree heat wave after an air conditioned train — "His flashy plaid coat seemed very uncomfortable in the baking sun, but that didn't keep Joe from signing numerous autographs. And with each autograph went a wisecrack."[20] His patience and good cheer in attending a hundred and one local events won him the stamp of "regular guy" and front page headlines like, "Joe E. Brown Is Truly Good Natured 'Boy,' He Shows At Peoria Reception."[21] Plus, here was an entertainer who could even pitch comic compliments based on the heat wave: "This has been a great reception — a warm reception — in fact, a hot reception. But I've enjoyed it as much as you."[22]

Brown's heartland premiere was a hit, but the most positive review for this frequently one-note picture came from a most unlikely source — the often hard-to-please *New York Times*. But as if recognizing the inherent weakness of this film, critic Bosley Crowther used his column space to wax poetic about the comedian in general, including one of the most affectionately long-winded tributes to Brown's comic face, with the oversized mouth. Though quoted at length in Chapter One, the poignant conclusion merits repeating: "But, for all [the face's] irregularities, it is also a face which has about it a certain rugged beauty, like the Maine coast."[23] Such a poetic Crowther comment is unusual, because as the later award-winning *New Yorker* critic Pauline Kael once comically observed, Crowther "can always be counted on to miss the point."[24] Be this as it may, while Crowther herein gets the point with his praise of Brown, there is one negative (between the lines) component to the piece, too. This quasi-review, which suddenly turns into random hosannas for Brown, could also double as a show business obituary. The chilling corollary to this implication — Crowther's timing was appropriate. That is, the comedian's streak of nearly non-stop quality pictures was derailed in 1936, with his forthcoming independent films often being deplorable. Thus, one could say, with a few exceptions (such as the much later *Some Like It Hot*, 1959), that a metaphorical Brown obituary was not inappropriate at this time.

The comedian's swan song for Warners, *Polo Joe*, returned him to a familiar scenario — masquerading as an athletic champion in a sport in which he was a novice. Brown's main memory of the picture in later years was linked to an uncited review which suggested that the performer was obviously a master horseback rider, despite the storyline.[25] One candidate for this critique would be the *New York Herald Tribune*'s take on *Polo Joe*: "[Brown] also tries to fool people into thinking he is no horseman; in this he does not succeed."[26] But the comedian enjoyed this tribute to his athleticism precisely because he had done *little* riding prior to *Polo Joe*. Routinely praised in reviews for the assorted athletic skills he brought to sports-orientated movies, especially related to baseball (see Chapter Six), Brown simply moved like an athlete, even if not skilled in a given sport. This was a physical grace he shared with friend and fellow comedian Buster Keaton, against whom he often played baseball. Of course, Brown might have been said to have inadvertently trained for his polo movie by taking part in a bizarre Hollywood diversion that swept the film community in 1934 — donkey baseball. This new approach to the national game had the batter hit the ball and then ride his mount to first base. All the fielders were on donkeys, too, and had to play the ball as closely to their animal as possible.[27]

The picture's most obvious liability for today's viewer is simply a flat script. The comedian had obviously gone this formula route before, but the proceedings had invariably been spiced up with new physical bits and fresh verbal repartee. There is none of that here. Indeed, one of the better sight gags, an overcrowded train compartment (as everyone attempts to close a window to alleviate the suffering of Joe's hay fever victim), is a direct steal from the Marx Brothers' famous "Stateroom Scene," that comedy seminar in overcrowding from the previous year's *A Night at the Opera* (1935). Whereas Brown material was getting lifted by others earlier in the decade, such as Joe's eccentric dance sequence from *Bright Lights* later resurfacing in Charlie Chaplin's *Modern Times* (1936), now Brown's films seemed more derivative.

Character actor Richard "Skeets" Gallagher plays the comedian's man Friday in *Polo Joe*, but there is not the chemistry exhibited here that was apparent between Brown and Eric Blore in a similar arrangement from *Sons o' Guns*. More effective in *Polo Joe* is supporting player Fay Holden, as the star's zany aunt. But like the rest of the script, her part is underwritten, and often simply calls for her to have long, drawn-out laughing attacks — which get old very quickly. Brown's love interest, Carol Hughes, is the most basic of romantic window dressing. While personality comedies seldom merit much more of a catalyst for change than a pretty face, even this part seems unduly thin.

The *Polo Joe* reviews were a mixed bag. *New York World Telegram* film critic and Brown fan William Boehnel was very positive in his critique: "Whether or not you happen to like Joe E. Brown, you're bound to have a good time watching his antics in *Polo Joe* ... which combines polo, love, and burlesque in an engaging and amusing manner."[28] Equally positive was Wanda Hale's *New York Daily News* review though, like Boehnel, she was quick to recognize that not everyone was a follower of the comedian: "Even though you're not a 'dyed-in-the-wool' Joe E. Brown fan we defy you to sit through *Polo Joe* without, intermittently, rolling in the aisles at the clown's capers. The Brothers Warner never have to worry over a Brown vehicle; the old one [Brown] is still good."[29]

In contrast, *The Hollywood Reporter*'s faint praise had a more diplomatically restrained tone:

> This last Brown comedy from the Burbank [Warner] lot is an adequate representation of the staple, reliable stuff that the exhibitors have come to expect from the cavern-mouthed comic. It will neither betray nor enhance the Brown box office draw.[30]

But there were no kid gloves from *Variety*, which bluntly panned the proceedings, "*Polo Joe* is one of the poorer of the comedian's vehicles and Brown's followers no matter how faithful, will be disappointed in him this time out."[31] *The New York Times* assumed a middle ground between *Variety* and *The Hollywood Reporter*, being unimpressed by the picture but deftly steering their disapproval away from the comedian: "For *Polo Joe* isn't

Mr. Brown's mistake but its script writers ... There isn't much any one can do with that [material], but the crater-mouthed comedian never stops trying and actually manages to win a few unreluctant chuckles."[32]

This latter *Time* review by Frank S. Nugent conjures up a reference to a stock figure in Italian comic theater — pantaloon (Pantalone), a foolish, pantaloons-wearing old man. Nugent treats him more as an abused god of comedy, "with the great pantaloon laughing hollowly at the picture's little jokes and wordlessly begging the audience to forgive the sins he is being forced to commit in the name of comedy."[33] While Nugent is treating the figure as no more than literary ornamentation, a tony *Times* garnishment, its usage makes one wonder how Brown might have explained the comic failure of *Polo Joe*. Granted, the comedian was not much for comedy theory, beyond his self-explanatory "downfall of dignity."[34] But he later made the most telling revelation when re-examining his favorite part, the baseball-playing title character of *Elmer the Great* (1933). Reflecting upon the touchingly comic authenticity of Elmer, Brown bemoaned the fact that "[t]oo often my roles had involved routines which had nothing to do with the characters, so that the laughs had to be artificially manufactured."[35] Though Brown's comments are obviously directed at the fall from comic grace which followed his exit from Warners, these symptoms are apparent in *Polo Joe*. His character in this picture is a mystery — an apparently wealthy young man returning to America after having spent years in China. Visiting his dotty but well-to-do aunt, a refugee from a screwball comedy, he meets a polo-crazed beauty and decides that mastering the sport will lead to romance. This covers the plot.

A thin narrative, however, does not necessarily hurt a personality comedy. Being thin on characterization does. The clown genre is all about establishing a humor hall tree upon which the comedian can "hang" his comic schtick — specific routines and/or variations of them which lend themselves to establishing the all-important screen comedy persona. By 1936, however, Brown had long ago established his personality comedian credentials. But this picture, and a number of the independently produced films to follow, did not allow Brown's humor hall tree of schtick (from that big-mouthed yell and athletic demeanor, to a propensity for eccentric dancing and the small-town milieu) to be showcased in a believable character. Brown had known and played baseball with an army of Elmers, and probably flirted with the egotism that drove (and sometimes derailed) this country fellow. What did he know, or care, about some shadowy figure visiting from China? *Polo Joe* suffered because of this.

Though most comedy depends to some degree upon exaggeration, the most memorable of merry moments are those with one foot in reality. That is why Elmer was Brown's favorite role. Moreover, such reality-touched comedy becomes not only a gift for the audience but a haven for the artist — an extension of who they are. I am reminded of an observation by author Ann Patchett on the nature of writing which also doubles as an insight on creativity in general: It "is a job, a talent, but it's also the place to go in your head. It is the imaginary friend you drink your tea with in the afternoon."[36]

The imaginary was about to leave the films of Joe E. Brown.

Ten

Creative Free Fall
and the Children's Advocate

One of the rare bright spots in Joe E. Brown's post–Warner films was *The Gladiator* (1938), in which a strength serum gives his college athlete unbelievable power. Thus, when someone offers to let him throw a javelin, Brown's incredulous character asks, "What's a matter, don't you want it?"

In July 1935, *The Hollywood Reporter* ran a short announcement that Brown would star in a Foreign Legion comedy as part of Warner Brothers' 1935–36 picture lineup.[1] Though this never came to pass, and the comedian left the studio by the end of 1936, one could metaphorically suggest that his film career then assumed a "Foreign Legion" posture, and *disappeared* for the rest of the decade. But it was not that the pictures stopped; the quality simply dropped off.

In 1936, Brown had signed a six-picture deal with independent producer David Loew.[2] While the comedian would later call this a "disastrous move" in his autobiography, with production standards not up to Warners levels, he would sometimes also hedge on this explanation, and cite health reasons.[3] But these threats to his well-being, a 1938 double hernia operation and a late 1939 automobile accident, occurred well after the majority of the mediocre movies were released. Indeed, as suggested in the previous chapter, the decline really started during his lame duck year (1936) at Warners.

An added quality control culprit was an increasingly frantic lifestyle. With his two older children (Don and Joe, Jr.) now at UCLA, Brown's wanderlust tendencies escalated even more, with wife Kathryn and the little girls (Kathryn Frances and Mary Elizabeth) joining him when possible. For instance, a 1937 press release revealed, "Joe and his wife are constantly away between pictures. Their present schedule ... calls for them to make a trip to Chicago, where Joe will do some [Cubs and White Sox radio] broadcasting ... [followed by] a long promised trip to the Orient."[4] (His 1936 foreign itinerary had included performing in London and accompanying the American Olympic team to Berlin.) It should be remembered that Douglas Fairbanks, Sr., the original filmland "King" (long before Clark Gable was accorded that title in the 1930s), had first established globetrotting as the epitome of Hollywood cool back in the silent era.

At home, Brown's busy dance card included an increased booster's attention to

UCLA, where his sons were on the football team, not to mention other local sports interests. For example, as a former racehorse owner and aficionado, he joined friend Bing Crosby and other entertainment celebrities in establishing a track at Del Mar, California. It was incorporated May 5, 1936; other founding members included Brown's close Warners buddy Pat O'Brien, Oliver Hardy, Gary Cooper and Leo McCarey.[5] Brown also had a controlling interest in professional boxer Lou Jallos, with newspaper columnist Mitchell Woodbury noting, as early as 1934, that "never a Friday night passes at the Hollywood stadium bouts but that [Brown] isn't forced into the ring for a bow or some bit of tomfoolery before the main event."[6] These pre-fight events became such a distraction, especially after a comic wrestling match with fellow screen clown Eddie Cantor, that Brown (with tongue firmly in cheek) had "himself suspended by the [local] athletic commission for unnecessary roughness."[7] Not surprisingly, the Brown fight fans were buying none of this, and the comedian was soon back in the pre-bout ring with an assortment of film-related foes, including a memorably merry encounter with silent star Richard Barthelmess.

Though Brown lost his studio-sponsored baseball team when he left Warner Brothers, the comedian immediately organized a new squad, drawing from his large network of diamond fans both in and out of the movie industry. Moreover, the comedian's naturally egalitarian nature took on a much more practical side in drafting a team. Never one to create a tony celebrity baseball nine, Brown was democratically more likely to choose no-name behind-the-scenes types ... *if* they were exceptional hitters and fielders! Remember, this was a man whose childhood hero had been baseball superstar Ty "win at all costs" Cobb. Consequently, Brown continued to squeeze in lots of participatory games, from various charities, to the annual West Coast spring training visits of the Chicago Cubs. And when he was not playing ball, he was watching a broad cross-section of athletic events. This was fueled by both a fan's fascination with the mythic sports hero, and Brown's need to ever expand his burgeoning personal hall of fame — the sports memorabilia den in his Beverly Hills home, which he called "My Room of Love." Though these treasures were dominated by legendary baseball artifacts, here are a few notable Brown items gathered by the late 1930s from other sports: the football jersey worn by the celebrated Red Grange in his last game (Chicago Bears vs. the Coast All-Stars), the track shoes worn by famed 1930s sprinter Frank Wykoff when he set the 100-yard dash record, a headband worn by pioneering automobile racer Barney Oldfield, a hockey stick used by the world champion India team in the 1932 Olympic games, and a horseshoe from Seabiscuit![8] As writer Jack Holland observed in the 1930s:

> Joe E ... has probably known more sports champs than any one person in the country. And there's nothing he likes better than to sit down in his big easy chair, pull out a baseball glove, George Coleman's swimming cap, Frank Hawks' [flying] helmet ... boxing gloves belonging to one of the greats ... and just think back over the vast number of [sports] experiences that have richly been his.[9]

Given this Brown fascination with all things athletic, it makes perfect sense that easily the best of the immediate post–Warner films was the sports comedy (focus on football) *The Gladiator*. Unfortunately, this was the fifth picture in the six-movie deal signed with Loew — quite the wait for a quality outing. The preceding films, which will be addressed shortly, were *When's Your Birthday, Riding on Air, Fit for a King* (all 1937) and *Wide Open Faces* (1938). But a brief examination of *The Gladiator* will explore just why this should have been the norm instead of the exception and how quickly the Brown reputation for quality comedy had been damaged.

The Gladiator anticipates, along comic lines, today's steroid issue. Brown plays an older Webster College student who had dropped out 12 years earlier because of financial problems. Both his father and grandfather had been Webster athletic stars. While he has no plans to play sports, a pretty coed (June Travis, his *Earthworm Tractors* co-star in 1936) encourages him to go out for football. She also provides the film with its title. Looking at the college's tributary pictures of Brown's relatives, she observes, "You should be a born gladiator." But his small-town milquetoast type, Hugo Kipp, has a disastrous first practice. Borrowing a scene from Harold Lloyd's *The Freshman* (1925), Brown is literally reduced to use as a tackling dummy. Worse yet, he is a victim of hazing. After Hugo is brought home to Prof. Danner's boarding house is a wheelbarrow, the old scientist takes pity and gives him a dose of an experimental strength drug.

The next day at practice, the proverbial worm turns. Brown scores a long touchdown run on a kick-off return in which he breaks tackle after tackle. Though football is the in-season sport, Hugo's newfound strength is also tested in track events, with amazing tosses for both the javelin and the discus. He has grown so powerful that the professor fears he will hurt someone: "It will be murder." So possible injury to others, rather than ethics, is what initially derails this early exercise in a steroid-like situation.

The age-old urgency to have a winning football team, though, results in the squad putting pressure on Brown's character to rejoin the group. Not knowing his strength is drug-induced, the team simply sees an amazing athlete. Travis' beautiful coed is elected to sweet-talk Hugo back. Naturally, she succeeds but he consciously decides to play carefully, like in his former job as a hospital aide at a children's hospital. With Hugo's participation, Webster College has a terrific fall, with the film utilizing newsreel footage from the oldest and most prestigious of amateur gridiron events, the Rose Bowl.

Travis' character is slowly falling in love, while Hugo has been smitten from day one. Yet, consistent with his small-town anti-heroic demeanor, he has trouble expressing his feelings to her. For example, when the youngster starts to quote the old romantic axiom, "In the spring a young man's fancy," she interrupts him by saying it is fall. Brown's frustrated fellow responds, "That's what makes it so tough." Unfortunately, he soon finds out that her initial involvement with him had been a ploy and, as occurred when he felt used in the baseball picture *Elmer the Great* (1933), he rebels. But *The Gladiator* then takes a new direction. Instead of eventually returning to football, where the picture has exhausted all its comic possibilities, Brown finds himself in a professional wrestling match against a 1930s icon in this sport — Man Mountain Dean (as himself). This is simply a variation on personality comedy's picaresque nature — maximize the humor at one location, and then move to another.[10] This phenomenon also allows our clown to interact with an ever-changing assortment of comic characters, such as Dean.

As is required of most personality comedies, all is resolved happily in *The Gladiator*. But because the strength serum wanes in mid-match, Brown's undersized wrestler has to win on his own skills. Or, more precisely, a lucky kick at the end of the competition. (Though Brown is superhuman in the picture, reality soon caught up with the actor. After several takes of lifting the 300-pound plus Dean, the 150-pound comedian needed surgery for a double hernia!)

This painful side of comedy notwithstanding, *The Gladiator* would be a

Brown as a fierce football player in *The Gladiator* (1938).

major critical and commercial hit — the last success of this magnitude in which he was the headliner. I sifted through over a score of reviews, and they were all ones Brown's mother might have written. From *The New York Times*:

> The slapstick tradition, which of late has been as much dishonored in the observance as in the breach, has achieved some kind of a jubilee this week in the new Joe E. Brown comedy at the Globe [Theatre]. Not since Chaplin have we behold so unbrokenly successful a pattern of pure cinematic clownery, or one that tickled us so hugely....[11]

The *New York Times* compared him to Chaplin! Too often, poorly researched contemporary criticism bemoans the fact that Brown was "shunned by [1930s] critics."[12] Nothing could have been further from the truth, although Brown's run of poor pictures both before and after *The Gladiator* threatened that positive critic-comedian relationship.

All-important *Variety* called this football-wrestling movie "[o]ne of the merriest stories which Joe E. Brown has done. Full of action. It's goofy, but a lot of fun, and it will help any bill on which it's included."[13] The *New York Post* called it "about as funny a picture as he or any other giggle-getter has offered in a season or so."[14] The *Brooklyn Eagle*, under the enthusiastic headline, "Joe E. Brown, With a Brightly Written Movie Called *The Gladiator* Under Him, Gallops Hilariously Across Globe's Screen," added, "So this is frisky comedy, the kind the sophisticated laugh at as well as the simple lovers of slapstick, and the children."[15]

Critics were also quick to document viewer response, such as the opening to the *Motion Picture Herald*'s review: "The preview audience was in general agreement that *The Gladiator* is one of Joe E. Brown's most amusing pictures."[16] And the *New York Daily News* described an audience that "approved noisily of every minute of it."[17] The response from critics and viewers alike was so strong that Brown's producer, David Loew, ran a full-page ad in *The Hollywood Reporter* citing 18 assorted raves.[18]

Digging deeper in the reviews, however, one finds a level of frustration with Brown's recent pictures. For instance, *The Hollywood Reporter*'s *Gladiator* critique said, "This is by far the best Joe E. Brown picture David Loew has turned out. Loew finally has hit on a combination of writers and director which has given the Brown fans something they will thoroughly enjoy."[19] More pointed still was a small-town theater owner's critique of the picture from the *Motion Picture Herald*'s "What the Picture Did for Me" small-market section. Writing from his Caney, Kansas, Liberty Theatre, C. R. Greg confessed:

> I made a mistake on this [film] and as the past few Joe E. Brown pictures were no good, I just played this one as a double-bill on Saturday. Don't make a mistake. Give *The Gladiator* two days [standard playing length] with plenty of billing and watch it go.[20]

Other mini-reviews from this small-theater section diplomatically implied the same, such as this comment from Sodus, New York: "We agree with our patrons that this is the best Joe E. Brown in some time. Very satisfactory ..."[21]

So what is wrong with the other Loew-produced Brown pictures — *When's Your Birthday?*, *Riding on Air*, *Fit for a King*, *Wide Open Faces* and *Flirting with Fate* (1938, which followed *The Gladiator*)? First, and most obvious, production values are not what they were at Warner Brothers. Even *The Gladiator* looks cheap compared to the college settings of *Local Boy Makes Good* (1931). The irony here is that Warners was hardly the Cadillac of studios during the 1930s. Among the majors, they were a poor cousin to MGM and Paramount. In fact, industry insiders used to kid that Warners excelled at the backstage musical because it was less expensive to produce. Still, they did right by Brown. The comedian's Warners sets consistently looked richly believable, with occasional impressive on-location shooting, such as in *Son of a Sailor* (1933). One might compare this drop-off in Brown's production values to the look of writer-director Preston Sturges' *The Sin of Harold Diddlebock* (1947), his first independently produced picture after leaving Paramount. While this underrated film merits a revisionist upgrading, the sets are strictly bargain basement in appearance.

The second problem plaguing the Loew-produced Brown movies is that the comedian is seldom given appropriate parts. *When's Your Birthday?* has him playing an astrologer. In *Fit for a King*, he is a newsman in Europe trying to thwart a royal assassination. And in *Flirting with Fate*, Brown is a suicidal manager of a theatrical troupe stranded in South America. None of these are remotely right for Brown, the most mainstream of American comedians. Both of his comedy types, the egotistical smart aleck and the milquetoast anti-hero, are small-town, sports-minded characters. He should never stray far from this foundation, let alone leave the country.

Wide Open Faces initially follows this principle, with Brown as a soda jerk in a backwater town. But once the picture introduces gangsters and tries to turn his character into a detective, the story falls outside the comfort zone of the comedian's dual personae. Only with *Riding on Air*, Brown's best Loew film after *The Gladiator*, is the comic's character consistency maintained. *Riding on Air* has the comedian playing the most American of small-town journalists — Elmer Lane, a character made famous by *The Saturday Evening Post* short stories of Richard Macaulay, who co-scripted the film. Fittingly, Lane was also a character obsessed by sports.[22] Though the trait was not drawn upon in *Riding on Air, Post* readers would have been aware of its connection to Brown, and the appropriateness of casting this comedian.

A third problem for the Loew-produced pictures was that Brown only "essayed" his milquetoast type. Warners had always been good about fluctuating between this anti-heroic figure and his smart aleck. Moreover, if truth be told, the comedian's best and favorite films, his baseball trilogy (see Chapter Six) and *Bright Lights* (1935) were decidedly from the smart-aleck camp. So why abandon this figure, not to mention making his anti-hero increasingly sappy, such as calling his *Wide Open Faces* soda jerk Wilbur Meeks? This failure to fluctuate anticipates a similar problem by Red Skelton in early 1950s television. After a highly rated first season on the small screen, his numbers suffered a precipitous drop for several years — an era of great network patience. When writer-troubleshooter Sherwood Schwartz was hired to right this comedy ship, one of his key corrections addressed the problem of over-exposing Skelton's troupe of characters. In the pre–Schwartz era, Red peppered each program with appearances by several of his comedy types. Schwartz changed the format to only one Skelton figure per show. This change, coupled with a more thematically tightened program, improved ratings dramatically.[23] Like Skelton, Brown's Loew pictures would have been assisted with some character type fluctuation, especially given that his strongest comedy persona (the egotistical wiseguy) was ignored.

A fourth weakness for Brown's films under the Loew label has to do with comedy character inconsistency, a fault which has to be laid at the comedian's feet. That is, his characters sometimes did and/or experienced things which were not in their normal humor perimeters. For example, given Brown's clown comedy puss, with that cavernous mouth and comic slits for eyes, he was no lady's man. Romantic interest in his screen characters was normally a drawn-out process related to a girl slowly succumbing to his inherent decency, such as Joe's bookstore co-worker in *Local Boy Makes Good*. But this was often not the case in the Loew pictures. The *New York Times* review of *Fit for a King* even called Brown to task for this, though it was done with comic affection:

> Incidentally, in [Brown's] last few films Joe (once the wallflower's delight) has shown signs of becoming a regular lady-killer, and this romantic cycle, which is continued in the present exhibit to a point where Joe might be mistaken for [handsome matinee idol] Tyrone Power Jr., is another thing we deplore, on behalf of Joe's loyal following among the frustrated.[24]

Coupled with this romantic inconsistency, Brown's characters under the Loew banner, and *after* his break with the producer, seemed to become progressively more dimwitted. While there was nothing new about Joe playing the fool, his earlier figures (with the exception of the inspired idiocy of Flute in *A Midsummer Night's Dream*, 1935) were usually not without some insights, such as the comments by his *Alibi Ike* (1935) title character on the nature of relationships between men and women: "Sometimes a fella don't know exactly what he's getting into. Take a good-lookin' girl and a fella does just what she wants him to do. When a fella gets to feeling sorry for a girl, it's off [he's hooked]."

Though tradition has long decreed that we transcend our comic favorites (indeed, the oldest of comedy theories is that of superiority), we still enjoy the odd comment from the fool which might make us reconsider our position on him. For instance, maybe his entertaining idiocy is something of a pose, and we label him a "wise fool," or "crazy like a fox." Or maybe the surprising observation is not so much insightfully wise, as revealing of an entirely different comedy agenda for our character. Then again, the fool's startling comment might only be an accidental exercise in comic absurdity. One such example, which could be bracketed under any of these umbrella explanations, would be Brown's much later closing line in *Some Like It Hot* (1959). After his fiancée (Jack Lemmon in drag) has gone through a litany of reasons on why they cannot marry, culminating with the fact that Lemmon is really a man, Brown observes, "Well, nobody's perfect." Now whether one interprets this as the height of comic absurdity or an eleventh-hour revelation that Brown's character is really a poser who swings both ways, the line does give wonderful pause to the picture — a close which does not close but rather opens new questions. This is the possible power of the fool — a potential for comic genius which Brown seems to abdicate, for a time, in the second half of the 1930s.

This sometime lack of character consistency by the comedian is surprising, given that Brown was a screen veteran by this time. Normally, this is something which plagues a comic figure early in his film career, such as Frank Capra's take on why Harry Langdon's career crashed and burned in the waning days of silent cinema — Langdon did not fully grasp the limitations of his screen persona.[25] Ironically, modern comedian Paul Reubens' most popular character, Pee-wee Herman, whose baby-faced persona resembles Langdon, also had an aborted film career plagued by this figure's inconsistency. Though normally written off today as the result of a series of sexual scandals, Pee-wee's movie career tanked well before this personal travail. After the brilliant *Pee-wee's Big Adventure* (1985, no doubt greatly assisted by gifted director Tim Burton), there would only be the disappointing *Big Top Pee-wee* (1988). Like Brown's films under Loew, one of Reuben's inconsistencies in the latter picture was a patently non-romantic figure (Pee-wee) suddenly becoming a ladies' man.

A final weak link in Brown's later films was that Father Time had started to catch up with the comedian who regularly played a young small-town hero or anti-hero. By 1940 he was nearly 50 and, though still boyish in appearance, he no longer passed as that fresh-faced kid from some stereotypical middle–American town. Brown's signature roles during his senior years, Captain Andy in *Show Boat* (1951) and the oversexed Osgood Fielding III of *Some Like It Hot*, had him playing characters his own age.

One should not leave this late 1930s tailspin totally demoralized. *The Gladiator* was a bona fide football hit, and *Riding on Air* had the most fitting of alter ego characters for Brown (the aforementioned Elmer Lane). In fact, period profiles of Lane creator Richard Macaulay reveal further parallels with Brown, especially involving athletics. Thus, while both men continued to regularly play a broad spectrum of sports which included tennis and golf, each individual's voyeuristic fan tendencies approached the obsessional. The following 1935 quote from Macaulay might just as easily have been taken from Brown:

> I am a football nut, one of the finest practicing Monday-morning quarterbacks in the business, and can tell you who ran how far in what game of 1927, even when you don't want to hear it. Basketball and baseball also claim my enthusiasm, and year after year I wait patiently for the White Sox to win another pennant. I've waited sixteen years, so I guess another few won't hurt me.[26]

Even when these late 1930s Brown vehicles were disappointing, the comedian still often managed respectable reviews — trading upon years of previous quality comedies. To illustrate, his *Wide Open Faces* was a real stinker. Yet, *The Hollywood Reporter* said of this picture:

[D]espite the shabby treatment which was accorded the excellent basic idea ... [and] the paucity of imagination displayed in developing the intrinsic plot, there is constant resort to sheer slapstick ... [that] remains funny enough and has sufficient sparkle ... to make it a good average Brown, which will please the Joe E. Fans.[27]

Quite possibly, this "can do no wrong" phenomenon might also have contributed to Brown's movie mediocrity at this time — the temptation to coast. Of course, not everyone was buying. Certain publications, such as *Variety*, were now categorizing Brown's weaker efforts as strictly child-oriented. Of the otherwise critically well-received *Riding on Air*, *Variety* opined, "[It] is out of the bottom of the basket. Will satisfy the Joe E. Brown addicts ... [N]one of it makes sense, but it's a natural for the juve [juvenile] matinees."[28]

Though radio audiences could not see the comedian's signature mouth, they could hear the yell — The *Joe E. Brown Show* (1938–1939).

As if taking this lead, the comedian, always conscious of youngsters, hosted the children-focused *Joe E. Brown Show* on CBS radio during the 1938–39 season. This half-hour comedy variety program was broadcast Saturday nights at 7:30 (EST), sponsored by Post Toasties. In the 1938 article "Post Toasties [Brown's program] A Natural for Kiddies Air Show," the comic wrote, "[W]hatever it was that each of us missed in our childhood we are likely to be more interested in as we grow up."[29] Since Brown entered show business at nine, he missed much of his childhood. Consequently, the comedian had always been driven to produce wholesome entertainment which youngsters could appreciate. Fittingly for this sports-obsessed entertainer, Brown likened the responsibility-legacy he felt towards children to the ongoing influence of his late friend Knute Rockne (1888–1931), the legendary football coach who built Notre Dame into a national gridiron power. Just as Brown could see Rockne's values continued in the young men he coached, the comedian also liked to think that the life lessons his comedy provided were positive. In addition, Brown's radio program was generously sprinkled with the feelgood populism so often linked to sports, since "the public likes to see an underdog eventually come out on top."[30]

While Brown's show received respectable ratings, it did not return for a second season.[31] But the comedian never stopped advocating for children. In 1939 he would be that rare public figure to speak out in favor of Congressional legislation which would permit 20,000 German-Jewish refugee children into the United States. Brown even flew to Washington to plead before the House Immigration and Naturalization Committee. Calling it a "simple act of humanity," the comic added, "We shouldn't be smug about things like this and say that we are getting along all right so let the rest of the world take care of itself."[32] When critics countered that there were plenty of poor children in America, Brown said that opening the gates of immigration "would lead to more interest in needy children here."[33] As the father of two adopted daughters, the comedian went on to say, "We shouldn't forget unfortunate children at home, but because these youngsters live across the sea I don't think we should forget them."[34]

While this wonderfully demonstrates Brown's compassion for the young and the oppressed, it also demonstrates his bravery and disregard for potential negative repercussions. These were conservative times when the subject was race relations. The same day (May 25, 1939) that *The New York Times* and other major newspapers keyed upon this House hearing regarding Jewish refugee children, the *Times* also ran an even more prominent article entitled "'Patriotic' Rally Has Anti-Semitic Tinge."[35] But one wonders about the qualifier term "Tinge," since the essay goes on to note that a featured speaker "was interrupted a dozen times by cries from the floor to 'throw the Jews out of Christian America.'"[36] More specifically, a number of isolationist and anti–Semitic groups banded together as the Allied Patriotic Societies to oppose the refugee bill. These conservative member organizations included the Veterans of Foreign Wars, the American Legion, the Society of Mayflower Descendants, the Daughters of the American Revolution, the Lord's Day Alliance of the United States, and the Daughters of the Confederacy. Francis H. Kinnicutt, president of the Allied Patriotic Societies, was perfectly blunt about the collective group's anti–Semitic agenda: "Strictly speaking, it is not a refugee bill at all, for by the nature of the case most of those admitted would be of the Jewish race."[37] As a final historical footnote to that era, the American Nazi Party had a political rally at Madison Square Garden as late as 1940. Plus, when Brown's comedy hero Charlie Chaplin did his satire of Hitler, *The Great Dictator* (1940), the diminutive comedian received hate mail.[38]

A further measure of these anti–Semitic times is indirectly found in the newspaper coverage of the refugee children. A survey of several major publications found only one newspaper (the *Des Moines Register* [39]) which even referred to them as Jewish. Otherwise, simply "refugee" was the optimal word, though *The New York Times* did get adventuresome and call the 20,000 youngsters "children of parents under persecution in Germany."[40] It was as if merely the term "Jewish" was something volatile. All this represents more evidence for the frightening validity of celebrated novelist Philip Roth's *The Plot Against America* (2004), which chronicles what might have occurred had the anti–Semitic aviator Charles Lindbergh been elected president in 1940.[41]

Brown was not alone in his support of the Wagner-Rogers bill which would have made it possible for these youngsters to come to America. Though in the minority, other prominent citizens also endorsed this legislation. But what is painfully obvious from period accounts is that the comedian was the only entertainer of note who made the effort, at his own expense, to fly to Washington and lobby for these at-risk youngsters. How paradoxical, that at a time when his movies were suffering through a creative nadir, Brown's "role" as a secular humanist should soar.

The Wagner-Rogers bill did not pass. In fact, it never moved beyond committee consideration level. Presumably, many of those Jewish children ended up in Nazi concentration camps.

Along related crusader lines, with much of the world at war by the following year (1940), the comedian used his love of children and tolerance for a metaphorical message on peace which played upon an old reference to grade school education: "The three R's are all right in their way but the three L's — Love, Learn and Laugh — are righter, especially right now. What we need to stop war is a crusade against hate — a crusade of laughter."[42] (His 1956 autobiography would be entitled *LAUGHTER Is a Wonderful Thing*.) As the following chapter will demonstrate, Brown lived up to his words in a multitude of ways after the United States' 1941 entry into World War II, from speaking out against the tragic relocation of Japanese-Americans to internment camps (more racial tolerance from the comedian), to entertaining tens of thousands of young American soldiers around the globe. Brown epitomizes the men and women whom *NBC Nightly News* anchor Tom Brokaw wrote about in his monumental tribute to World War II Americans, *The Greatest Generation* (1998).[43] Flash-forward to the 1950s, when America's youth were being attacked as juvenile delinquents; Brown's consistency as an advocate for the young remained constant:

> Our boys and girls are the finest people on earth. It's the older generation that has lost faith and hope — and we'd better start rebuilding immediately. If we want better kids, we have to have better grownups.[44]

While Brown's commitment to the young stretched back a lifetime to his own lost childhood, he had several months of unplanned introspection forced upon him in December of 1939. Driving along Sunset Boulevard near UCLA's "Joe E. Brown [baseball] field," the comedian was involved in a two-car accident in which his station wagon rolled end over end for 75 feet and then dropped down a 35-foot embankment.[45] Though Brown and the media tended to treat the accident casually, such as a *Chicago Tribune* headline about the comic being in "stitches," or Joe's widely quoted comment to his doctor, "Might have been a good idea to have sewed up part of my [cavernous] mouth while you were at it," Brown's injuries proved more serious.

What is unclear is whether the original report was a faulty diagnosis, or a smoke screen to protect Brown (in an era when health problems were considered a potential career liability). The comedian's oldest son, Don, initially told reporters that his father was "shaken and bruised and had minor cuts, but that no bones were broken."[46] But it was soon clear that the elder Brown had broken his back for the second time. (Like the comic's baseball buddy and fellow screen funnyman Buster Keaton, Brown had unknowingly broken his back as a young entertainer, only to immediately go back on stage and soldier through the pain. It was only years later that an unrelated x-ray revealed the break.)

During surgery to stitch up facial lacerations, his heart stopped. But the comedian was a fatalist and simply felt his "number hadn't come up."[47] While having no desire to die, he was all right with what he saw as a preordained book of life. Still, two things bothered him during his long convalescence. One was basic father-love; his six-year-old daughter Kathryn had suffered a skull fracture three days before Joe's accident. She had been thrown from a horse, and it is possible he might have felt somehow responsible, since he had become fascinated with riding after making *Polo Joe* (1936). Thankfully, Kathryn had a rapid and complete recovery.

This recovery gave Brown more time to brood over concern number two—his slumping career. Though the comedian had been in something of a creative free-fall since his lame duck year (1936) at Warners, Joe's latest films before the accident, *$1,000 a Touchdown* and *Beware Spooks* (both 1939), had been especially disappointing. *Touchdown* had been the real *coup de grace* to his comedy confidence. As the first movie after his unfortunate teaming with independent producer David Loew, *Touchdown* seemed to have everything going for it. Normally, sports stories were a sure thing for Brown, and *Touchdown* was another college football saga, just a year after his gridiron hit *The Gladiator*—a rare success under Loew. *Touchdown* also featured what should have been ideal casting—Brown co-starred with fellow big-mouth comedienne Martha Raye. But as the *New York Daily News* critic noted, "It is inevitable that these two players, on whose mouths nature's knife slipped, would get together for at least one picture. The idea itself is very funny but the result isn't. Paramount failed to take advantage of the possibilities."[48] *The New York Times* was even more pointed in its criticism, including a comic broadside close to its review: "It ends with Joe E. scoring the last-second touchdown by being thrown over the goal posts. They threw the wrong man: Delmer Daves, who wrote it, would be our choice—and we'd insist on a field goal."[49] Brown's later take on the picture was much more succinct: "it was terrible."[50]

Failure is always frustrating, but for a man whose personal philosophy was the old axiom, "If it is worth doing, it is worth doing well," this development must have been especially galling.[51] Brown decided that once he physically recovered, the best gauge for the real state of his acting would be to briefly return to the stage. With a live audience he could get immediate feedback on his thespian skills, which he had begun to doubt by late 1939. In 1940 Brown would return to regional theater with a revival of his beloved *Elmer the Great*, the Ring Lardner-George Cohan play which Joe had played so successfully on stage and screen in years past. Not surprisingly, he was a resounding success in New Haven, Connecticut, with *The New York Times* even covering his first-night audience-demanded curtain speech. Brown's lengthy remarks began comically (he referred to his return to the "illegitimate stage") but he soon dovetailed into a perspective consistent with his aforementioned "Three L's": "In his speech he said his aim was to get 'decent laughs,' no matter how far he had to go for them, and that these were what the world needed more than anything else today."[52]

Brown was getting back his live audience comedy confidence at the most opportune of times, for he was on the verge of an extended one-man tour of unprecedented dimensions. And it would be an inspired mix of his twin passions — the healing nature of laughter, in the support of the young. With World War II as a catalyst, and American soldiers around the globe, Brown's "theater" was about to become the world at large.

ELEVEN

"G. I. Joe" for *Your Kids and Mine*

When you have lost your own boy all other lads become your sons.
— Joe E. Brown (1944)[1]

While Brown would later call the 1930s his most satisfying decade, the 1940s would qualify as his most bittersweet.[2] From the agonizing loss of his beloved oldest son, Don Evan, in a war-related plane crash (1942), to Joe's groundbreaking and revitalizing entertaining of American troops (1942–45) around the globe during World War II, the comedian was on a proverbial rollercoaster of emotions during the first half of the decade.

As if following that stereotypical script that plots scenes of quiet before the inevitable storm, the 1940s began on an upbeat note for Brown, privately and professionally. The comedian and his wife Kathryn renewed their vows at Hollywood's St. Thomas Church on Christmas Eve 1940 — the twenty-fifth anniversary of their marriage. The original 1915 ceremony had been a simple affair at the New York City Courthouse. But the financially pinched Brown had promised his bride "some day we'll have a real wedding, in a church, with organ music and flowers and all the rest."[3] An added catalyst for this romantic event might have been the September 1940 marriage of Joe and Kathryn's younger son, 21-year-old Joe LeRoy, with brother Don as best man.[4] (Of course, one should add that Brown was always decidedly sentimental. Just the year before, he had been so moved by the poignant close to the romantic comedy *Love Affair* that he would later write about it as "My Favorite Movie Scene."[5])

Regardless, as noted earlier in the text, Joe and Kathryn's silver anniversary wedding was a celebration of family. Don gave the "bride" in marriage. Joe LeRoy was best man. Elementary school–aged daughters Mary Elizabeth and Kathryn Frances were the flower girls, and daughter-in-law Virginia Newport Brown was matron of honor. Back in 1915, the comic and Kathryn had to limit their wedding trip to a subway ride. As a tongue-in-cheek commemoration of that event, they followed their second ceremony with a short bus ride — since the Los Angeles area did not have a subway system at that time.

Professionally, Brown was able to get his confidence back as a performer, after some less-than-memorable movies, by returning to the stage in the early 1940s. While

The two Browns of *So You Won't Talk* (1940), the mild-mannered Joe (under the bed) and the gangster (picture insert).

his autobiography simply keys upon a 1942 regional revival of the George Kelly comedy *The Show-Off*, there was also a late–1940 tailored-for-Brown production of *Elmer the Great* in New Haven, Connecticut, and a 1941 star turn in a Los Angeles production of the light comic opera *Rio Rita*.[6]

Even before recharging his creative batteries with the stage production of *Elmer*, his single film release for the year, *So You Won't Talk* (1940), was a decided improvement upon such earlier screen outings as *$1,000 a Touchdown* and *Beware, Spooks* (both 1939). Though *So You Won't Talk* was nowhere near Brown's mid–1930s glory days, it cast the comedian in an often entertaining dual role. He plays both a bearded milquetoast type and an escaped killer, with the former character being a dead ringer for the gangster after he loses the whiskers. Though a variation of this story had been done more creatively in John Ford's *The Whole Town's Talking* (1935, with Edward G. Robinson), the similarly titled *So You Won't Talk* still had its own comic twist.

The charm of the better-budgeted Ford picture is seeing signature tough guy

Robinson playing a meek anti-hero as well as a gangster. While Brown "essays" the same two types, the hook this time is seeing the often mild-mannered Joe as a Robinson-style killer. Besides breaking Brown out of a milquetoast rut (after once alternating this figure with his patented smart aleck), it is simply a revelation to see Brown as a gangster. Though not always laugh-out-loud funny, there is still a sudden appreciation of his broad range of abilities. This experience is not unlike the first time I viewed the comic outtakes at the close of the satire *Being There* (1979). For two-plus hours, Peter Sellers had played the vacuous gardener Chance with the deadpan mask of Buster Keaton's Great Stone Face. I had too easily accepted the great restraint of the Sellers performance. But the multiple miscues entertainingly added at the end act as a funny reminder — metaphorical footnotes — to the degree of difficulty of Sellers' role in this picture.

Despite comparable merits by the comedian in *So You Won't Talk*, his performance went largely underappreciated. Worse yet, it was sometimes seen as merely derivative of the Robinson film.[7] *Variety* was that rare publication which found more to praise about the picture, calling the dual roles "rather cleverly concocted," though it bemoaned the fact that neither part provided an "opportunity for him to use that wide mouth in the familiar way."[8] Timing-wise, Brown's movie was also hurt by the simultaneous release of Charlie Chaplin's greatest commercial hit *The Great Dictator* (1940). Ironically, that movie showcased Chaplin in dual roles, also. He played a variation of his standard Tramp figure as the Jewish barber, and a satirical take on Adolf Hitler as the dictator Hynkel.[9]

Despite the entertainment improvements on exhibit in *So You Won't Talk*, compared to Brown's late–1930s run of movie mediocrity, his gangster parody was not able to dissipate the general sense of decline now associated with his screen career. Thus, the following year (1941) would be the first time since the silent era (1927) that the comedian did not have at lease one film in general release. *So You Won't Talk* had been a Columbia picture, as was the preceding *Beware, Spooks*. Brown would make two more Columbia comedies, with a Republic picture sandwiched between them. Republic was a minor studio, which underlined the fact that he had fallen to "B" movie status.

The paradox of pictures is that these preserved pieces of time became Brown's comedy legacy, and his much-longer but ever so ephemeral stage career — both before and after his movie star period — is limited to sketchy descriptions and yellowing programs. Perhaps that is the reason Brown devotes so much more space to his stage work in both a 1945 *New Yorker* profile and his 1956 autobiography.[10] Reading these chronicles of the clown, one occasionally fears that film-related pages have somehow become lost in the editing process. If the comedian were not already on record as crediting his movie-blessed 1930s as the most satisfying of decades, there is a tongue-in-cheek line from yet another stage-slanted profile of Brown which would merit further consideration: "He then gave up acting — he went into pictures."[11] But beyond the joy of a live audience giving a performer immediate feedback on how he is doing, there is never a sense that the comedian felt one medium was superior to the other. Like most of us, he simply went where the work was. And World War II was about to redefine the term "workload."

Despite the pre-war power of various isolationist groups in the United States (see previous chapter), there were numerous indicators which suggested the country might soon be drawn into a conflict which had already engulfed much of the world. War signs ranged from the initiation of the first peacetime military draft in American history (September 1940), to Congress' passage of President Franklin D. Roosevelt's Lend-Lease Act (March 1941), which enabled this country to assist Great Britain in her battle with Nazi Germany. Add to this a marked increase in the production of American armaments, and it was obvious that war was inescapable.

Consistent with this atmosphere, the Brown family was involved in an assortment of patriotic activities. The comedian's sons were in the Army Air Corps, a product of their father's aforementioned interest in flying. Joe's wife Kathryn was active in the local Red Cross, and Joe, Sr., was entertaining at stateside military bases. His desire to rediscover his live audience performing roots could not have come at a better time. He was about to set records as a one-man show for American boys in uniform around a war-torn world.

His initial foray into full-time "G. I. Joe" mode began in early 1942, just weeks after the Japanese attack on Pearl Harbor officially put the United States into World War II. With many of Brown's surrogate "boys" from UCLA (friends and Bruin classmates of the comedian's two sons) now in the military, Joe was beginning to receive overseas correspondence from them. One particularly moving letter came from snowy Alaska, requesting that Brown "come up and put on a show."[12] While any veteran trouper loves to perform, this request was coupled with a need to boost morale. The sports-obsessed comedian had sometimes been invited to give pep talks to UCLA athletic groups, and this Army correspondent was now requesting a combination entertainer and half-time motivator. Joe was up to the task.

One could say that during World War II, Brown achieved a populist Will Rogers–like status as America's *Self-Made Diplomat*, to borrow part of the title of one of Rogers' humor books.[13] Rogers had become famous earlier for his comic globetrotting, traveling the world as a humorous reporter and an American troubleshooter in areas in need of assistance. During World War II, this seemed an apt characterization of Brown. Indeed, the comedian's own description of his wartime status, "Ambassador without portfolio," has a direct link to Rogers.[14] This is the same phrase Rogers applied to himself on the frontispiece page of his aforementioned 1926 text. Brown and Rogers had long been friends before the older comedian's tragic death in a 1935 plane crash. Both had shared a love of baseball, flying and, most importantly, a belief in the common man (populism). But well before Brown's use of the "ambassador" reference, the period press was applying variations of that moniker to the wartime entertaining of the cavernous-mouthed comedian. For example, after his 34-day tour of Alaskan military camps and outposts, the July issue of *Photoplay* magazine called him "Hollywood's ambassador of good citizenship." And eventually the media even linked Brown to Rogers' number one populist disciple, director Frank Capra. Capra helped fill the cinema void created by Rogers' death with a series of classic populist pictures like *Mr. Deeds Goes to Town* (1936) and *Mr. Smith Goes to Washington* (1939). Consequently, when *The New York Times* attempted to cover Brown's later extensive war tour of the Pacific Theatre, the newspaper entitled their April 12 story about one leg of that trip "Mr. Brown Goes to Australia."

The comedian's Alaskan trip established several precedents for his future military tours. First, he "ignored all restricting red tape and went on his own initiative."[15] When the government finally cleared him to go to Alaska, Brown was already there entertaining troops — at his own expense! (On subsequent trips, the comedian and the government came closer to working on the same page.) Brown was a perpetual trailblazer for performers in and around war zones. He was also the first entertainer to bring a show into the Pacific Theatre. Though other stars (such as Bob Hope) are better known for lightening the load of American troops, during World War II Brown was both the groundbreaker and the workhorse.

The comedian was apt to go anywhere to perform, regardless of the terrain and/or climate and irrespective of audience size. Probably Brown's most rewarding experience on this first tour was his visit to a tiny outpost in the Eskimo village of Gambell, on the isolated, primitive St. Lawrence Island. Ever the populist, he made the trip, in part, for some Eskimo-American soldiers from this small town. The comedian had met them after a show in Nome. The young men had never before been away from home and felt their parents would be concerned. Consequently, after meeting with Gambell's one missionary family and the local government official, Brown sought out the parents of these soldiers. Such sensitivity undoubtedly contributed to an Eskimo leader later presenting a proclamation to the comic that March 17 (the day he arrived) would henceforth be known in Gambell as the Joe E. Brown holiday!

Brown's Alaskan adventure called attention to the fact that men and women in uniform need some well-deserved distractions and the assurance that they are not forgotten. Bob Hope made an Alaskan troop tour two years after Brown; in his World War II memoir *I Never Left Home*, Hope observed, "General Buckner said our trip up there was a tonic to the men's spirits that money couldn't buy. In other words, what they needed was ... just some sign from home that they weren't forgotten."[16]

A week after Brown's return from Alaska, his tour was in the news again: The Japanese bombed one of the camps (Dutch Harbor) where he had put on a show.[17] This development put the comedian in demand as a speaker on the war effort, including a June talk to the Hollywood Women's Press Club at the film colony's celebrated Brown Derby restaurant. But Brown had been speaking out on issues for some time, from his 1933 Los Angeles Breakfast Club talk on the government's NCR (National Recovery Administration) film code, which would limit actors' salaries, to his 1939 pleading before a Congressional Committee to allow 20,000 Jewish-German refugee children into the United States.[18] Though one might not readily link Brown with contemporary actor-activist Tim Robbins, a recent comment by the latter sounds very much like the comedian. When asked why he remains outspoken, Robbins said, "The bottom line is, if you're compromising your beliefs because you think it's going to hurt, you're not living in a free society."[19] Neither Brown's stance on the Jewish children nor his criticism of Japanese-American internment camps (which will be addressed shortly) were then popular with the general public, but the comedian still spoke out.

Not surprisingly, after Brown's return from Alaska, he resolved to soon "start out again to other battlefronts where our kids needed giggles and guffaws. I had found my war work."

For the immediate time being, however, Brown, like most stateside Americans, had to earn a living. The comedian was hoping to build upon the modest success of his latest Columbia comedy, *Shut My Big Mouth* (1942), which had opened during his Alaskan army base tour. With a title which played upon his signature comedy component, this Western parody would prove to be one of his stronger "B" pictures. *Variety*'s February 25 review was right on target: "Better-than-average Joe E. Brown comedy programmer."

One could make a case for *Mouth* being the best of Brown's Columbia comedies. As with his earlier gangster parody for the studio, *So You Won't Talk*, the comedian has a dual role in this Western spoof. He is a smart-aleck sheriff, whose alternations between false bravado and cowardice (*á la* Bob Hope) often have him masquerading as a feisty Western woman. Add to this an extended comic dance number in drag, and his adoption by an Indian tribe who christen him Chief Cave-in-the-Face, and one has an often diverting picture.

In mid–April 1942, Brown began production on his first Republic film, *Joan of Ozark* (1942), which had the working title *Lazybones*.[21] Though this studio represented a drop in the Hollywood pecking order, with publications like *The New York Times* often not even reviewing its films, *Joan of Ozark* would be a pleasant surprise. As film historian Leonard Maltin later observed, "Republic had no pretensions about art, but when that studio made a B [picture] it was fast-paced and efficient. The studio had little background in comedy but found itself with a major attraction in hillbilly comedienne Judy Canova...."[22] Canova's broad humor and comic singing was very big in the small town rural market.

Republic felt that teaming Canova with Brown would be a natural, since his strength was also the small town rural audience. Moreover, since his "A" star had fallen, Republic could now afford him — always an important consideration for a poor studio. Their topical story for the duo has Canova's title character, Joan of Ozark, uncovering a Nazi spy ring in the United States. "Naturally," the German gang uses a New York nightclub as a cover. Paradoxically, when they lure Joan to the club in order to try to bump her off, she becomes a hit attraction, and they have to rethink their options. Brown is her agent and general partner in all spy shenanigans. Brown and Canova are often very funny together. *The Hollywood Reporter's* headline for its review nicely summarizes the duo's success together — "*Joan of Ozark* Hit Teams Canova-Brown in Top Form."[23] Borrowing a page from Chaplin's *The Great Dictator*, Brown's most inspired routine in the film is his Hitler impersonation, which the *Reporter* called a "panic." *Variety* added, "Here, in combination, their [Canova and Brown] pull is extended beyond [the] ordinary in a picture which measures up fully to what [their fans] expect."[24]

Joan opened only three months after its first day of production; by the time it was released, Brown was already at work on his last Columbia comedy, *Daring Young Man* (1942). Though his Western parody for Columbia, *Shut My Big Mouth*, might have raised expectations for *Daring Young Man*, the movie was a major disappointment. Brown is again battling Nazi spies in America, but the script gives him little opportunity for humor. Unlike Bob Hope's *My Favorite Blonde* (also from 1942), which brilliantly works German spies to an American parody of Alfred Hitchcock's *The 39 Steps* (1935), Brown's picture is reduced to Nazi agents sending secret transmissions via an electronically controlled bowling ball!

As with most of his Columbia pictures, Brown again plays dual parts in *Daring Young Man*— his standard milquetoast type and the character's free-spirited grandmother. Just as the best thing about *Shut My Big Mouth* had been Brown's take-charge Western heroine, the comedian's portrayal of a gambling grandmother steals the show in *Daring Young Man*. With a screwball comedy mindset and topical lines like, "Mr. Roosevelt's been president ever since I was a little girl," "she" makes all of "her" scenes amusing. But unlike the Western parody, where Brown spends most of his time in drag, his *Daring Young Man* grandmother is a minor character who cannot rescue the picture. The film's only other footnote to funny is the witty throwaway reference to Brown's signature mouth: "Looks like you bit off more than you can chew ... but that hardly seems possible." If there had only been more of the same. This would further cement his demotion to a second-tier studio like Republic.

Upon completing *Daring Young Man*, Brown began entertaining troops at stateside military camps.[25] This was to be followed by the comedian starring in a road show production of the stage play *The Show-Off*. The revival opened in Detroit in September 1942, and Brown's older son Don and several other Army pilots were able to visit the comedian that autumn. As members of the Ferrying Division of the Air Transport Command stationed in Long Beach, California, they made a flying layover to assist Joe in a Detroit war bond drive. It was a great visit for father and son. Don was excited about being assigned to the Pacific, and pleased his dad by telling him that he wished the comedian could come along. Joe's response was that maybe they would meet up — each doing his job.

On October 8, 1942, Brown was still performing *The Show-Off* in Detroit and (like many old-school entertainers who enjoyed interacting with the public) was briefly manning the box office window — selling tickets! He enjoyed the reaction of surprised patrons. Brown was expecting to hear from Don, so he was not surprised to receive a call from the Air Transport Command. Exhilarated to take the call, while still kidding with fans, the comedian suddenly heard, "We want to reach Joe E. Brown to tell him that his son has just been killed in a routine flight ... Will you get the message to him?"[26] For a time, the world simply ended:

> Later [during World War II] when I was out there alone [entertaining troops] ... I sometimes thought of that thing we had said to each other [about meeting in the Pacific] ... I'd see a lad down in the audience who looked like my son, and I'd remember. I did meet him out there hundreds of times...[27]

Capt. Don Brown, who had saved his own money to take flying lessons long before he joined the Army Air Corps, was 25. The former UCLA varsity football player and student-body president had joined the Army Reserve in 1939, the same year another scholar athlete, Iowa quarterback Nile Kinnick, spoke for America in his Heisman Trophy acceptance speech, "I thank God I was warring on the gridirons of the Midwest and not on the battlefields of Europe."[28] But a global war could not be avoided. Four hundred thousand Americans would die in service — including Don Brown and Nile Kinnick. (Pilot Kinnick's death was also in a non-combat military plane crash.)

Joe E. Brown would call his next American armed forces entertainment tour, to the Pacific Theatre, a "memorial" to his son.[29] After Don's military funeral service (October 10, 1942) at Los Angeles' famed Forest Lawn Cemetery, a film obligation kept the comedian in the United States through the end of the year. But in early January 1943, Brown was off for three months of shows big and small. He would work so closely to the ever-changing front lines that the sketchy press coverage of the trip would be purposely vague about his whereabouts. For instance, note the location cited in a *New York Times* dateline for an article about Brown — "AN ADVANCED SOUTH PACIFIC BASE, Feb. 18."[30]

So what constituted a show for the comedian? While there was never a set program (Brown liked to improvise), one can piece together a good idea from period articles and Joe's aforementioned World War II memoir *Your Kids and Mine.* The show would often begin with a group singing of "God Bless America." Then, following a tradition which dated back at least to his 1936 London Palladium performance, he would construct a comedy collage, both discussing and drawing from his films. Given that the comedian loved baseball and felt that his best movies were the diamond trilogy of *Fireman, Save My Child* (1932), *Elmer the Great* (1933) and *Alibi Ike* (1935), it should come as no surprise that a major source of his live comedy was baseball-related. Of all this diamond material, an especially popular Brown sketch on his military tour was to pantomime the Elmer pitching routine, including a comic corkscrew wind-up.

Baseball went beyond just a source of entertainment material for the tour. Brown also spent a great deal of time with soldiers and sailors in small group sessions, from visiting hospitals to eating with the men in mess hall settings. Though small talk was never a problem with a born raconteur like Brown, he found his typical baseball fan knowledge of the game was a natural ice breaker and a good subject of conversation with men in uniform. After all, this was a time when the sport was truly the *national* pastime; Japanese soldiers would attempt to bait American forces by yelling, "To hell with Babe Ruth."[31] Brown also modestly saw himself as merely a visiting symbol of home — a poignant reminder of a native land that also defined itself, in part, by baseball:

> I'd know it wasn't just me talking ... It was home itself; it was the days when he was a high school kid and the neighborhood theater was showing one of my pictures. It was the old lost times when everything was right, and Mom was baking an apple pie ... and the kids on his block were getting up a baseball team....[32]

But Brown was so internationally synonymous with baseball that even the Japanese prisoners he encountered wanted baseball material from the comedian![33]

Because Brown's act also involved his eccentric dancing and comic songs, he was accompanied on this tour by musician-singer-composer Johnny Marvin. Given Brown's recent successful film teaming with hillbilly comedienne Judy Canova in *Joan of Ozark*, it was hardly a coincidence that Marvin's specialty was hillbilly music. *Joan* also provided another popular sketch for Brown's military audiences: his extended imitation of Hitler. The comedian's lack of a regular entertainment troupe allowed Brown to travel light, taking his intimate show to the most inaccessible of locations, where he might only be performing for a handful of people.

Still, individual shows often had audiences of several thousand. At such times, the most popular makeshift stage was fashioned by placing a 16 x 16 tent floor on several 55-gallon oil drums.[34] Sometimes the men in uniform would completely surround Brown, turning his temporary stage into a theater in the round:

> Take the night at Milne Bay [New Guinea]. Four thousand kids were out there in the pouring rain. They were all around the stand. I'd tell one joke facing one way and then turn around and tell another. Even when they couldn't hear me they'd laugh.[35]

Photoplay magazine poignantly suggested that these men's desperate need to laugh might be explained by calling Brown "a link in a chain of hope and courage and love between them and the folks back home."[36] Link or not, Brown would sometimes perform as many as eight shows a day, and each audience might number as many as 5,000. Given that a program ran a minimum of an hour or more, Brown's old multiple-show vaudeville roots were severely tested, especially since he was now over 50.

As Brown traveled thousands of miles criss-crossing the Pacific, his military shows were not all recycled movie material. The programs were also peppered with jokes about popular targets, from kidding officers to the dreaded armed forces chow. For example, Brown enjoyed observing, "One reason I had to come over here was that I just couldn't get any good Spam in the States."[37] The comedian was also adept at what is now called "observational humor." He had fun with the newly constructed jungle rough roads, the Pacific's most awkward creature (the slapstick-orientated Gooney Bird) and those giant tropical mosquitoes. This was Brown's favorite insect story from the Pacific tour: "Say, fellas, did you hear about the mosquito that landed on the bomber strip at the airfield yesterday? The boys put in ninety gallons of gas before they realized it wasn't a P-38."[38]

Other easy joke material could be mined from just a plane passing overhead. Brown might feign fear and say, "I hope those are our boys!" Or the comedian could just give the plane a casual glance and observe, "Ah ... here comes Eleanor" — a reference to President Franklin D. Roosevelt's wife, who often went on fact-finding missions for her physically handicapped husband. On other occasions, Brown could be more politically pointed, as when he told a large audience of soldiers and sailors in the Pacific that he was there to entertain them "and to check [Wendell] Willkie's expense account."[39] (Willkie, the Republican candidate for President in 1940, had later been sent around the world by Roosevelt on a good will tour of allied military bases.)

Brown doubled as an armed forces representative, getting the word back to the United States from their young men in uniform. During this first Pacific tour, the comedian reported from New Zealand that morale on the islands was "even higher than the folks back home believe and I guess I have been in every place in the Pacific where there is a man."[40] Two years later (1945), after yet another Pacific tour, he said that American fighting men did not agree with the persecution of American-born Japanese in the United States: "They think it's terrible. They think it's horrible. I know. I've had a number of round-table discussions with them on that subject alone."[41]

The comedian's 1943 three-month tour of Pacific bases ended in late April of that year. He had covered over 30,000 sea and land miles, from bombers and Jeeps to jungle footpaths.[42] Signed for a supporting role in an "A" picture, the Betty Grable Technicolor musical *Pin Up Girl* (1944), Brown promised from the set, "I'm going out again [entertaining troops] soon. I hope to get to Italy this time."[43]

In July, *Chatterbox* (1943), the comic's second Republic picture, opened. Shot in late 1942, just prior to the start of Brown's Pacific tour, it again teamed him with Judy Canova. Drawing upon her hillbilly schtick and his then-recent Western parody success with *Shut My Big Mouth*, *Chatterbox* was yet another six-gun spoof. Brown plays a radio cowboy with few real Western skills. Signed to star in a sagebrush film, Brown's cowboy is rescued by Canova's character, producing negative publicity for him. She is teamed with this pretend Western star to avoid further embarrassment. Compared to their amusing antics in *Joan of Ozark*, *Chatterbox* is much weaker film fare. *Variety* complained that the Brown-Canova antics "fail to lift the shoddy material provided in the script."[44] Still, it is not without a certain charm today. The shoot was both an emotional challenge and a welcome activity, since it directly followed the funeral of Joe E.'s son Don. (The comedian's younger son and namesake, Joe, Jr., had followed his brother into the Army Air Corps, but remained stationed in California for the duration of the war.)

America's favorite big mouth comics reteam in *Pin Up Girl* **(1944).**

Even though Brown had spent the early part of 1943 entertaining troops in the Pacific, he was chomping at the bit to continue his one-man crusade for American men in uniform. But before leaving again in November of 1943, the comedian appeared in a supporting role in the aforementioned *Pin Up Girl* and played his last starring part for Republic, *Casanova in Burlesque* (1944). The former film again teamed him with fellow big-mouth comic Martha Raye, last seen with him in their disappointing *$1,000 a Touchdown* (1939). But while *Pin Up Girl* was a step-up in quality, Brown and Raye were still mere support in what is now seen as a weak Betty Grable film.

Casanova is back to "B" movieland, but it is a genuinely diverting comedy with Brown leading a double life as a Shakespeare professor at a small-town college and a burlesque comic. Featuring everything from Brown's inspired eccentric dancing to a parody performance of *Taming of the Shrew*, the movie has much to recommend it. Republic had successfully worked a variation of the Columbia Brown pictures, where the comedian often played two parts. But his Republic films were more consistently entertaining. In addition, *Casanova* has the novelty for modern audiences of showcasing Dale

Brown in *Casanova in Burlesque* (1944), with Dale Evans (left) and June Havoc.

Evans in a non-cowgirl part. The actress now synonymous with Roy Rogers Western films and television programming appears here as an active fan of the period's jump jive music!

By the time *Casanova* reviews appeared, Brown was well into his third tour of American military installations outside the United States. Having left the previous November, the comedian flew east from New York for an ultimate destination of India and China. Given Nazi Germany's then-occupation of continental Europe, Brown's plane had first flown to South America in order to cross the Atlantic to North Africa. After a series of shows in the Far East, he entertained his way back to his original target site of Italy.

Brown's Thanksgiving shows (1943) in New Delhi, India, made him the "first entertainer from home to reach this 'end of the line' theatre [of war]."[45] By early December, the comedian was setting another tour precedent: "Entertainment-starved American forces in China, who have heard, remotely, of Stage Door Canteens and USO shows back home, are seeing Hollywood in the flesh for the first time [thanks to

Brown]."[46] By the mid–February 1944 completion of this three-month tour, the comedian had given 200–300 shows and traveled a minimum of 47,000 miles.[47] In a trip that took Brown to 19 countries, "his most appreciative audience was 35 wounded Americans in an Italian hospital. His largest was 15,000 G. I.'s in India. Treasured possession was a list of names of American soldiers who had asked Joe to remember them to Mom, Dad and friends."[48]

Ever the representative for the man in uniform, Brown entertained closest to the front lines in Italy, about which he later stated, "Our American kids are making a lot of friends for us in Italy, especially among the younger generation. They [American soldiers] hand out food and candy and play with the youngsters, and the old folks like it."[49]

While Brown continued to tour as an ongoing tribute to the memory of his son Don, he confessed shortly after returning from Italy, "Just one guy leaning back in a wheelchair laughing pays me for any hardships I'll ever encounter."[50] Brown's "reviews" for his many military shows often came by way of the many appreciative letters he received from men in uniform and from their grateful parents. Their "thank yous" covered everything from the comedian's sacrifices to his commitment to *clean* material.

Needless to say, Brown also received more official "reviews" or "thank yous" after returning from this most ambitious of tours. For example, the comedian's New York homecoming was sweetened by the presence of his family (wife Kathryn, surviving son Lt. Joe, Jr., and daughter-in-law Virginia) and the special welcoming ceremony staged by beloved Gotham mayor Fiorello La Guardia, who directed the city from 1934 to 1945. Next, a grateful President Roosevelt invited Brown and his family to the White House for a personal recognition of the highest order — a gesture the comedian would later use as a memorable close to his World War II memoir *Your Kids and Mine.*

Back home in Hollywood, the film industry, as well as civic and military leaders, paid tribute to Brown at a special testimonial dinner on May 3, 1944. Officially sponsored by the Independent Motion Picture Producers' Association, the gala was at the Ambassador Hotel, with comic Henny Youngman as master of ceremonies. The evening's entertainment included Abbott and Costello, Jimmy Durante, Edward G. Robinson, Freddie Bartholomew, Arthur Treacher, John Carradine and Billy Gilbert.[51] The high point of the night was Brown's acceptance of a special scroll in recognition of his public service. Fittingly, he remained an advocate for American men in uniform with his closing remarks:

> I accept this honor especially on behalf of the millions of G. I.'s all over the world who I wish could be here tonight. They, not a man like me, are the men to whom honors should be directed. They are our heroes today and I trust and pray that when they return they will be treated as such — as they deserve — by the American people.[52]

The event was broadcast to 23 Western stations of what was then called the Blue Network — the American Broadcasting Company (ABC).[53] In the next few years, Brown would receive a number of additional war-related honors, including a Bronze Star (the highest military award then available to a citizen).[54]

While 1944 now found Brown with a need to get back to the job of earning a living, one of his war-related charities continued to assist men in uniform. Appropriately for the sports-obsessed comedian, Joe had founded the All-Pacific Recreation Fund, which supplied athletic equipment to American military men serving in the Pacific Theatre. By 1944, over $50,000 worth of sports supplies had found their way to the troops.[55] Consistent with this sports perspective, Brown also continued to raise military relief funds stateside throughout the war by sponsoring charity baseball games and other athletic events. When possible, Brown would put his corkscrew wind-up delivery, dating from his first stage production of *Elmer the Great*, to use in these games. (By this time, the comedian's signature way of acknowledging public recognition of his presence at an event was to pantomime that zany Elmer delivery.)

In the summer of 1944, Brown returned to his home studio, Warner Brothers, for the first time since *Polo Joe* (1936). The picture was *Hollywood Canteen*, an all-star tribute to World War II servicemen set in the film colony's real-life haven for men in uniform. Besides featuring the co-founders of the original Hollywood Canteen (Bette Davis and John Garfield), the essentially variety show format included a cinema "who's who" in cameo appearances, including Barbara Stanwyck, Joan Crawford, Sydney Greenstreet, Peter Lorre and a host of comics. Besides Brown, the funnymen included Jack Benny, Eddie Cantor and Jack Carson. While this return of the prodigal film son (Brown) to Warner Brothers might have been a bittersweet experience for the comedian (given his now "B" star status), he rose to the occasion. As was the case with the all-star film production of *A Midsummer Night's Dream* (1935), where Brown and his fellow comics stole the critical kudos, Joe and the other *Canteen* funnymen again eclipsed the dramatic stars.[56]

Brown could be heard that autumn on ABC radio's *Stop or Go* quiz show. But this was a quiz program only in the sense that Groucho Marx's later *You Bet Your Life* (first on radio in 1947) was a quiz show. Both programs were merely entertaining excuses to showcase the comic shenanigans of these funnymen. Consistent with this humor accent, Brown's most memorable *Stop or Go* program came late that year (November 26, 1944), when the comedian celebrated his forty-fourth anniversary in show business. His guests for this program included Orson Welles, Jack Benny, Dorothy Lamour, Rudy Vallee and Hedda Hopper.[57] This coast-to-coast, 30-minute program aired Sunday nights at 8:30 EST. (Early in 1945 it was moved to Thursday evening at 10:30 EST). As with the comedian's earlier radio program, CBS' *Joe E. Brown Show* (1938–39), *Stop and Go's* ratings were respectable but it was not renewed.

For the patriotically driven Brown, maybe it was just as well. He was anxious to return to the Pacific war theater and entertain more troops. Most individuals would have used the best-seller status the previous autumn (1944) of his World War II memoir *Your Kids and Mine* as the logical finis to his tours for servicemen. But Brown was anything but typical. After the May 1945 cancellation of *Stop and Go,* the comedian left on another grueling Pacific trip (covering 38,000 miles) for his boys in uniform.[58]

Well before his last World War II tour, however, Brown was contemplating America's obligation to these young people who had sacrificed so much. In a late 1944 interview with New York's *PM* newspaper, the comedian observed, "We spent billions for war. We should spend billions for those who have fought this war, not as a charitable thing, but as our duty and their right to fill up that void of two or three years taken right out of their lives."[59] When the interviewer suggested taxpayers might squawk at such expense, Brown, the compassionate liberal, revealed a rare public display of anger:

> It's just too damned bad about them, just too damned bad. I pay taxes, too. I'll be perfectly satisfied to pay taxes the rest of my life. If anybody comes out of this with more money than he went in with, he is not a good American.[60]

In Tom Brokaw's book celebrating the young Americans who were instrumental in winning World War II, *The Greatest Generation* (1998), he writes that getting to know them was a "life-changing experience."[61] Yet, that is precisely the way most Americans of that period, from battlefield warriors, to stateside workers, felt about Joe E. Brown. He was, in his own modest way, just that important.

❖ TWELVE ❖

The Last Act

"It's Saturday night forever!" This Joe E. Brown "happy ending" comment was triggered by the return of Howard Keel's character in *Show Boat* (1951).

The student of Joe E. Brown is tempted to recycle the comedian's above-noted line as a joyful moniker for the man's career. Certainly, most Americans felt this way during the second half of the 1940s, when Brown was taking home a broad assortment of awards. Of course, the catalyst for a great deal of this recognition came from his tireless entertaining of American troops during World War II. The awards and praise for the comedian actually started well before the close of the conflict, from a tributary scroll presented to him by the Independent Motion Picture Association, to *Photoplay* columnist Cal York heralding Brown as "The man who gives of himself completely to our cause and the boys behind it" (both May 1944).[1] But the postwar 1940s saw a host of additional honors. A veritable avalanche occurred on a single day (December 7, 1945) in his hometown of Toledo, Ohio. This date, ironically the fourth anniversary of the Japanese bombing of Pearl Harbor, was christened "Joe E. Brown Day," with the funnyman receiving no less than 16 awards! These ranged from a University of Toledo honorary degree to a Gold Medallion of Achievement previously given to only five other persons. The *Toledo Times* stated that this "First Citizen" was being "recognized ... as an actor, a sportsman, an author [for his war memoir], and — a great American."[2] Stating that his greatest ambition was to be called a "citizen of the world," the comedian modestly added, "I have no great talents, but I do have a great love of what I'm doing and a great love for people."[3]

Three special guests Brown made point of including in this memorable day were his beloved widowed mother, Anna Brown, the comedian's fifth-grade teacher Lillian Schroeder, and acrobat William (Billy) Ashe, who first introduced an elementary school–aged Brown to show business as part of the Marvelous Ashtons. The baseball fanatic's diamond friends taking part in the festivities included Richard C. Muckerman, president of the St. Louis Browns (now the Baltimore Orioles). The comic would later describe this Toledo tribute as the "biggest day of my whole life."[4]

Toledo Mayor Lloyd E. Roulet proclaimed, "He has traveled more than 200,000 miles and [made] 732 personal appearances to entertain members of our armed forces in all parts of the world and in this country."[5] Roulet also noted that the Eskimo village of Gambell, Alaska, had already established the wise precedent of honoring Brown with a special day. Following the entertainer's 1942 war-related visit to that isolated community, the town council proclaimed, "We ... make rule that every March 19 must be holiday called Mr. Joe E. Brown day because he make happy this day."[6] But after all, this was a comic *Look* magazine had already labeled the "Favorite pin-up boy of the Army" (May 30, 1944), and for whom that same Army had given (October 24, 1945) its highest civilian award, the Bronze Star, for meritorious achievement.[7]

The *Toledo Times* would kiddingly chronicle Brown's special December 7 (1945) by observing, "Most of the day will be spent in heaping awards upon the hometown boy whose oversized mouth and heart have made him a beloved comedian throughout the world."[8] But this affectionate quote might also have served as a harbinger of the many additional awards which would come Brown's way in the next few years. For instance, in 1946 he would receive a special citation from the Military Order of the Purple Heart for his "meritorious and conspicuous service" entertaining servicemen and women.[9] In 1948, the comedian's war work was honored with a roast by the show business organization Fall Guys:

> One skit portrayed Mr. Brown as a baseball player who "struck out three times" in a game shortly after the Civil War. Mr. Brown rose, did a handstand and a somersault and asked his hecklers: "Who is this old guy you're talking about?"[10]

Reminiscing at another point during the roast about his wartime entertaining, Brown self-deprecatingly observed, "When I opened my mouth in the South Pacific, 8,000 mosquitoes flew in."[11]

While these acts of recognition would continue into the 1950s, the most memorable follow-up to Brown's many war-related accolades would fittingly occur on Memorial Day 1949. On that date, his birthplace of Holgate, Ohio, would honor him with yet another "Joe E. Brown Day" and the dedication of a new baseball stadium named after him. The keynote speaker at this event was no less a diamond celebrity than the commissioner of Major League Baseball, A. B. "Happy" Chandler. In accepting a special plaque on this occasion, Brown acknowledged both his mother and his wife, and said "sports should stress the fight not only to win, but to win honestly."[12] During a ceremony that attracted an audience of 10,000 to this Ohio village, Army jets performed a fly-by, dipping their wings, and Brown entertained the audience with comedy schtick from *Elmer the Great* that had been especially popular with his armed services audiences. This 1949 return to his home state resulted in additional recognition, including an honorary degree of Doctor of Humanities from Ohio's Bowling Green State University. The citation read, in part, "In acknowledgment of a renowned and brilliant career as an actor on stage, screen and radio; [and] in sincere appreciation of your great contribution to the servicemen of World War II...."[13]

Given Brown's gung-ho attitude about *Your Kids and Mine* (the title of his war memoir), it should come as no surprise that the comedian periodically put himself in harm's way during the fighting. These activities ranged from getting permission from Gen. Douglas MacArthur to go on aerial bombing missions, to actually manning a rifle when his ground position came under fire during an Allied advance. The latter situation led to the amazing postwar disclosure that his sharpshooting abilities had resulted in the death of two enemy soldiers during fighting on the main Philippine island of Luzon. This patriotic revelation (December 22, 1945) came by way of an onstage reunion between Brown and close friend Major General Robert S. Beightler, commander of the 37th (Ohio) division. In Columbus, Ohio, where the comedian was touring with a stage production of *Harvey*, the major general said, "[Brown] had more personal courage than any other entertainer from the United States whom I met."[14]

The comedian confessed at the time, "I've never mentioned it before. Maybe some people will think I shouldn't have done it. I was only doing what everyone else was doing — trying to help win the war. Besides, the Japs were shooting at me."[15] While Brown had crossed a line normally verboten for non-combatants in a war zone, most postwar Americans endorsed the comic's knee-jerk response. For example, when Major General Beightler first revealed Brown's deadly marksmanship to that *Harvey* audience in Columbus, it "brought an ovation that exceeded any applause for Joe's stage performance."[16] *The New York Times'* supportive print coverage of the incident fell under the diplomatic title, "Screen Comedian Who Turned Serious."[17]

Like the battlin' preacher common to American pop culture as late as Ward Bond's central character in the celebrated Western *The Searchers* (1956), Brown was capable of compartmentalizing compassion and combat. The comedian best defined this position in a war-related talk he gave in 1946. The occasion was an American Legion Gold Star ceremony, where mothers who had lost a child in the conflict were given a special certificate. Brown was chosen for the ceremony since he had lost his son Don to the war. In a speech which pleaded for postwar tolerance he said in part, "I hated everything the Nazis and Japs stood for while there was war, but now they are no longer enemies, they are just human beings."[18] But this was consistent with an interview Brown had given even before the end of the war, when he was raising a lonely voice against the interment camps for Japanese-Americans: "We're going to have to stop hating. As long as we hate, there will be wars." When his agent volunteered the comment, "You mean blind hate, Joe," the comedian said, "Any hate is blind."[19]

Brown mixed his postwar pleas for tolerance with an ongoing advocacy for men and women in uniform who were about to re-enter the civilian world. In fact, he spoke to the California legislature about jobs for vets even before the end of the war. He coupled this particular lobbying with an appeal to politicians to understand all that the veterans had experienced.[20] The comedian's advocacy also embraced military personnel whose tours of duty would keep them overseas well past the conclusion of the war. In an interview entitled "Joe E. Brown Tells What's Ailing G.I. Abroad," the entertainer shared their fears — "scared of his future as a breadwinner and is frantic to get home...."[21]

Fittingly, given Brown's populist outreach tendencies, he spent much of the post-war 1940s touring in the aforementioned play *Harvey*. This Pulitzer Prize–winning fantasy comically chronicled the life of the benevolent alcoholic Elwood P. Dowd and his title character companion, Harvey, a six-foot, 1 1/2 inch "rabbit" visible only to Dowd. Though Dowd was far from the sharpest tool in the shed, he was the ultimate advocate for a good-neighbor policy. In Brown's autobiography he later stated the perfect argument for why this mildly pickled character spoke so well to the period. According to Joe, the fan of the play is forced to "re-examine his concept of normalcy, that make him wonder if, in the case of Dowd vs. the world, the former hasn't won out in the sanest, most logical way open to him, not in being an alcoholic, but in keeping whatever proof he can that human beings are good guys who like to get along."[22]

Brown garnered rave reviews everywhere he went with *Harvey*, particularly in his second hometown — Hollywood. One such kudo, from the *Hollywood Citizen-News*, also documented the comedian singing the play's timely postwar message:

> Joe E. Brown makes of his role a sheer delight. He catches the wonderful philosophy of Mary Chase's noted character, and he projects it with commendable skill. In a little talk after the curtain, he paid tribute to Miss Chase and commented upon the fine philosophy of Elwood as a basis for perpetual brotherhood.[23]

Elwood P. Dowd's philosophy was consistent with the populist *esprit de corps* nature of Brown's small-town milquetoast type character, grown to middle age. Dowd's signature line, "I always have a wonderful time wherever I am and whomever I am with," would be right at home in a Brown comedy like *Local Boy Makes Good* (1931). This added connection of Brown to Dowd undoubtedly further fueled the especially warm 1946 filmland reception the comedian received in the play. For instance, the *Los Angeles Times* observed:

> [H]e makes the interpretation his own and quite believable. It was an evening of acclaim for him, and he was held on the stage for many minutes after the close, giving a speech and telling stories. Many professional folk were in the audience, and it was ... one of the biggest openings from the Hollywood standpoint.[24]

The critic for the *Los Angeles Examiner*, under the headline, "'Joe E.' Great in *Harvey*," literally waxed poetic about the play: "There is much sense in its nonsense, much gleeful commentary on the foibles of human nature ... it sets off a sort of laughter that seemed to have vanished from the theater: Laughter without malice...."[25]

Given this kind of acclaim, and Brown's special rapport for the part, it is no wonder that the comedian toured in *Harvey* (with occasional breaks) for several seasons. A better idea of his life on tour with *Harvey* can be gathered from a more focused look at a typical heartland stop during this time — a week's engagement in Indianapolis, Indiana, during February 1948. The comedian arrived in town a day early and mixed his love of sports with good publicity by immediately attending an Indianapolis Caps hockey

Brown's *Local Boy Makes Good* (1931) character is a second cousin to Elwood P. Dowd of *Harvey*.

match. Brown's companion for the event was his invisible co-star, Harvey. Moreover, "at the end of the second period ... Brown and Harvey went to the Caps' dressing room and gave a little pep talk. The [come from behind winning] Caps were all over the ice for the last period — like scared rabbits, maybe."[26]

Besides such invaluable "news items" for the show, local writers praised the comedian's return, based upon a brief *Harvey* run the previous autumn (1947). For example, the *Indianapolis News* critic described the event as "a repeat engagement of one of the season's entertainment highlights."[27] Moreover, there was a practical Midwestern appreciation of the comic's standard bonus material for the same price:

> Mr. Brown is famous for his curtain speeches and for the droll stories he tells. Monday night, as usual, no one made the slightest effort to leave the theater at the end of the play, for everyone was waiting for this informal and charming afterpiece.[28]

The comedian's rambling curtain speeches were known to be entertainingly eclectic, though they never failed to emphasize the play's gentle message of tolerance and kindliness. But the *Indianapolis News* chronicled a rarely documented post-show Brown comic story. The set-up for the bit involved four film comedians who met regularly, but their conversation was simply an excuse to try to top each other:

> Mostly, they didn't listen to what anyone was saying, for they were so intent on what they were going to say next. Anyway, one day one of them finished a story, there was automatic laughter and another said, "You may wonder why I'm so quiet, but today I had news that has just about knocked me out. My father and I were very close. We corresponded regularly until I came out here and then I sort of drifted away. Today I heard — he died last night." The man paused for a second, and immediately another comic burst in with, "If you think that's funny, listen to this."[29]

Brown's after-the-curtain talks had proven so popular that the comedian also periodically gave speeches to special interest groups, mixing a message of tolerance with a lifetime of sports and show business anecdotes. Thus, the comedian would make room during his 1948 Indianapolis engagement of *Harvey* for one such talk — speaking at DePauw University "on his pet theories regarding co-operation and understanding."[30]

Though the play had originated on Broadway (1944) with Frank Fay as Dowd, Brown had toured so extensively with the production that he was becoming equally synonymous with *Harvey*. One contrast between Brown's take on Dowd, versus Fay's, undoubtedly played more effectively for heartland audiences — teetotaler Joe never puts a bottle to his signature cavernous mouth during the production:

> Brown explains that he believes the power of suggestion is enough to indicate Elwood P. Dowd's drinking habits in this scene. He professes not to be prudish about the drinking matter, but is deeply impressed with the influence a popular entertainer has on his followers, particularly the young ones....[31]

Brown (center) during his 1948 *Harvey* visit to Indianapolis. The local dignitaries include Frank Paul (far left), manager of the Lyric Theatre.

Brown would eventually own the record for the most stage appearances as the character Dowd—1305 and counting by the early 1950s.[32] Brown's roadshow production of *Harvey* generated both great business and notices throughout the United States (including a Broadway revival) and abroad (a London engagement and an Australian tour). His teaming with a giant invisible "rabbit," a mischievous "Pooka," had become a special phenomenon of the modern theater, a throwback to an earlier time when stage careers were sometimes tied to a single property. (*Harvey* author Mary Chase has described a "Pooka" as a "very big animal, any kind, who scrapes up an acquaintance with people he happens to take a liking to, and I have known several such [Pookas]."[33] In Irish myth the lighthearted "Pooka" can take any form. In this case, Harvey chooses to appear to Dowd as a large rabbit.)

Brown once expressed concern about being too associated with the property ("I don't want to have another 'Mousie' on my hands"), but he kept returning to the play.[34] One of his late career disappointments was not getting to play Dowd in the eventual screen adaptation of *Harvey* (1950). The part went to Jimmy Stewart, whom Brown had once recommended (1947) to replace Fay as the stage Dowd, when the Broadway actor needed a vacation! But as was Brown's nature (his Dowd-like nature), the comic was magnanimous about the lost opportunity: "Stewart was a hot attraction for younger movie fans, so maybe he was a logical choice. He was fine in the movie."[35] (Stewart, like Brown, would also log a great deal of *Harvey* revival stage time late in his career. It proved to be a pivotal play for both populist performers.)

While Brown dearly loved *Harvey* as both a work of theatrical art and a postwar philosophy, he also stayed with the play because his film career had all but dried up. Brown's B-movie run during the war years was not without a few neglected gems, which was partly fueled by Hollywood's expanded film production during World War II. But the box office largely disappeared after the conflict. Following "an all-time peak in ticket sales" in 1946, movie attendance steadily dropped between 1947 and 1963.[36] The "villains" included an assortment of distractions (from America's mass migration to the suburbs, to the popularity of night baseball), but the continued decline in the 1950s was all about the power of television to keep potential fans home.

Unfortunately for Brown, those bookend dates of filmland's box office decline (1947–63) also represented the framing years for the remainder of the comedian's scaledback movie career, from 1947's *The Tender Years* to 1963's *The Comedy of Terrors*. Given Hollywood's fragmented audience during this time period, the film colony's production ploy was to give viewers something they could not receive at home with television's small screen and conservative values. Brown's occasional screen appearances during this era perfectly reflected this development. For example, in 1951 he would co-star in MGM's lavish Technicolor remake of *Show Boat*. In 1956, the comedian was one of over three dozen stars to make a cameo appearance in producer Michael Todd's epic widescreen (Todd-AO) Technicolor adaptation of Jules Verne's classic *Around the World in 80 Days*. Brown next played a featured part in writer-director's Billy Wilder's groundbreaking adult sex comedy *Some Like It Hot* (1959), a picture which the American Film Institute would later (2000) christen the greatest comedy ever made. Then, the comedian played another cameo in producer-director Stanley Kramer's super-comedy *It's a Mad Mad Mad Mad World* (1963), another mammoth movie which featured countless funnymen in parts big and small.

Even Brown's last picture, a cameo in the low-budget horror parody *The Comedy of Terrors*, reflected the period's diminishing returns for Hollywood. This B-production was a product of American International Pictures, a company that emerged during Hollywood's tough economic times in the postwar era. Recognizing early that movieland's one remaining loyal demographic group was the teenage dating crowd, AIP specifically catered to this young audience. Quickly and inexpensively made, the company's films were often in exploitative genres such as horror, and sometimes featured former A-stars. Thus, *Terrors'* cast also included Vincent Price, Peter Lorre, Boris Karloff and Basil Rathbone.

Brown's first postwar picture, *The Tender Years*, was unconventional, however, in ways unlike the aforementioned movies. It was neither a big-budget extravaganza, nor an inexpensive exploitation film. *Years* was a modestly funded family drama which celebrated a Henry David Thoreau–like act of "Civil Disobedience": An 1880s minister (Brown) fights to outlaw organized dog fighting. Just as the fellowship moral of *Harvey* resonated with the comedian, the animal rights message of *Years* also reflected the comedian's deeply felt beliefs (born of childhood carrying for circus animals). But beyond that, *Years* was also consistent with Brown's war-era conviction that the young were the promise of the future. That is, in *The Tender Years*, Brown's character initially feels that the dog his film son has rescued from a man who stages pit fights needs to be returned. But the youngster (Richard Lyon, son of former screen stars Ben Lyon and Bebe Daniels) reminds Brown's minister that not all laws are just, and that sometimes civil disobedience is the only way to address a greater evil.

Brown's character realizes that if he does not follow through on this act of conscience, his son's "tender years" will be forever compromised, and the boy will be lost to both his father and himself. Consequently, the minister puts himself at risk, and (as the saying goes) this made all the difference. Given the storyline, the unique slant provided by *The Tender Years* involved both a problem film subject, and a rare non-comedic part for Brown.

The comedian received some of the best notices of his career. *Variety* said he deserts "his customary buffoon character to give an able and moving performance as a country preacher who believes in the value of faith, goodwill and honesty...."[37] The *Los Angeles Times* added, "Brown deserves plaudits for the reserve of his performance in an unusual role, as remote from his former exuberance as might be imagined."[38] But his greatest praise came from the insider publication *Film Daily*:

> He acquits himself of a fine, human performance replete with dignity and good taste. He does it with such skill that he will stop the spectator cold. As he builds his role he creates a warmth that will make itself immediately felt.[39]

Consistent with Brown's rave reviews, the picture was equally well-received. The *Hollywood Citizen News* stated, "A certain quiet simplicity and sincerity are the film's distinguishing features ... [with] a rustic setting almost poetic in its charm."[40] But given *Tender Years'* "problem film" nature, the movie was not without some controversy. For instance, while *The Hollywood Reporter* felt Brown played "the kindly minister with charm and a gentle sense of humor," the publication questioned "[t]he wisdom and taste of showing sequences on the screen such as the [canine] beatings and the dog fights...."[41] Such qualms were unfounded. The movie played especially well in the heartland, where the *Indianapolis News* observed, "*The Tender Years* is a mighty film produced with sparse capital and emerging as excellent family entertainment."[42]

The Tender Years' family values would have undoubtedly also played well with

Brown's old armed forces audience, given that they were a major catalyst for what has come to be known as the "baby boom" phenomenon. In fact, as the comedian toured the country in *Harvey*, he was able to reconnect with many veterans who had now returned to civilian life. The only negative legacy of that World War II experience was Brown's periodic hospitalization for recurrences of the malaria he had first contracted while entertaining troops in the Pacific. His fourth and most severe attack occurred in early 1949, canceling his Philadelphia opening of *Harvey*.[43] New malaria-related medication at this time greatly lessened the severity of future attacks for Brown and other victims of this disease.[44]

Memorable postwar 1940s moments for the comedian and his wife Kathryn included two 1947 events. First, that summer the romantic couple renewed their wedding vows for the second time. Their original ceremony (1915) was a simple affair at the New York City courthouse. Brown's promise of an eventual church wedding followed in 1940. But whereas that was an Episcopal service (Joe's religion), the third exchange of vows was a Catholic ceremony for his wife. The wedding was largely a family affair, including their son Joe LeRoy, daughters Mary Elizabeth and Kathryn Frances, and a special UCLA "son," Mike Frankovich, who also acted as the comedian's pilot and military liaison during the days of World War II entertaining. Joe and Kathryn's third ceremony also featured Joseph Breen and his wife standing up with them.[45] (Reflective of Brown's belief in "clean comedy," family friend Breen was the head of Hollywood's Production Code Administration — filmland's self-censorship department.) Also in 1947, Joe and Kathryn donated money for a lodge in memory of their late son Don Evan. The building would be a special addition to an ongoing UCLA student summer camp for underprivileged children.[46]

In the late 1940s-early 1950s, Brown, the former film star, scrambled to remain active, from TV guest shots on the suspense anthology *Hand of Mystery* (1949–51) and *The Ed Wynn Show* (1949–50, the first regular television program to originate from the West Coast), to starring in the brief Broadway run of *Courtin' Time* (1951). His most high-profile success at the time was appearing as Captain Andy in the aforementioned hit film *Show Boat*. *The New York Times* called his characterization "as true as you could wish," while the *Los Angeles Times* quoted legendary movie musical producer Arthur Freed as saying "Joe E. Brown was the ideal choice for Cap'n Andy."[47] The *Saturday Review of Literature* even flirted with controversy by stating, "Brown is a remarkable improvement on Charles Winninger [who was critically well-received as the captain in the 1936 screen adaptation of the play]."[48] The 1951 *Show Boat*, with such classic Jerome Kern–Oscar Hammerstein II songs as "Old Man River" and "Can't Help Lovin' That Man," was a major box office hit. Even the movieland premiere was described as causing "a stir in Hollywood ... such as has not been known since the good old days ... [and restoring] old-time glamour."[49] The gala opening attracted such iconic film colony figures as Clark Gable, Norma Shearer, Joan Crawford, Alan Ladd and Irene Dunne, who starred as Magnolia (Captain Andy's daughter) in the 1936 screen version of *Show Boat*.

Besides Brown, the 1951 remake featured Kathryn Grayson in the Dunne part, Howard Keel as her gambler husband and the sensual, scene-stealing Ava Gardner as the mulatto Julie Laverne. Brown was born to play the veteran entertainer–Mississippi River show boat captain, whose scenes fittingly include yet another inspired example of the comedian's signature eccentric dance routine. Though Brown's part is strictly in support of the stars, the comic is so good that one wonders why he did not generate more period press. *Saturday Evening Post* writer Keith Moore posed a variation of this very question in the first installment of a two-part profile of Brown in December 1951: "The fact that movie reporters have scarcely mentioned his work as Cap'n Andy in the current MGM version of *Show Boat*, while expending much linage on younger stars in this color confection, cannot have overjoyed him."[50]

Though such neglect would have upset many one-time stars, such was not the case with Brown. While not a religious man in the traditional sense of the word, he was a devotee of the eleventh chapter of Ecclesiastes, the Biblical lesson that encourages casting bread on the waters: If one gives generously, good things will eventually happen to you. The definitive example of this for Brown involved a 1944 automobile accident in which his daughter Mary Elizabeth was critically injured. Tragically, so many other car crashes had occurred that evening that the emergency room could not take care of the girl. A frantic Brown raced through the hospital trying to find someone to help his child. He finally cornered an exhausted doctor about to go home after a double shift. The physician, Dr. Lawrence Leidig, initially begged off, but stayed on when he realized it was Brown. Lawrence treated the girl for seven hours and literally saved her life. After this medical miracle, the comedian shyly asked if the doctor was a fan, since he was not going to help until he recognized the comedian. Lawrence explained, "Fifteen years ago I asked movie stars to come to the Children's Orthopedic Hospital and cheer up the patients on Christmas Eve. The only ones who came were [acclaimed song-and-dance man] Bill Robinson and you."[51]

A story like this, or the previous chapter's chronicling of Brown's ongoing sacrifices to entertain American troops, document the comedian's longtime humanitarianism. But the comedian had seen so many hurtful things by the early 1950s, many related to World War II, that he felt concern over his ability to be the stereotypical brash comic:

> I'm not the comedian I once was. A comedian has to be slightly insulting, comedy has to be 70 per cent insults and I'm afraid today when I say something funny it may hurt someone. If another comic makes some crack about my [big] mouth, I just can't insult him back. I've lost something there, but I'm not sorry ... I know I've become too sensitive and I worry about it.[52]

Adding to Brown's anxiety was his increased involvement in television. The often "live" nature of the programming had him especially concerned over his comedy timing. Plus, the production chaos reminded him of an earlier technological wasteland — the confusion which accompanied the birth of talking pictures. Though hopeful that the dust would eventually settle, he was amazingly open about his small screen fears: "I don't mean [TV] shouldn't have [developed, with all its complexity], but I'm a fellow who is simple as hell—came from nowhere and got my education from people [the school of hard knocks]—and I don't like the [medium's] increased tempo...."[53]

Despite this anxiety, Brown did not hide his head in the sand. During the early 1950s he was no stranger to television. In addition to the guest appearances already mentioned, he substituted for Arthur Godfrey as the host of *Arthur Godfrey's Talent Scouts* (1948–58) during the summers of 1951 and 1952. This was no small accomplishment. Though Godfrey is forgotten today, he was a huge star in the 1950s. His *Talent Scouts* was the top-ranked television program of 1951–52, and second only to *I Love Lucy* (1951–57) the following season.[54] Moreover, Godfrey also had a second popular television show during this period—*Arthur Godfrey and His Friends* (1949–59). He was the "only personality in TV history to have two top-rated programs running simultaneously in prime time for an extended period (eight-and-a-half seasons)."[55]

The high visibility Brown received courtesy of *Arthur Godfrey's Talent Scouts* undoubtedly led to the comedian's only regular television program, *The Buick Circus Hour* (1952–53). The musical drama aired every fourth week on NBC (Tuesday 8:00–9:00 PM, EST). The time slot was normally filled by comedian Milton Berle's groundbreaking *Texaco Star Theatre* (1948–56), a variety show so popular that Berle came to be known as "Mr. Television." "Uncle Miltie," as Berle was also affectionately nicknamed, was often credited with being the greatest single catalyst for getting families to buy their first television. Occupying Berle's television spot once a month was another great boon to Joe's small screen career.

The Buick Circus Hour, showcasing Brown as an aging clown, co-starred popular Broadway stars John Raitt (as the circus owner) and Dolores Gray (as a young singer in love with the big top owner). *Variety's* review of the series first installment was mixed. On the negative side, the critic felt Brown merited more screen time, and that the story had too many loose plot points. But conversely, the critique was an extended rave for the comedian:

> Brown opened with a cute sight gag, involving a big dog and a tiny pooch. He had a sock [great] number midway in the layout [show], as a tramp clown giving a marksmanship exhibition, revealing his mastery of pantomime and his early circus training. Another amusing turn [routine] found Brown togged [dressed] out as a gal's guardian angel....[56]

The Buick Circus Hour originated live from New York, at a time when the majority of American television was being broadcast from the proverbial Gotham City. But Brown would leave the program after a year to become a play-by-play television announcer for the New York Yankees' 1953 home games. As if this were not exciting enough for baseball fanatic Brown, he was replacing baseball legend Joe DiMaggio. While no explicit explanation for the switch was made, the answer was probably later available in reviews of the comedian's interview skills. For example, "Brown is relaxed before the camera. Shy, diffident ball players loosen up for him as they never did for his predecessor, the illustrious Joe DiMaggio."[57] (The only problem for this film funnyman was that some viewers just wanted him to crack wise throughout the games!) The happy new baseball announcer said "he did not get into show business until he was nine but he was a confirmed baseball fan at four."[58]

Paralleling this Yankee appointment was Brown's 1953 acceptance of the presidency of the Pony League—an organization directing the 200-plus teams coast-to-coast of 13- and 14-year-old baseball players.[59] Two years later, his equally diamond-obsessed son, Joe LeRoy, would become the general manager of the Pittsburgh Pirates. The *New York Times* article announcing his appointment would be entitled, "Rickey Successor Pledges Pennant."[60] For longtime Yankee fan Brown, his son's eventual fulfillment of that pennant promise would involve upsetting the "Bronx Bombers" in one of baseball's most storied World Series (1960)!

Busy 1953 had already gotten off to a special start with Brown's daughters being married in an elaborate double wedding on Valentine's Day. The ceremony, witnessed by 800 guests, took place at St. Martin's of Tours Church, Brentwood, California. Mary Elizabeth, 23, married Steven Kenneth Fair, Jr., and Kathryn Frances, 20, exchanged vows with Armond Lloyd Lisle. Brown escorted Mary down the aisle first, then left by way of a side aisle and repeated the process with Kathryn. Mary carried a prayer book which her mother had held at *her* wedding.[61] After a reception at the Bel Air Hotel, the two couples left for honeymoons in Hawaii, a longtime favorite vacation destination for the Brown family.

When the proud papa returned to his entertainment career, the focus remained on both television and regional theater. Brown's additional small screen credits included appearances on *Schlitz Playhouse of Stars* (1951–59), *Screen Director's Playhouse* (1955–56), *General Electric Summer Originals* (1956), *The Ann Southern Show* (1958–61), *Five's a Family* (1961, a Brown pilot not picked up by NBC), *Route 66* (1960–64) and *The Greatest Show on Earth* (1963–64). This Brown list does not include talk show appearances and the *This Is Your Life* on which he was spotlighted.

Two of these credits merit special attention. First, Brown's installment of *Screen Director's Playhouse*, "The Silent Partner" (broadcast December 21, 1955), was a funny quality production about an oldtime comedy duo: Joe and the great Buster Keaton. *Variety* stated, "Whenever the performers break away from a high-moisture-content [sentimental] script and display their deft and engaging slapstick under George Marshall's understanding direction, they show that they still retain the ability to garner boisterous yocks." The cast also included ZaSu Pitts, Jack Elam and, in a cameo, Bob Hope. Second, Brown's pilot *Five's a Family* (aired July 14, 1961) was widely considered to be strong enough to make it as a series. For instance, the *Los Angeles Mirror* critic, in a review entitled, "Joe E. Brown Just Misses," observed, "Brown was easily the center of attraction as he did a little pantomime, and it seems the show could have held its own against some of the series which made the grade. A weekly diet of Joe E. Brown couldn't hurt TV...."[62] The pilot mixed comedy and drama as Brown played a retired detective-grandfather living with his policeman son and family.

The comedian's real-life grandpa status had received a great deal of press attention back in 1954 when his two daughters, of the double wedding ceremony, had both given birth within 48 hours of each other ... and at the same hospital! Brown cancelled all engagements to be on hand for the arrival of his first grandchildren. As if delivering in order of their ages, Mary's baby was born first — a daughter named after the comedian, Jo Leslie Fair. Brown told Hollywood columnist Louella Parsons, "She looks just like Mary and ... doesn't have my mouth and funny face."[63] Two days later, daughter Kathryn gave birth to a son, James L. Lisle. With the sisters on opposite ends of the hospital, medical attendants reported that the comedian "put in an astonishing amount of mileage in getting back and forth between them."[64]

During the remainder of the 1950s and early 1960s, Brown would also continue to surface in regional stage revivals of such plays as his standby *Harvey*, *Show Boat*, *Courtin' Time* and *Father of the Bride*. In late 1959 the comedian turned night club performer, teaming with Dorothy Shay in an act at Las Vegas' Tropicana.[65] The "Las Vegas supper club belt," as it was then being called, had already attracted many of Brown's 1930s screen comedy contemporaries, including Chico and Harpo Marx, the Ritz Brothers and George Burns. Brown's Tropicana stint was no doubt assisted by his movie-stealing supporting role in *Some Like It Hot*, the third highest-grossing picture of 1959, after *Auntie Mame* and *The Shaggy Dog*.[66] *Hot*, which will be addressed further in the epilogue, was an inspired capstone to a significant comedy career. The picture returned Brown, however briefly, to the humor heights he had known in the first half of the 1930s.

While he would continue to perform well into the 1960s (with his death coming on July 6, 1973, after a long illness), there was a sense of a career winding down in the 1950s. This was especially punctuated by the writing of his autobiography, LAUGHTER *Is a Wonderful Thing* (1956, with Ralph Hancock). Though all memoirs are an attempt, at some level, to present a summing up, rare is the autobiography which so succeeds at that task. As a longtime biographer, I have spent the better part of my life researching and chronicling the lives of others. But with the exception of the first half of Charlie Chaplin's redundantly entitled *My Autobiography* (1964), no other show business–related memoir comes close to Brown's. Appropriately, the book was critically well-received. His hometown paper, the *Toledo Times*, praised its "ring of honesty," and *The New York Times* celebrated "its homespun hero ... [as someone who has] an entertaining and absorbing success story to spin."[67] But the *Variety* reviewer best encapsuled Brown's introspective accomplishment:

> The same good humor, matched by an innate concept of decency, successfully skirts the Pollyanna, tells a full-blown story of a showman whose predilection for laughter was eclipsed only by his love of baseball, his family and his country.[68]

After the publication of the comedian's memoir, Ohio Governor Frank J. Lausche set aside November 20, 1956, as "Joe E. Brown Day." Lausche's proclamation said, in part, that it was fitting and proper that the state honor "a world-famous son who has brought happiness and goodwill to millions."[69] But this was just another of the many awards and recognitions which continued to come Brown's way, including being selected Humanitarian of the Year (1958) on behalf of the American Medical Center. (The Humanitarian scroll was presented to the comedian by his baseball buddy Walter O'Malley, president of the Los Angeles Dodgers.)

Some of the final news articles on Brown came courtesy of a tragic 1961 fire which destroyed his home and a lifetime collection of sports memorabilia and special thank yous, displayed in his "Room of Love." But like the comedy genre at which he so excelled, Brown was all about resilience. Plus, the comic was moved yet again by many organizations replacing his awards, such as a grateful American government giving him another Bronze Star.

Within a few years, Brown had converted a small guest house on his grounds into a new trophy room. But with typical self-deprecating humor he christened it "the outhouse." And in a reflective mood, he told a *Los Angeles Times* reporter, "There's been tragedy [in my life, such as] when we lost our boy. But I've had the chance given every other citizen in a free country of living my life as I wanted to live it and becoming what I wanted to become."[70]

And we are all the richer for it.

Afterword: "Zowie!"

For all the originality of the Billy Wilder and I. A. L. Diamond screenplay, *Some Like It Hot* (1959), supporting player Joe E. Brown made a script contribution, too. His character's pet phrase, "Zowie!," a term for anything which excited him, had been a regular part of Brown's 1930s vocabulary.[1]

As one comes to the close of writing a biography, there is often an eclectic assortment of stories about one's subject which for any number of reasons have not yet found their way into the finished manuscript. Of course, much of one's extensive research never makes it into the biography. Like a metaphorical detective, the profiler has many "leads" which do not pan out, and historic "witnesses" who are often redundant. Yet, the conscientious biographer is always sifting and resifting through a file cabinet of materials, looking for that story which suddenly has either new relevance, or, if truth be told, has previously been neglected in that proverbial cabinet — where documents become lost ... alphabetically. If the profiler is lucky, the final winning anecdotal candidates for the biography form a pattern that assists in summing up a memorable life. Three such items for Brown, involving a robbery, a ranking and a ribald role, do just that — help paint a more complete picture of the comedian.

First comes the robbery, or more correctly, the robbery attempt. In 1938, a transient put a gun in Brown's ribs and demanded that he hand over his money. The comedian talked him out of it — "What's the use of getting in a lot of trouble — are you broke?"[2] When his question received an affirmative, the comedian *gave* the man some money. Later, when the individual was apprehended, Brown did not press charges.

The ranking involves a 1943 *Photoplay* article which called Brown one of "the ten best husbands in Hollywood."[3] Author Hedda Hopper, the famed filmland columnist, noted that when the comedian and his wife renewed their wedding vows on their twenty-fifth anniversary, "[m]any Hollywood sophisticates went to laugh. [But] they stayed to weep a bit, because it was a moving occasion."[4]

Third, in writer-director Cameron Crowe's inspired book-length interview with legendary writer-director Billy Wilder, the Hollywood veteran gives Brown the highest marks, both as a person and a comic, for their collaboration on *Some Like It Hot*:

177

He did the part and was an absolute [brilliant] surprise to people, to young people, because they'd never *seen* him. He had the biggest mouth in the *world*. He was the nicest guy. You have to be alert [in casting], you know? You have to sit there, always, and say, "Is that the best I can do?"[5]

Yet another reference to how nice and funny Brown was — so what's news about that? Well, Wilder, like so many of his movies, is entertainingly cynical about most subjects. It was no accident that his films were often a showcase for dark comedy, such as *Some Like It Hot* being predicated upon two musicians (Tony Curtis and Jack Lemmon) witnessing the St. Valentine's Day Massacre. Wilder, this most gifted writer of both biting satire and broad parody, neither suffered the fool, nor easily gave comedy compliments. Consequently, it is startling to have him turn almost sentimental when the subject of Brown comes up.

This teaming of Wilder and Brown was also fitting on several additional levels for the comedian. First, while his *Some Like It Hot* character is wealthy dirty old man

Brown and Jack Lemmon during the celebrated conclusion of *Some Like It Hot* (1959).

Osgood Fielding, the part is built upon a foundation of Brown's nice guys. That is, Wilder was concerned that the public might find Osgood in poor taste. Thus, another reason for casting Brown was his lifetime reputation of always being a real mensch, both on screen and off. Second, *Some Like It Hot* fits under a number of comedy umbrellas, starting with parody, from spoofing gangster films, to stars kidding their personae. Thus, while George Raft parodies his tough guy image, Brown has fun with the squeaky-clean characterization for which he was famous. Third, with *Some Like It Hot* set in the late 1920s, Wilder wanted supporting players synonymous with the period. By casting Brown, Raft and Pat O'Brien (as an undercover cop), Wilder had both that period performer ambience and a historical footnote for students of film: Here are some veteran performers whose earlier work merits reconsideration. Fourth, while Wilder was probably not cognizant of the fact, *Some Like It Hot* also taps into provocative plot points with direct links to Brown's early career. For example, just as his Osgood character falls for a man in drag (Jack Lemmon), Brown's title character in the hit picture *The Circus Clown* (1934) does the same thing—he is smitten by a female-impersonating bareback rider.

Some Like It Hot's dark comedy status, a comic picture based upon two guys witnessing a murder and disguising themselves as women, also has parallels with Brown's earlier screen career. For instance, part of the catalyst for Joe to play a woman in the popular *Shut My Big Mouth* (1942) was safety, also. And while neither *A Very Honorable Guy* (1934) nor *Flirting with Fate* (1938) was a hit, both of these Brown vehicles had decidedly dark comedy plots. *A Very Honorable Guy* is a Damon Runyon story involving an anti-heroic gambler who sells his body to science to cover his debts! *Flirting with Fate* has Brown again in need of cash, and willing to commit suicide for the insurance money. But naturally, every comic attempt fails. Therefore, while Brown is best categorized as a personality comedian, he had flirted with black humor prior to *Some Like It Hot*.

A fifth tie between Joe's 1930s heyday and the Wilder classic involves Brown's propensity for comic dance material. This staple of the comedian's repertoire found new fruition during Osgood's seminal tango with Lemmon as Daphne. Though Brown's imaginatively funny film footwork dates from the pre-war era, especially his eccentric numbers from *Bright Lights* (1935), the comic's amusing strutting had also been show-cased in closer proximity to *Some Like It Hot*—1951's *Show Boat*. After Joe's famous big mouth, a hallmark of his humor was the eccentric dance routine.

A final comic connection of quintessential Brown to *Some Like It Hot* involves Osgood's show-stopping closing comment to Lemmon in drag, after it is revealed "she's" a he: "Well, nobody's perfect." This crack, which the American Film Institute (AFI) recently (2005) designated one of cinema's 100 most memorable lines, is a gem of absurdity—perfectly fitting for a comic whose signature verbal routine is a drunken "Little Mousie" nonsense story, told in a high-pitched, cartoon rodent voice.

These many Brown couplings to *Some Like It Hot* seem to demonstrate a

Brown in *A Very Honorable Guy* (1934).

cross-section of everything central to Joe but baseball. However, even there, a link exists. Both Brown and Wilder were baseball fanatics; they kept meeting at Los Angeles Dodgers games during the team's inaugural West Coast season (1958). With *Some Like It Hot* being shot late that same year, baseball was yet another factor in Brown's casting. Moreover, "[a]s long as Joe E. Brown was on the set, Billy conveniently had the inside track on all the player's, managers, and umpires in the [Dodgers'] National League."[6]

Since it drew from so many Brown basics, it should come as no surprise that his *Some Like It Hot* characterization was universally praised, from the *Motion Picture Herald* calling Osgood a "delightfully cockeyed millionaire," to *The Hollywood Reporter* stating that the "wacky playboy [is] enacted with a wonderful idiot zest by Joe E. Brown."[7] And as so often happened in past all-star productions, Brown tended to shine brightest. To illustrate, *Boxoffice* magazine observed, "Lemmon's [in-drag] scenes with Brown, playing a middle-aged enamored playboy, are the picture's comic high spots."[8]

The definitive Wilder biographer, Ed Sikov, has even drawn a key connection from the Osgood-Daphne "romance": "Brown's trademark gesture, a nearly silent laugh effected by stretching his huge orifice as wide as possible, is infectious—Daphne does it, too. These two are clearly made for each other."[9] One might further argue that Osgood and Daphne are also linked by both being "lovable fools," to borrow a phrase from Bernard F. Dick's analytical biography of Wilder.[10] That is, both characters are sending out patently mixed sexual messages. Osgood's line, "Well, nobody's perfect," could be "read" as openly gay, or simply the philosophical casualness of a benevolent

boob. And Daphne, at times, seems to be genuinely succumbing to Osgood's attention. After all, Lemmon's sidekick, Tony Curtis (Joe/Josephine), has to remind "her,"
"Just keep telling yourself you're a boy. You're a boy." Still, Lemmon (Jerry/Daphne)
muses, "I tell you, I will never find another man who's so good to me." Wilder keeps
it unclear as to whether it is Jerry or Daphne who is falling for Osgood. Indeed, years
later, Curtis would imply that Daphne and Osgood had a better chance of living on as
a duo, versus the coupling of his Joe/Josephine and Marilyn Monroe's Sugar: "That's
why the picture doesn't end on Marilyn and me. [It closes on Daphne and Osgood.]
Billy knew that [Joe and Sugar would not last]. As soon as that toothpaste would have
been empty, he'd be gone."[11]

Put another way, Osgood and Josephine are the nicest characters in the picture,
which brings one full circle back to the moral of the three stories which open this section — from a robbery, to the ribald, Brown's inherent decency always seems to shine
through. Moving beyond Joe's amazing comedy legacy, one admires all the more the
stellar person behind the laughter. Contemporary pop culture often feeds upon revisionist biographies that relish finding the unsavory in their subjects. I was reminded of
this recently when novelist Francine Prose wrote that too many biographers "choose to
spend years exposing the despicable secrets of such apparently vile subjects."[12]

A variation of this modern biography as a dishing phenomenon was brought home
to me by a *New York Times* article by a 2002 profiler of the celebrated Los Angeles
Dodgers pitcher, Sandy Koufax. Author Jane Leavy was feeling like a failure as a
researcher, because all her evidence suggested Koufax was nearly as flawless as the perfect game he once pitched — which was the framing device of Leavy's book. She needed
a friend to remind her, "It is a privilege to write about someone you actually like."[13]

Though I never needed such a reminder about either Brown, or any of my other
biography subjects, I did relate to Leavy's position — the paradox of modern biography,
where it is daring to chronicle niceness. Plus, Dodgers fan Brown would have undoubtedly appreciated this baseball connection. Of course, the celebration of great accomplishments in the arts, or on the diamond, do no necessitate that we admire the ethics
of a particular gifted performer. But it is a pleasant bonus when a performer's actions
behind the scenes are as admirable as his turns in the spotlight.

When diamond star Wade Boggs was inducted into the Baseball Hall of Fame
(2005), he said in part, "Our lives are not determined by what happens to us, but how
we react to what happens."[14] I thought immediately of Brown turning the loss of his
son during World War II into a legacy of love — entertaining American servicemen
around the globe, throughout the long conflict. His simple message was summarized
in the title of his later memoir, *LAUGHTER Is a Wonderful Thing*. The comedian was
always reacting "to what happens" in the most admirable of ways.

Brown might have said, "Well, nobody's perfect," but at times, he came awfully
close.

Joe E. Brown Filmography

Contrary to the popular belief that Joe E. Brown was simply a beloved B-star, for much of his screen career the comedian was an A-picture performer. However, due to some low-budget Brown films in the late 1920s and early 1940s, movies often not widely reviewed, the comic's later filmographies were often incomplete. What follows is a comprehensive Brown filmography — all feature-length fiction films. The comedian also appeared in a Vitaphone short subject (*Joe E. Brown in Don't Be Jealous*, 1928) and a documentary about entertaining the troops (*Cassino to Korea*, 1950).

Brown's 54 features found him working with a proverbial who's who of Hollywood. Interestingly, four of his screen love interests were played by performers destined to take home a Best Actress Oscar: Ginger Rogers, Olivia de Havilland, Jane Wyman and Susan Hayward. Though Brown never won an Academy Award, he appeared in two films which were Oscar-nominated for Best Picture — *A Midsummer Night's Dream* (1935) and *Around the World in 80 Days* (1956), with the latter movie winning the statuette.

May 1928   *Crooks Can't Win* (FBO, 60 minutes).
     Director: George M. Arthur. Stars: Thelma Hill, Sam Nelson, Joe E. Brown, Eugene Strong, Charles Hall, James Eagle.

July 1928   *Hit of the Show* (FBO, 60 minutes).
     Director: Ralph Ince. Story ("Notices"): Viola Brothers Shore. Stars: Joe E. Brown, Gertrude Olmstead, William Norton Bailey, Gertrude Astor, Ole M. Ness, Lee Shumway.

October 1928   *Take Me Home* (Paramount, 60 minutes).
     Director: Marshall Nellan. Screenplay: Ethel Doherty. Story: Harlan Thompson and Grover Jones. Stars: Bebe Daniels, Neil Hamilton, Lilyan Tashman, Doris Hill, Joe E. Brown.

December 1928   *The Circus Kid* (FBO, 65 minutes).
     Director: George B. Seitz. Screenplay: Story: James Ashmore Creelman. Stars: Frankie Darro, Joe E. Brown, Helene Costello, Poodles Hanneford, Sam Nelson, Lionel Belmore, John Gough.

1929   *Molly and Me* (Tiffany-Stahl, 60 minutes).
                Director: Albert Ray. Screenplay: Lois Leeson, Fred and Fannie Hat-
                ton. Stars: Belle Bennett, Joe E. Brown, Alberta Vaughn.

                My Lady's Past (Tiffany-Stahl, 60 minutes).
                Director: Albert Ray. Screenplay: Fred and Fannie Hatton and Frances
                Hyland. Stars: Belle Bennett, Joe E. Brown, Alma Bennett.

May 1929   *On with the Show* (Warner Bros., 120 minutes).
                Director: Alan Crosland. Screenplay: Robert Lord. Story: Humphrey
                Pearson. Stars: Betty Compson, Louise Fazenda, Sally O'Neil, Joe E.
                Brown, Purnell B. Pratt, William Bakewell.

                Painted Faces (Tiffany-Stahl, 60 minutes).
                Director: Albert Rogell. Screenplay: Frederick and Fanny Hatton.
                Story: Frances Hyland. Stars: Joe E. Brown, Helen Foster, Lester
                Cole.

December 1929   *Sally* (Warner Bros., 100 minutes).
                Director: John Francis Dillon. Screenplay: Waldemar Young, from
                the musical comedy of that name (Jerome Kern score). Stars: Mar-
                ilyn Miller, Alexander Gray, Joe E. Brown, T. Roy Barnes, Pert Kel-
                ton, Ford Sterling.

February 1930   *Song of the West* (Warner Bros., 82 minutes).
                Director: Ray Enright. Screenplay: Harvey Thew, from the Laurence
                Stallings and Oscar Hammerstein, 2nd, operetta *Rainbow*. Stars: John
                Boles, Vivienne Segal, Marie Wells, Joe E. Brown, Sam Hardy, Mar-
                ion Byron.

April 1930   *Hold Everything* (Warner Bros., 78 minutes).
                Director: Roy Del Ruth. Screenplay: B. G. DeSylva and John
                McGowan, from the stage musical of the same name. Stars: Joe E.
                Brown, Winnie Lightner, Georges Carpentier, Sally O'Neil, Edmund
                Breese, Bert Roach.

August 1930   *Top Speed* (Warner Bros., 71 minutes).
                Director: Mervyn LeRoy. Screenplay: Humphrey Pearson and Henry
                McCarty, from the musical by Bert Kalmar, Guy Bolton and Harry
                Ruby. Stars: Joe E. Brown, Bernice Claire, Jack Whiting, Frank
                McHugh, Laura Lee, Rita Flynn.

October 1930   *Maybe It's Love* (Warner Bros., 71 minutes).
                Director: William Wellman. Screenplay: Mark Canfield. Dialogue:
                Joseph Jackson. Stars: Joan Bennett, Joe E. Brown, James Hall, Laura
                Lee, Anders Randolf, Summer Getchell, the 1929 All-American foot-
                ball team.

November 1930   *The Lottery Bride* (United Artists, 85 minutes).
Director: Paul Stein. Screenplay: Horace Jackson. Story: Herbert Stothart. Dialogue: Howard Emmett Rogers. Stars: Jeanette MacDonald, John Garrick, Joe E. Brown, Zasu Pitts, Robert Chisholm, Joseph Macaulay.

January 1931   *Going Wild* (Warner Bros., 70 minutes).
Director: William A. Seiter. Story ("The Aviator"): James Montgomery. Stars: Joe E. Brown, Lawrence Gray, Laura Lee, Walter Pidgeon, Ona Munson, Frank McHugh.

February 1931   *Sit Tight* (Warner Bros., 77 minutes).
Director: Lloyd Bacon. Story-Screenplay: Rex Taylor. Stars: Winnie Lightner, Joe E. Brown, Claudia Dell, Paul Gregory, Lotti Loder, Hobart Bosworth.

July 1931   *Broad Minded* (Warner Bros., 65 minutes).
Director: Mervyn LeRoy. Story-Screenplay: Harry Ruby and Bert Kalmar. Stars: Joe E. Brown, Ona Munson, William Collier, Jr., Marjorie White, Holmes Herbert, Margaret Livingston, Thelma Todd, Bela Lugosi.

November 1931   *Local Boy Makes Good* (Warner Bros., 67 minutes).
From the J. C. Nugent–Elliott Nugent play *The Poor Nut*. Stars: Joe E. Brown, Dorothy Lee, Ruth Hall, Edward Woods, Eddie Nugent, Wade Boteler.

February 1932   *Fireman, Save My Child* (Warner Bros., 67 minutes).
Director: Lloyd Bacon. Story-Screenplay: Ray Enright, Arthur Caesar and Robert Lord. Stars: Joe E. Brown, Evalyn Knapp, Guy Kibbee, Lillian Bond, George Ernest, George MacFarlane, George Meeker.

May 1932   *The Tenderfoot* (Warner Bros., 70 minutes).
Director: Ray Enright. From the George S. Kaufman play *The Butter and Egg Man*. Stars: Joe E. Brown, Ginger Rogers, Lew Cody, Vivian Oakland, Robert Greig, Spencer Charters, Ralph Ince (Brown's director on *Hit of the Show*).

November 1932   *You Said a Mouthful* (Warner Bros., 75 minutes).
Director: Lloyd Bacon. Screenplay: Robert Lord and Bolton Mallory. Story: William B. Dover. Stars: Joe E. Brown, Ginger Rogers, Preston Foster, Sheila Terry, Farina, Joe Holt (swimming champion).

May 1933   *Elmer the Great* (Warner Bros., 74 minutes).
Director: Mervyn LeRoy. Screenplay: Tom Geraghty and Whitney Bolton, from the Ring Lardner–George M. Cohan play. Stars: Joe E.

Brown, Patricia Ellis, Claire Dodd, Sterling Holloway, Preston Foster, Frank McHugh.

November 1933　*Son of a Sailor* (Warner Bros., 70 minutes).
Director: Lloyd Bacon. Story-Screenplay: Al Cohn and Paul Gerrard Smith. Additional dialogue: Ernest Pagano and H. M. Walker. Stars: Joe E. Brown, Jean Muir, Frank McHugh, Thelma Todd, Johnny Mack Brown.

May 1934　*A Very Honorable Guy* (Warner Bros., 62 minutes).
Director: Lloyd Bacon. Screenplay: Earl Baldwin. Story: Damon Runyon. Stars: Joe E. Brown, Alice White, Robert Barrat, Alan Dinehart, Irene Franklin.

June 1934　*The Circus Clown* (Warner Bros., 63 minutes).
Director: Ray Enright. Story-Screenplay: Bert Kalmar and Harry Ruby. Stars: Joe E. Brown, Patricia Ellis, Dorothy Burgess, Donald Dilloway.

November 1934　*6-Day Bike Rider* (Warner Bros., 69 minutes).
Director: Lloyd Bacon. Story-Screenplay: Earl Baldwin. Stars: Joe E. Brown, Maxine Doyle, Frank McHugh, Gordon Westcott, Arthur Aylesworth.

July 1935　*Alibi Ike* (Warner Bros., 73 minutes).
Director: Ray Enright. Screenplay: William Wister Haines. Story: Ring Lardner. Stars: Joe E. Brown, Olivia de Havilland, Ruth Donnelly, Roscoe Karns, William Frawley.

August 1935　*Bright Lights* (Warner Bros., 82 minutes).
Director: Busby Berkeley. Screenplay: Bert Kalmar and Harry Ruby. Story: Lois Leeson. Adaptation: Ben Markson and Benny Rubin. Stars: Joe E. Brown, Ann Dvorak, Patricia Ellis, William Gargan, Arthur Treacher, William Demarest, The Maxellos.

October 1935　*A Midsummer Night's Dream* (Warner Bros., 117 minutes).
Director: Max Reinhardt and William Dieterle. Screenplay: Charles Kenyon and Mary McCall, Jr., from the William Shakespeare play. Stars: James Cagney, Joe E. Brown, Hugh Herbert, Frank McHugh, Victor Jory, Olivia de Havilland, Ross Alexander, Grant Mitchell, Nini Theilade, Verree Teasdale, Dick Powell, Jean Muir, Ian Hunter, Anita Louise, Mickey Rooney, Dewey Robinson, Hobart Cavanaugh, Otis Harlan, Arthur Treacher, Billy Barty.

May 1936　*Sons o' Guns* (Warner Bros., 79 minutes).
Director: Lloyd Bacon. Screenplay: Jerry Wald and Julius J. Epstein,

from the Fred Thompson–Jack Donahue play. Stars: Joe E. Brown, Joan Blondell, Beverly Roberts, Eric Blore.

July 1936   *Earthworm Tractors* (Warner Bros., 69 minutes).
Director: Ray Enright. Screenplay: Richard Macauley, Joe Traub and Hugh Cummings, from William Hazlett Upson's stories. Stars: Joe E. Brown, June Travis, Guy Kibbee, Carol Hughes.

November 1936 *Polo Joe* (Warner Bros., 62 minutes).
Director: William McGann. Screenplay: Peter Milne and Hugh Cummings. Stars: Joe E. Brown, Carol Hughes, Richard "Skeets" Gallagher, Joseph King, Gordon [Bill] Elliott, Fay Holden.

March 1937   *When's Your Birthday?* (RKO, 77 minutes).
A David L. Loew Production. Director: Harry Beaumont. Screenplay: Harry Clark, from the Fred Ballard play. Stars: Joe E. Brown, Marian Marsh, Fred Keating, Edgar Kennedy, Maude Eburne, Suzanne Kaaren, Margaret Hamilton.

June 1937   *Riding on Air* (RKO, 70 minutes).
A David L. Loew Production. Director: Edward Sedgwick. Screenplay: Richard Flournoy and Richard Macaulay, from Macaulay's Elmer Lane stories. Stars: Joe E. Brown, Guy Kibbee, Florence Rice, Vinton Haworth.

October 1937 *Fit for a King* (RKO, 73 minutes).
A David L. Loew Production. Director: Edward Sedgwick. Screenplay: Richard Flournoy. Stars: Joe E. Brown, Helen Mack, Paul Kelly, Harry Davenport, Halliwell Hobbes, John Qualen.

April 1938   *Wide Open Faces* (Columbia, 67 minutes).
A David L. Loew Production. Director: Kurt Neumann. Screenplay: Earle Snell, Clarence Marks and Joe Bigelow. Story: Richard Flournoy. Additional dialogue: Pat C. Flick. Stars: Joe E. Brown, Jane Wyman, Alison Skipworth, Lyda Roberti, Alan Baxter, Berton Churchill.

August 1938   *The Gladiator* (Columbia, 70 minutes).
A David L. Loew Production. Director: Edward Sedgwick. Screenplay: Charlie Melson and Arthur Sheekman, from the Philip Wylie novel. Stars: Joe E. Brown, Man Mountain Dean, June Travis, Dickie Moore, Lucien Littlefield.

December 1938 *Flirting with Fate* (MGM, 67 minutes).
A David L. Loew Production. Director: Frank McDonald. Screenplay: Joseph Moncure March, Ethel La Blanche, Charlie Melson and

Harry Clork. Stars: Joe E. Brown, Leo Carrillo, Beverly Roberts, Wynne Gibson, Steffi Duna.

October 1939   *$1,000 a Touchdown* (Paramount, 71 minutes).
Director: James Hogan. Story-Screenplay: Delmer Daves. Stars: Joe E. Brown, Martha Raye, Eric Blore, Susan Hayward.

November 1939   *Beware, Spooks!* (Columbia, 65 minutes).
Director: Edward Sedgwick. Screenplay: Richard Flournoy, Albert Duffy and Brian Marlow, from the Flournoy play. Stars: Joe E. Brown, Mary Carlisle, Clarence Kolb, Marc Lawrence.

October 1940   *So You Won't Talk* (Columbia, 68 minutes).
Director: Edward Sedgwick. Screenplay: Richard Flournoy. Stars: Joe E. Brown, Frances Robinson, Vivienne Osborne, Bernard Nedell, Tom Dugan, Dick Wessel, Anthony Warde.

February 1942   *Shut My Big Mouth* (Columbia, 71 minutes).
Director: Charles Barton. Screenplay: Oliver Drake, Karen DeWolf, Francis Martin, from a Drake story. Stars: Joe E. Brown, Adele Mara, Victor Jory, Fritz Feld, Don Beddoe.

July 1942   *Joan of Ozark* (Republic, 80 minutes).
Director: Joseph Santley. Screenplay: Robert Harari, Eve Greene and Jack Townley. Additional dialogue: Monte Brice and Bradford Ropes. Stars: Judy Canova, Joe E. Brown, Eddie Foy, Jr., Jerome Cowan.

Daring Young Man (Columbia, 70 minutes).
Director: Frank R. Strayer. Screenplay: Karen DeWolf and Connie Lee. Stars: Joe E. Brown, Marguerite Chapman, William Wright, Claire Dodd, Lloyd Bridges.

July 1943   *Chatterbox* (Republic, 75 minutes).
Director: Joseph Santley. Screenplay: George Carleton Brown and Frank Gill, Jr. Stars: Joe E. Brown, Judy Canova, Rosemary Lane, John Hubbard.

January 1944   *Casanova in Burlesque* (Republic, 74 minutes).
Director: Leslie Goodwins. Screenplay: Frank Gill, Jr. Story: John Wales. Stars: Joe E. Brown, June Havoc, Dale Evans, Marjorie Gateson, Lucien Littlefield.

May 1944   *Pin Up Girl* (Twentieth Century–Fox, 85 minutes).
Director: Bruce Humberstone. Screenplay: Robert Ellis, Helen Logan and Earl Baldwin. Story: Libbie Block. Stars: Betty Grable, John Harvey, Martha Raye, Joe E. Brown, Eugene Pallette.

December 1944   *Hollywood Canteen* (Warner Bros., 124 minutes).

Director-Screenplay: Delmer Daves. Stars: all-star cast includes: Bette Davis, John Garfield, Barbara Stanwyck, Joan Crawford, Jack Benny, Joe E. Brown, Jack Carson, Sydney Greenstreet, Peter Lorre.

December 1947　*The Tender Years* (Alperson–Twentieth Century–Fox, 81 minutes). Director: Harold Schuster. Screenplay: Jack Jungmeyer, Jr., and Arnold Belgard. Story: Jack Jungmeyer, Jr. Adaptation: Abem Finkel. Stars: Joe E. Brown, Richard Lyon, Noreen Nash, Charles Drake.

July 1951　*Show Boat* (MGM, 107 minutes). Director: George Sidney. Screenplay: John Lee Mahin, from the Jerome Kern–Oscar Hammerstein, 2nd, musical play and the Edna Ferber novel. Stars: Kathryn Grayson, Ava Gardner, Howard Keel, Joe E. Brown, Marge Champion, Gower Champion, Robert Sterling, Agnes Moorehead, Leif Erickson.

October 1956　*Around the World in 80 Days* (United Artists, 175 minutes). A Michael Todd Production. Director: Michael Anderson. Screenplay: S. J. Perelman, from the Jules Verne novel. Stars: all-star cast includes: David Niven, Shirley MacLaine, Charles Boyer, Joe E. Brown, Charles Coburn, Ronald Colman, Noël Coward, Marlene Dietrich, Trevor Howard, Buster Keaton, Peter Lorre, Jack Oakie, George Raft, Frank Sinatra, Red Skelton.

March 1959　*Some Like It Hot* (United Artists, 120 minutes). Director: Billy Wilder. Screenplay: Wilder and I. A. L. Diamond. Story: R. Thoeren and M. Logan. Stars: Marilyn Monroe, Tony Curtis, Jack Lemmon, George Raft, Pat O'Brien, Joe E. Brown, Nehemiah Persoff.

November 1963　*It's a Mad Mad Mad Mad World* (United Artists, 192 minutes). Director: Stanley Kramer. Story-Screenplay: William and Tania Rose. Stars: all-star cast: Spencer Tracy, Milton Berle, Sid Caesar, Buddy Hackett, Ethel Merman, Mickey Rooney, Dick Shawn, Phil Silvers, Terry-Thomas, Jonathan Winters, Edie Adams, Dorothy Provine, Jimmy Durante, William Demarest, Buster Keaton, Joe E. Brown, Jerry Lewis.

December 1963　*The Comedy of Terrors* (American-International, 88 minutes). Director: Jacques Tourneur. Screenplay: Richard Matheson. Stars: Vincent Price, Peter Lorre, Boris Karloff, Basil Rathbone, Joe E. Brown.

Chapter Notes

Preface and Acknowledgments

1. Joe E. Brown (as told to Ralph Hancock), *Laughter Is a Wonderful Thing* (New York: A. S. Barnes, 1956).

2. Leonard Maltin, *The Great Movie Comedians: From Charlie Chaplin to Woody Allen* (New York: Crown, 1978): 130.

3. See the author's *Charlie Chaplin: A Bio-Bibliography* (Westport, Connecticut: Greenwood, 1983).

4. William T. Vollmann, "The Constructive Nihilist," *The New York Times* (August 14, 2005): Book Review: 8.

5. See the author's *Mr. Deeds Goes to Yankee Stadium: Baseball Films in the Capra Tradition* (Jefferson, North Carolina: McFarland, 2004).

Chapter One

1. A 19th-century circus axiom of which Brown was fond.

2. Joe E. Brown (with Margaret Lee Runbeck), *Your Kids and Mine* (Garden City, New York: Doubleday, Doran, 1944): 12.

3. Bosley Crowther, *Wide Open Faces* review, *The New York Times* (April 15, 1938): 23.

4. "Brown, LeRoy and Story Highlights," *The Hollywood Reporter* (March 23, 1933): 3; *Going Wild* review, *The New York Times* (January 26, 1931): 21.

5. Marguerite Tazelaar, *Sit Tight* review, *New York Herald Tribune* (February 19, 1931): 17.

6. Rose Pelswick, *Local Boy Makes Good* review, *New York Evening Journal* (November 27, 1931): 29.

7. Bosley Crowther, *Earthworm Tractors* review, *The New York Times* (July 25, 1936): 16.

8. Donald C. Manlove (ed.), *The Best of James Whitcomb Riley* (Bloomington: Indiana University Press, 1982): 69.

9. Joe E. Brown (as told to Ralph Hancock), *Laughter Is a Wonderful Thing* (New York: A. S. Barnes, 1956): 30.

10. Leonard Maltin, *The Great Movie Comedians: From Charlie Chaplin to Woody Allen* (New York: Crown, 1978): 123.

11. Brown, *Laughter Is a Wonderful Thing*: 7.

12. Wes D. Gehring, *Seeing Red: The Skelton in Hollywood's Closet* (Davenport, Iowa: Robin Vincent, 2001).

13. Wes D. Gehring, *The Marx Brothers: A Bio-Bibliography* (Westport, Connecticut: Greenwood, 1987).

14. Nicholas Dawidoff (ed.), *Baseball: A Literary Anthology* (New York: Library of America, 2002): 1.

15. John Bowman and Zoel Zoss, *Diamonds in the Rough: The Untold History of Baseball* (New York: Macmillan, 1989): 3.

16. "Japanese Captives Wanted Baseball Talk," *The New York Times* (April 25, 1943): Section 1: 13.

17. "Baseball Post to Joe E. Brown," *The New York Times* (April 1, 1953): 38.

18. Sheila Wolfe, "Joe E. Brown Grins, Waits for Surgery," *Chicago Tribune* (April 16, 1965): Section 1: 3.

19. "Ricky Successor Pledges Pennant," *The New York Times* (October 26, 1955): 36.

20. Fred C. Kelly, *The Life and Times of Kin Hubbard: Creator of Abe Martin* (New York: Farrar, Straus and Young, 1952): 52.

21. Sara Hamilton, "Whooie! Here Comes Joe E.," *Photoplay* (November 1932).

22. Brown, *Laughter Is a Wonderful Thing*: 37.

23. Michael Chabon, *Wonder Boys* (New York: Picador, 1995): 251.

24. Jim Knipfel, *Slackjaw: A Memoir* (1999; rpt. New York: Berkley Books, 2000): 180.

Chapter Two

1. Joe E. Brown (as told to Ralph Hancock), *Laughter Is a Wonderful Thing* (New York: A. S. Barnes, 1956): 225.

2. "Rowe's Hand Mashed by Joe Brown," *New York Herald Tribune* (October 9, 1934): 20.

3. Ibid.

4. "Lusty Shake: Joe Brown's Grip May Have Cost Game," *Toledo Times* (October 9, 1934): 2.

5. Will Rogers, "Mr. Rogers Makes His Official Report on the World Series Finale and the Riot" (October 10, 1934, syndicated daily newspaper telegram), in *Will Rogers' Daily Telegrams, Vol. 4, The Roosevelt Years: 1933–1935*, ed. James M. Smallwood (Stillwater: Oklahoma State University Press, 1979): 228.

6. Charles W. Dunkley, "Cards Go Wild in Dressing Room," *Toledo Times* (October 10, 1934): 7.

7. "Dizzy Calls Self 'Lousy' But Paul Will Thump 'Em," *Toledo Times* (October 4, 1934): 1.

8. Paul A. Schroder, "Dizzy Dean Is Not So Dizzy When Currency Is Involved, Stage Contract Shows," *Toledo Times* (October 14, 1934): 3-B; Brown, *Laughter Is a Wonderful Thing*: 212.

9. "Sporting Life," *Time* (April 27, 1953).

10. Vince Staten, *Ol' Diz: A Biography of Dizzy Dean* (New York: Harper Collins, 1992): 145.

11. Hy Gardner, "'We Need Better Grownups...' So Says Joe E. 'Grin,' Who Defends Our Kids," *Parade* (July 6, 1952): 13.

12. Dunkley, "Cards Go Wild in Dressing Room."

13. "St. Louis Acclaims Cardinals on Return Home," *Toledo Times* (October 11, 1934): 7.

14. "Sporting Life," *Time*.

15. Mitchell Woodbury, "Strolling Around [:Series Trophies Given Joe Brown]," *Toledo Times* (October 14, 1934): 5-D.

16. Brown, *Laughter Is a Wonderful Thing*: 213–14.

17. Lowell Reidenbaugh, *Baseball's Hall of Fame: Cooperstown: Where the Legends Live Forever* (1983; rpt. New York: Crescent Books, 1997): 52.

18. Ted Williams and Jim Prime, *Ted Williams' Hit List* (1995; rpt. Indianapolis: Masters Press, 1996): 82.

19. Red Smith, *Red Smith on Baseball* (Chicago: Ivan R. Dee, 2000): 130.

20. Ty Cobb (with an introduction by John N. Wheeler), *Busting 'Em and Other Big League Stories* (1914; rpt. Jefferson, North Carolina: McFarland, 2003): 25.

21. Ibid.,: 25–26.

22. C. Wann Woodward, "Political Stalemate and Agrarian Revolt, 1877–1896," in *The National Experience: A History of the United States*, John M. Blum, ed. (New York: Harcourt Brace, 1968): 513.

23. "Joe E. Brown," in *Current Biography 1945*, ed. Anne Rothe (New York: H. W. Wilson, 1946): 76.

24. Brown, *Laughter Is a Wonderful Thing*: 75.

25. Joe E. Brown (with Margaret Lee Runbeck), *Your Kids and Mine* (Garden City, New York: Doubleday, Doran, 1944): 191–92.

26. Alva Johnston, "Profiles: Comedy [Joe E. Brown]," *The New Yorker* (July 7, 1945): 29.

27. Brown, *Laughter Is a Wonderful Thing*: 87.

28. See the author's *Laurel & Hardy: A Bio-Bibliography* (Westport, Connecticut: Greenwood, 1990).

29. "Sidelights of the Week," *The New York Times* (December 29, 1940): Section 4:2.

30. For instance, see: "Joe E. Browns Wed Again on the 25th Anniversary," *The New York Times* (December 25, 1940): 32.

Chapter Three

1. Joe E. Brown (as told to Ralph Hancock), *Laughter Is a Wonderful Thing* (New York: A. S. Barnes, 1956): 125.

2. Ibid., 123.

3. "Joe Evan Brown," in *Current Biography 1945*, ed. Anna Rothe (New York: H. W. Wilson, 1946): 76.

4. For more on the Marx Brothers and Broadway, see the author's *The Marx Brothers: A Bio-Bibliography* (Westport, Connecticut: Greenwood, 1987): 28–30.

5. Louis Cook, "Who Said Joe's Mouth Was Big? You Can Blame It All on Lester...," *Detroit Free Press* (July 12, 1964): 10-D.

6. "*Jim Jam Jems* Noisy But Funny," *New York Herald* (October 5, 1920): 11.

7. "*Jim Jam Jems* Takes Front Ranks on Broadway," *New York Tribune* (October 5, 1920): 8.

8. For more on the significance of Harry Langdon's silent film career, see the author's *Personality Comedians as Genre: Selected Players* (Westport, Connecticut: Greenwood, 1997): 5–6.

9. James Agee, "Comedy's Greatest Era" (1949), in *Agee on Film, Volume 1* (1969; rpt. New York: Grosset & Dunlap, 1972): 14.

10. See both Frank Capra's *Frank Capra: The Name Above the Title* (New York: Macmillan, 1971): 62–71, and William Schelly's *Harry Langdon* (Metuchen, New Jersey: Scarecrow Press, 1982).

11. See the author's *Laurel & Hardy: A Bio-Bibliography* (Westport, Connecticut: Greenwood, 1990).

12. Mark Twain, *A Connecticut Yankee in King Arthur's Court* (1889; rpt. Scranton: Chandler, 1963): 54.

13. Brown, *Laughter Is a Wonderful Thing*: 154.

14. See the author's *The Marx Brothers: A Bio-Bibliography*: 30.

15. "Sporting Life," *Time* (April 27, 1953).

16. Joe E. Brown questionnaire, circa 1930s, in the Joe E. Brown files, Margaret Herrick Library, Academy of Motion Picture Arts and Sciences, Beverly Hills, California.

17. *Greenwich Village Follies* review, *The New York Times* (September 21, 1923): 4.

18. "Pleasing Bill at Palace," *The New York Times* (October 23, 1923): 18.

19. "*Betty Lee* Premiere," *The New York Times* (December 26, 1924): 18.

20. "*Betty Lee* Tuneful, Gay, Speedy Musical Comedy," *New York Herald Tribune* (December 26, 1924): 8.

21. "*Captain Jinks* Comes to Town and Charms Everybody," *The New York Post* (September 9, 1925): 14.

22. "Colorful *Captain Jinks* Here With Wit and Song," *New York Herald Tribune* (September 9, 1925): 14.

23. Brown, *Laughter Is a Wonderful Thing*: 169.

24. See the author's *The Marx Brothers: A Bio-Bibliography*: 28–56.

25. *Twinkle Twinkle* review, *The New York Times* (November 17, 1926): 22.

26. "*Twinkle Twinkle* Sparks at the Liberty Theatre," *The New York Post* (November 17, 1926): 8.

27. Richard Watts, Jr., "*Twinkle Twinkle* Tells of Film Star and Hollywood 'Sin,'" *New York Herald Tribune* (November 17, 1926): 21.

28. Ibid.

29. Brown, *Laughter Is a Wonderful Thing*: 178.

Chapter Four

1. See the author's *W. C. Fields: A Bio-Bibliography* (Westport, Connecticut: Greenwood, 1984): 91.

2. Joe E. Brown (as told to Ralph Hancock), *Laughter Is a Wonderful Thing* (New York: A. S. Barnes, 1956): 179.

3. *Crooks Can't Win* review, *Variety* (May 30, 1928).

4. "A Tragic Comedian," *The New York Times* (July 9, 1928): 25.

5. *Hit of the Show* review, *Variety* (July 11, 1928).

6. *Take Me Home* review, *Variety* (October 24, 1928).

7. Bob Brooks, "'Circus Is Greatest' Says Joe E. Brown," *Los Angeles Mirror* (March 20, 1961).

8. "Winter and the Circus," *The New York Times* (December 17, 1928): 23; *The Circus Kid* review, *Variety* (December 19, 1928).

9. Brown, *Laughter Is a Wonderful Thing*: 187.

10. "Going to Movies Is Social Obligation in Hollywood," *Toledo Times* (September 2, 1934): 4-D.

11. Joe E. Brown, "My Favorite Movie Scene," *The Saturday Evening Post* (March 31, 1945).

12. Mordaunt Hall, *On With the Show* review, *The New York Times* (May 29, 1929): 28; *On With the Show* review, *Variety* (June 5, 1929).

13. *Sally* review, *Variety* (December 25, 1929).

14. Regina Crewe, "*Hold Everything* Marvel in Comedy as Seen on Screen," *New York American* (April 23, 1930): 17.

15. Marguerite Tazelaar, "*Hold Everything* Opens New Hollywood Theater," *New York Herald Tribune* (April 23, 1930): 16.

16. *Hold Everything* review, *Variety* (March 26, 1930).

17. John S. Cohen, Jr., "The Warners' Hollywood Theater Opens With *Hold Everything*," *New York Sun* (April 23, 1930): 23.

18. "Notable Audience Views Picture of *Hold Everything*," *New York American* (April 23, 1930): 17.

19. Jim Dent, *Monster of the Midway* (New York: St. Martin's Press, 2003): 60.

20. Mordaunt Hall, "Joe E. Brown and Patricia Ellis in a Film of a Baseball Comedy by Ring Lardner," *The New York Times* (May 26, 1933): 24.

21. Bland Johaneson, *Alibi Ike* review, *New York Daily Mirror* (July 17, 1935).

22. Leonard Maltin, *The Great Movie Comedians: From Charlie Chaplin to Woody Allen* (New York: Crown, 1978): 125.

23. Roger Kahn, *A Flame of Pure Fire: Jack Dempsey and the Roaring '20s* (New York: Harcourt Brace, 1999): 231.

24. Mordaunt Hall, "*Hold Everything* Opens New Theatre," *New York Times* (April 23, 1930): 24; Irene Thirer, "*Hold Everything* Opens Hollywood," *New York Daily News* (April 23, 1930): 38.

25. Cohen, Jr., "The Warners' Hollywood Theater Opens With *Hold Everything*"; Crewe, "*Hold Everything* Marvel in Comedy as Seen on Screen."

26. *Hold Everything* review, *Variety*.

27. Ibid.

28. Bert Lahr letter, "Bert Lahr Labels Joe Brown 'Lifter,'" *Variety* (March 28, 1930).

29. Brown, *Laughter Is a Wonderful Thing*: 195.

30. Ibid.

31. John Lahr, *Notes on a Cowardly Lion: The Biography of Bert Lahr* (1969; rpt. New York: Ballantine Books, 1970): 126.

32. Ibid., 127–28.

33. See the author's *Leo McCarey: From Marx to McCarthy* (Lanham, Maryland: Scarecrow, 2005): 30–32.

34. David Robinson, *Chaplin: His Life and Art* (New York: McGraw-Hill, 1985): 354.

35. Brown, *Laughter Is a Wonderful Thing*: 195.

Chapter Five

1. Cobbett Steinberg, *Reel Facts: The Movie Book of Records* (New York: Vintage Books, 1978): 403–04.

2. "The Palladium: Mr. Joe E. Brown in Person," *London Times* (August 19, 1936): 8.

3. "*Top Speed* with Joe Brown," *Harrison's Reports* (September 6, 1930); *Top Speed* review, *Variety* (September 3, 1930).

4. Mordaunt Hall, "Joe E. Brown in Comedy: Laura Lee Also Amuses in *Top Speed* at the Strand," *The New York Times* (August 30, 1930): 7.

5. Henry Jenkins, *What Made Pistachio Nuts? Early Sound Comedy and the Vaudeville Aesthetic* (New York: Columbia University Press, 1992): 149.

6. Ibid.: 283.

7. See the author's *The Marx Brothers: A Bio-Bibliography* (Westport, Connecticut: Greenwood, 1987) and *Groucho and W. C. Fields: Huckster Comedians* (Jackson: University Press of Mississippi, 1994).

8. See the author's *Leo McCarey: From Marx to McCarthy* (Lanham, Maryland: Scarecrow, 2005).

9. John S. Cohen, "*Let's Go Native*, Wherein Jack Oakie and Others Spread Mirth on a Tropical Island," *New York Sun* (August 30, 1930): 4.

10. Hall, "Joe E. Brown in Comedy: Laura Lee Also Amuses in *Top Speed* at the Strand."

11. *Broad Minded* review, *Variety* (July 7, 1931).

12. Joe E. Brown (as told to Ralph Hancock), *Laughter Is a Wonderful Thing* (New York: A. S. Barnes, 1956): 112.

13. Regina Crewe, "*Going Wild* Hits High Laugh Mark; Joe E. Brown Star," *New York American* (January 27, 1931): 17.

14. "Skylarking," *The New York Times* (January 26, 1931): 21.

15. *Broad Minded* review, *Variety*.

16. *Top Speed* review, *Variety*.

17. See especially Lori Van Pelt's detailed biography *Amelia Earhart: The Sky's No Limit* (New York: Tom Doherty Associates Book, 2005).

18. *Maybe It's Love* review, *Variety* (October 22, 1930).

19. William Wellman interview by the author, Los Angeles (June 1975), author's files; see also the author's "The Last William Wellman Interview," *Paper Cinema* (vol. 1, no. 1, 1982): 9–13.

20. *The Lottery Bride* review, *New York Evening Journal* (November 29, 1930): 9.

21. "Music by Mr. Frimi," *The New York Times* (November 29, 1930): 21; *Lottery Bride* review, *Variety* (December 3, 1930).

22. *Sit Tight* review, *Variety* (February 25, 1931).

23. "*Sit Tight* A Sad Film," *The New York Times* (February 19, 1931): 20.

24. *Local Boy Makes Good* review, *The New York Post* (November 27, 1931): 21.

25. William Boehnel, *Local Boy Makes Good* review, *New York World Telegram* (November 28, 1931): 21.

26. *Local Boy Makes Good* review, *New York Herald Tribune* (November 27, 1931): 21; Regina Crewe, "Joe E. Brown Climbs to New Heights in Picture Hilarity," *New York American* (November 27, 1931): 15.

27. Rose Pelswick, *Local Boy Makes Good* review, *New York Evening Journal* (November 27, 1931): 29.

28. Harold Lloyd (with Wesley W. Stout), *An American Comedy* (1928; New York: Dover, 1971): 59.

29. Gerald Mast, *Howard Hawks, Storyteller* (New York: Oxford University Press, 1982): 136; see also the author's *Romantic vs. Screwball Comedy: Charting the Difference* (Lanham, Maryland: Scarecrow, 2002).

30. John S. Cohen, Jr., *Local Boy Makes Good* review, *New York Sun* (November 27, 1931): 43.

31. Mae Tinée, "Sparkling Role Helps Joe Brown in Film Comeback," *Chicago Tribune* (January 31, 1932): Part 9: 1.

32. Leonard Maltin, *The Great Movie Comedians: From Charlie Chaplin to Woody Allen* (New York: Crown, 1978): 127.

33. Joe E. Brown Press Release, Paramount studio biography (July 5, 1939), in the Joe E. Brown file, Margaret Herrick Library, Academy of Motion Picture Arts and Sciences (Beverly Hills CA).

34. Grace Kingsley, "Screen's Comedians Make Best Fathers," *Los Angeles Times* (May 27, 1934): Part 2: 1.

35. Ibid.

36. Joe E. Brown, untitled essay in uncited Los Angeles newspaper (March 3, 1934), in the Joe E. Brown file, Margaret Herrick Library.

37. Joe E. Brown, "Post Toasties a Natural for Kiddies' Air Show," *Rim Monthly* (December 1938): 17.

38. Joe E. Brown Press Release, RKO studio biography [ca. 1937], in the Joe E. Brown file, Margaret Herrick Library.

Chapter Six

1. See the author's *Mr. Deeds Goes to Yankee Stadium: Baseball Films in the Capra Tradition* (Jefferson, North Carolina: McFarland, 2004).

2. Joe E. Brown, "The Role I Liked Best…," *The Saturday Evening Post* (November 9, 1946); "Joe E.

Brown to Stage," *The Hollywood Reporter* (November 26, 1930): 2.

3. Ring Lardner, *You Know Me Al: A Busher's Letters* (1914; rpt. New York: Collier Books, 1991).

4. See especially Walter Blair's *Native American Humor* (1937; rpt. Scranton, Pennsylvania: Chandler Publishing, 1960).

5. For example, see Richard Watts, Jr., *Fireman, Save My Child* review, *New York Herald Tribune* (February 19, 1932): 12; *Fireman, Save My Child* review, *New York Sun* (February 20, 1932): 6.

6. Lowell Reidenbaugh, *Baseball's Hall of Fame: Cooperstown, Where the Legends Live Forever* (1983; rpt. New York: Crescent Books, 1997): 280.

7. "Joe Brown Wants to Play Rube Waddell," *The Hollywood Reporter* (December 28, 1942): 3.

8. See the author's *Seeing Red: The Skelton in Hollywood's Closet: An Analytical Biography* (Davenport, Iowa: Robin Vincent, 2001).

9. *Fireman, Save My Child* review, *Film Daily* (February 21, 1932).

10. *Fireman, Save My Child* review, *Variety* (February 23, 1932).

11. William Boehnel, "*Fireman, Save My Child* Called Joe Brown's Best," *New York World Telegram* (February 19, 1932): 24.

12. "*Fireman* Corking Comedy," *The Hollywood Reporter* (January 27, 1932): 3.

13. Sol Polito, *Fireman, Save My Child* review, *International Photographer* (March 1932).

14. Ibid.

15. *Fireman, Save My Child* review, *Variety*.

16. Watts, Jr., *Fireman, Save My Child* review.

17. Boehnel, "*Fireman, Save My Child* Called Joe Brown's Best."

18. *Fireman, Save My Child* review, *New York Sun* (February 20, 1932): 6.

19. Cobbett Steinberg, *Reel Facts: The Movie Book of Records* (New York: Vintage Books, 1978): 403.

20. "Joe E. Brown in *Fireman, Save My Child*," *Film Daily* (February 21, 1932).

21. "*Fireman* Corking Comedy," *The Hollywood Reporter*.

22. "Brown and Keaton in Ball Game Sunday," *The Hollywood Reporter* (February 27, 1932): 2.

23. John Thorn and Pete Palmer, eds., *Total Baseball* (New York: Warner Books, 1989): 1979–80.

24. Jonathan Yardley, *Ring: A Biography of Ring Lardner* (1977; rpt. New York: Rowman & Littlefield, 2001): 81–82.

25. Joe E. Brown (as told to Ralph Hancock), *Laughter Is a Wonderful Thing* (New York: A. S. Barnes, 1956): 202.

26. Thorn and Palmer, eds., *Total Baseball*: 1651.

27. Brown, *Laughter Is a Wonderful Thing*: 202.

28. See the author's *Seeing Red: The Skelton in Hollywood's Closet: An Analytical Biography*.

29. Lucius Beebe, "*Elmer the Great*— Radio City Music Hall," *New York Herald Tribune* (May 26, 1933): 18; Regina Crewe, "*Elmer the Great* Is Hilarious Film of Lardner-Cohan Play," *New York American* (May 26, 1933): 13.

30. "*Elmer the Great* Gives Plenty of Belly-Laughs," *The Hollywood Reporter* (March 23, 1933): 3.

31. Mordaunt Hall, "Joe E. Brown and Patricia Ellis in a Film of a Baseball Comedy by Ring Lardner," *The New York Times* (May 26, 1933): 24.

32. Rose Pelswick, "Baseball Hero Wins," *New York Evening Journal* (May 26, 1933): 20.

33. *Elmer the Great* review, *New York Sun* (May 27, 1933): 27.

34. William Dabb, *Elmer the Great* mini-review, *Motion Picture Herald* (May 13, 1933): 53.

35. Carl Veseth, *Elmer the Great* mini-review, *Motion Picture Herald* (July 22, 1933): 69.

36. L. Weber, *Elmer the Great* mini-review, *Motion Picture Herald* (July 8, 1933): 47; R. W. Hickman, *Elmer the Great* mini-review, *Motion Picture Herald* (May 27, 1933): 39.

37. Brown, *Laughter Is a Wonderful Thing*: 214.

38. Joe E. Brown, "The Role I Liked Best...," *The Saturday Evening Post* (November 9, 1946).

39. Ibid.

40. "Engagement of Joe E. Brown to Be Limited," *Los Angeles Times* (November 24, 1932).

41. Corbin Patrick, "Victor Varies Musical Output With Joe Brown Baseball Album," *Indianapolis Star* (May 16, 1947): 25.

42. "Japanese Captives Wanted Baseball Talk, Says Joe E. Brown on Return From Pacific," *The New York Times* (April 25, 1943): Section 1: 13.

43. Ring Lardner, "Alibi Ike," in "*Haircut*" *and Other Stories* (1922; rpt. New York: Scribner's, 1954): 36.

44. "Me 'n Paul" (cover story), *Time* (April 15, 1935): 52.

45. Regina Crewe, "*Alibi Ike*, Amusing Ring Lardner Tale, Stars Joe Brown," *New York American* (July 17, 1935); "*Alibi Ike* Comedy Home Run," *The Hollywood Reporter* (June 8, 1935): 3.

46. Richard Watts, Jr., *Alibi Ike* review, *New York Herald Tribune* (July 17, 1935): 10.

47. Larnder, *You Know Me Al: A Busher's Letters*: 46.

48. Ibid., 72.

49. Brown, *Laughter Is a Wonderful Thing*: 213.

50. Lardner, *You Know Me Al: A Busher's Letters*: 45.

51. Reidenbaugh, *Baseball's Hall of Fame: Cooperstown, Where the Legends Live Forever*: 193.

52. *Alibi Ike* review, *Los Angeles Times* (June 7, 1935).

53. Thorn and Palmer, eds., *Total Baseball*: 261.

54. "*Alibi Ike* Comedy Home Run," *The Hollywood Reporter*.

55. "Ring Lardner Story Offers Joe Brown Familiar Material," *The New York Post* (July 17, 1935).

56. "Joe E. Brown Returns in a Merry Film Version of Ring Lardner's *Alibi Ike*, at the Cameo," *The New York Times* (July 17, 1935): 22.

57. Eileen Creelman, "Joe E. Brown as a Ring Lardner Ball Player in 'Alibi Ike,'" *New York Sun* (July 17, 1935).

58. Wanda Hale, "'Alibi Ike' Cheers Joe E. Brown Fans," *New York Daily News* (July 17, 1935).

59. Brown, *Laughter Is a Wonderful Thing*: 222.

Chapter Seven

1. Laura Moser, *Bette Davis* (London: Haus Publishing, 2004): 23.

2. *You Said a Mouthful* review, *Variety* (November 22, 1932); Eileen Creelman, *The Circus Clown* review, *New York Sun* (June 2, 1934): 15.

3. Joe E. Brown (as told to Ralph Hancock), *Laughter Is a Wonderful Thing* (New York: A. S. Barnes, 1956): 199.

4. See A&E's *Biography* segment on Groucho, first televised June 15, 1993.

5. Joe E. Brown Warners biography, circa 1932, in the Joe E. Brown files, Margaret Herrick Library, Academy of Motion Picture Arts and Sciences, Beverly Hills, California.

6. "Joe Brown Raisin King," *The Hollywood Reporter* (September 8, 1934): 4.

7. Keith Monroe, "The Battling Buffoon Named Brown," *The Saturday Evening Post* (December 8, 1951): 23.

8. For instance, see "Joe E. Brown in Hospital Role," uncredited Los Angeles newspaper (May 11, 1932); "Joe E. Brown Operated Upon," uncredited Los Angeles newspaper (May 26, 1932), both in the Joe E. Brown files, Margaret Herrick Library; "Joe E. Brown in Hospital," *The New York Times* (May 8, 1936): 21.

9. "Joe E. Brown Hurt in Auto Accident," *Indianapolis Star* (December 7, 1939): 4.

10. Carl Veseth, *Elmer the Great* mini-review, *Motion Picture Herald* (July 22, 1933): 69; Gladys E. McArdle, *Elmer the Great* mini-review, *Motion Picture Herald* (July 15, 1933): 79.

11. Bert Silver, *Son of a Sailor* mini-review, *Motion Picture Herald* (January 27, 1934): 59; W. E. O'Brien, *Son of a Sailor* mini-review, *Motion Picture Herald* (March 3, 1934): 57; H. M. Johnson, *Son of a Sailor* mini-review, *Motion Picture Herald* (March 31, 1934): 61.

12. S. H. Rich, *You Said a Mouthful* mini-review, *Motion Picture Herald* (April 29, 1933): 37.

13. Henry Reeve, *Son of a Sailor* mini-review, *Motion Picture Herald* (June 2, 1934): 59.

14. Herman J. Brown, *You Said a Mouthful* mini-review, *Motion Picture Herald* (May 19, 1934): 87.

15. Monroe, "The Battling Buffoon Named Brown": 108.

16. Hy Gardner, "We Need Better Grownups...," *Parade* (July 6, 1952): 13; also implied in period pieces, such as "Joe E. Brown Arrives; Gets Auto from Missus," *The Hollywood Reporter* (October 14, 1931): 3.

17. Joe E. Brown Warners biography, circa 1932.

18. E. A. Reynolds, *Elmer the Great* mini-review, *Motion Picture Herald* (September 30, 1933): 50.

19. *You Said a Mouthful* review, *Variety*.

20. Mitchell Woodbury, "Strolling Around: Cup O' Chatter," *Toledo Times* (August 12, 1934): 5-D.

21. Keith Monroe, "The Battling Buffoon Named Brown (Part Two)," *The Saturday Evening Post* (December 15, 1951): 128.

22. "Joe E. Brown to Report Baseball on Radio at Chicago," *The Hollywood Reporter* (January 29, 1937): 2; "Joe E. Brown on Hop to Fulfill Radio Spots," *The Hollywood Reporter* (April 14, 1937): 4; "Joe E. Brown Returns from Milking Ball Games," *The Hollywood Reporter* (May 22, 1937): 5.

23. "Notre Dame Grid Banquet Done Up Good and Brown," *Indianapolis News* (December 13, 1938): Section 2: 2.

24. William Boehnel, "At the Strand [*The Tenderfoot*]," *New York World-Telegram* (May 21, 1932): 19.

25. *The Tenderfoot* review, *Variety* (May 24, 1932).

26. Rose Pelswick, "Delightful Picture," *New York Evening Journal* (May 21, 1932): 10.

27. Mordaunt Hall, "Joe E. Brown in a Boisterous Film Conception of the Stage Comedy, *The Butter and Egg Man*," *The New York Times* (May 25, 1932): 23.

28. Stephen Rathbun, "Joe Brown Plays a Texan in *The Tenderfoot*," *New York Sun* (May 23, 1932): 29.

29. *The Tenderfoot* review, *Variety*; *Tenderfoot* opening announcement, *New York Times* (May 22, 1932): Section 8: 4.

30. See the author's *Parody as Film Genre: Never Give a Saga an Even Break* (Westport, Connecticut: Greenwood, 1999).

31. Marguerite Tazelaar, "*You Said a Mouthful*—Winter Garden," *New York Herald Tribune* (November 18, 1932): 16.

32. William Boehnel, *You Said a Mouthful*

review, *New York World Telegram* (November 18, 1932): 28.

33. Quoted in a *You Said a Mouthful* ad, "That's Saying a Mouthful! About Joe E. Brown in *You Said a Mouthful*."

34. Ibid.

35. "An Aquatic Hero," *The New York Times* (November 18, 1932): 23; "*You Said a Mouthful* Funny," *New York Daily News* (November 18, 1932): 54.

36. William Boehnel, "Joe Brown Sets New Mark in Slapstick," *New York World Telegram* (December 1, 1933): 34.

37. Mordaunt Hall, *Son of a Sailor* review, *The New York Times* (November 30, 1933): 38; "Latest 'Joe E.' Typical," *The Hollywood Reporter* (November 1, 1933): 3.

38. S. H. Rich, *Son of a Sailor* mini-review, *Motion Picture Herald* (February 24, 1934): 51.

39. Bert Silver, *Son of a Sailor* mini-review.

40. Peter Bylsma, *Son of a Sailor* mini-review, *Motion Picture Herald* (March 31, 1934): 61.

41. Sammie Jackson, *Son of a Sailor* mini-review, *Motion Picture Herald* (June 23, 1934): 131.

42. Henry Jenkins, *What Made Pistachio Nuts? Early Sound Comedy and the Vaudeville Aesthetic* (New York: Columbia University Press, 1992): 148.

43. See the author's: *W. C. Fields: A Bibliography* (Westport, Connecticut: Greenwood, 1984) and *Groucho & W. C. Fields: Huckster Comedians* (Jackson: University Press of Mississippi, 1994).

44. *The Circus Clown* review, *Variety* (July 3, 1934).

45. Jenkins, *What Made Pistachio Nuts? Early Sound Comedy and the Vaudeville Aesthetic*: 149.

46. Donald Phelps, "*Golden Boy*: The Life, Times, and Comedic Genius of Joe E. Brown," *Film Comment* (November-December 1994): 31.

47. "*Circus Clown* Grand Fun," *The Hollywood Reporter* (May 5, 1934): 3.

48. William Boehnel, "Joe Brown Amusing in *The Circus Clown*," *New York World Telegram* (July 3, 1934): 4.

49. "*The Circus Clown*: Romance, Comedy, Drama," *Motion Picture Herald* (May 13, 1934).

50. *The Circus Clown* review, *Variety*.

51. Robert Edgren, "Miracles of Sport," *Toledo Times* (August 13, 1934): 6.

52. "9 Hurt in Film Crash," *Los Angeles Examiner* (August 8, 1934): 1.

53. Mitchell Woodbury, "Strolling Around Hollywood," *Toledo Times* (September 15, 1934): 6.

54. "Lion Claws Film Comic Joe Brown," unnamed Los Angeles newspaper (February 25, 1934), in the Joe E. Brown files, Margaret Herrick Library, Academy of Motion Picture Arts and Sciences, Beverly Hills, California.

55. André Bazin, "The Virtues and Limitations of Montage," in *What Is Cinema?*, vol. 1, ed./trans. Hugh Gray (1958; rpt. Los Angeles: University of California Press, 1967): 52; see also the author's *Charlie Chaplin: A Bio-Bibliography* (Westport, Connecticut: Greenwood, 1983): 143–44.

56. "Scared Lion Scares Brown," unnamed newspaper (February 16, 1934), in the Joe E. Brown files, Margaret Herrick Library, Academy of Motion Picture Arts and Sciences, Beverly Hills, California.

57. "*Six-Day Bike Race* Amusing Farce," *The Hollywood Reporter* (September 28, 1934): 2.

58. Rose Pelswick, "Joe E. Brown Has Amusing Gags," *New York Evening Journal* (November 3, 1934): 15.

59. Regina Crewe, "*6-Day Bike Rider* Hilarious Comedy," *New York American* (November 3, 1934): 9; "Invoking the Gag Rule," *The New York Times* (November 3, 1934): 20.

60. "Joe Brown Comedy at Rivoli," *Toledo Times* (November 3, 1934): 6.

61. For example, see "Free $50,000 Worth of Bicycles" (ad), *Toledo Times* (September 23, 1934): n.p.

62. Mitchell Woodbury, "Strolling Around Hollywood," *Toledo Times* (September 16, 1934): 5-D.

Chapter Eight

1. Cobbett Steinberg, *Reel Facts: The Movie Book of Records* (New York: Vintage Books, 1978): 403–04.

2. Rose Pelswick, "*Midsummer Night's Dream* Shakespearean Fantasy Molded by Reinhardt Makes Film History," *New York Evening Journal* (October 10, 1935): 25.

3. Roy W. Adams, *Alibi Ike* mini-review, *Motion Picture Herald* (December 21, 1935): 67.

4. "Leo McCarey Is Guarded After Kidnapping Attempt," *Los Angeles Evening Herald* (May 29, 1934); see also the author's *Leo McCarey: From Marx to McCarthy* (Lanham, Maryland: Scarecrow, 2005): 114–15.

5. "Cinema Stars' Homes Under Heavy Guard," *Los Angeles Examiner* (May 12, 1934).

6. "Joe Brown to Hawaii," *The Hollywood Reporter* (May 26, 1934): 3.

7. Mitchell Woodbury, "Strolling Around [Note Book]," *Toledo Times* (August 5, 1934): 5-D.

8. Carlisle Jones, "Most of Filmdom's Biggest Stars Have Lived Horatio Alger Stories" (syndicated), *Toledo Times* (October 21, 1934): 5-D.

9. See especially "The Palladium: Mr. Joe E. Brown in Person," *London Times* (August 19, 1936): 8; "Dave Loew Sets Joe E. Brown Pix on RKO Program," *The Hollywood Reporter* (April 30, 1936): 2.

10. Keith Monroe, "The Battling Buffoon Named

Brown [Part 2]," *The Saturday Evening Post* (December 15, 1951): 30, 126.

11. Ibid., 126.

12. Michael Shapiro, "It's 1942: The Bronx Bombers Play and U. S. Bombers Attack," *The New York Times* (March 30, 2003): Section 4: 1.

13. Louella Parsons, "Joe E. to Do Song, Dance" (syndicated), *Toledo Times* (August 11, 1934): 6.

14. Eileen Creelman, *Bright Lights* review, *New York Sun* (August 15, 1935): 9.

15. *Bright Lights* review, *The New York Times* (August 15, 1935): 15.

16. Wanda Hale, "New Brown Musical Is Field Day for Star," *New York Daily News* (August 16, 1935): 43.

17. Frederick L. Collins, "Old Brown Joe," *Liberty* (September 28, 1940): 25.

18. *Bright Lights* review, *Time* (August 26, 1935); "Strand Shows Joe E. Brown in Gay Film," *New York Evening Journal* (August 15, 1935): 14.

19. See the author's *Charlie Chaplin: A Bio-Bibliography* (Westport, Connecticut: Greenwood, 1983).

20. Joe E. Brown Press Release, Warner Studio biography (ca. 1932), in the Joe E. Brown file, Margaret Herrick Library, Academy of Motion Picture Arts and Sciences, Beverly Hills, California.

21. Hale, "New Brown Musical Is Field Day for Star."

22. *Bright Lights* review, *Variety* (August 21, 1935).

23. "One of Best Joe E. Brown Films," *The Hollywood Reporter* (July 24, 1935): 3.

24. *Bright Lights* review, *The New York Times* (August 15, 1935): 15.

25. Ibid.; "*Bright Lights* at Strand," *New York World Telegram* (August 15, 1935): 14.

26. G. A. Troyer, *Bright Lights* mini-review, *Motion Picture Herald* (October 12, 1935): 55.

27. E. J. McLurg, *Bright Lights* mini-review, *Motion Picture Herald* (October 5, 1935): 59.

28. Joe E. Hewitt, *Bright Lights* mini-review, *Motion Picture Herald* (October 26, 1935): 89.

29. Troyer, *Bright Lights* mini-review; Robert Wile, *Bright Lights* mini-review, *Motion Picture Herald* (November 16, 1935): 68.

30. "Reinhardt's Production of *Dream* Superbly Beautiful," *The Hollywood Reporter* (September 18, 1934): 2.

31. Ibid.

32. *Dream* was one of the top-grossing pictures of 1935. See Cobbett Steinberg, *Reel Facts: The Movie Book of Records* (New York: Vintage Books, 1978): 339–40.

33. Stanley Cavell, *Pursuits of Happiness: The Hollywood Comedy of Remarriage* (Cambridge, Massachusetts: Harvard University Press, 1981): 49.

34. Ibid., 49–51; See also Northrop Frye, *Anatomy of Criticism: Four Essays* (1957; rpt. Princeton, New Jersey: Princeton University Press, 1973): 183; Northrop Frye, *A Natural Perspective* (New York: Columbia University Press, 1965): 128.

35. Cavell, *Pursuits of Happiness: The Hollywood Comedy of Remarriage*: 49.

36. See the author's *Screwball Comedy: A Genre of Madcap Romance* (Westport, Connecticut: Greenwood, 1986): 48–49, and his *Romantic vs. Screwball Comedy: Charting the Difference* (Lanham, Maryland: Scarecrow, 2002).

37. Harold C. Goddard, *The Meaning of Shakespeare, Volume 1* (1951; rpt. Chicago: University of Chicago Press, 1970): 79.

38. Joe E. Brown (as told to Ralph Hancock), *Laughter Is a Wonderful Thing* (New York: A. S. Barnes, 1956): 207.

39. Ibid.: 209.

40. Henry W. Simon, Ph.D, "Supplement to *Photoplay* Studies: For 'Midsummer Night's Dream'" *Photoplay* [and Warner Brothers] (September 1935): 9.

41. *A Midsummer Night's Dream* review, *Screenland* (October 1935).

42. Andre Sennwald, *A Midsummer Night's Dream* review, *New York Times* (October 10, 1935): 31.

43. Thornton Delehanty, "*A Midsummer Night's Dream* Has Premiere on Broadway," *The New York Post* (October 10, 1935): 21.

44. Richard Watts, Jr., *A Midsummer Night's Dream* review, *New York Herald Tribune* (October 10, 1935): 17.

45. "*Midsummer Night's Dream* Triumph for All Concerned," *The Hollywood Reporter* (October 9, 1935): 3.

46. Otis Ferguson, "Shakespeare in Hollywood," *The New Republic* (October 16, 1935).

47. Steinberg, *Reel Facts: The Movie Book of Records*: 368.

48. Ferguson, "Shakespeare in Hollywood."

49. *A Midsummer Night's Dream* review, *Variety* (October 16, 1935).

50. Louella Parsons, "'Puck' Found By Producer" (syndicated), *Toledo Times* (September 13, 1934): 6.

51. "Chaplin to Play in Shakespeare at Bowl," *The Hollywood Reporter* (June 27, 1934): 4.

52. Parsons, "Joe E. to Do Song, Dance."

53. Patrick McGilligan, *Cagney: The Actor as Auteur* (1975; rpt. New York: Da Capo Press, 1979): 61.

54. Brown, *Laughter Is a Wonderful Thing*: 210.

55. "Joe E. Brown, Comedian of Movies and Stage, Dies," *The New York Times* (July 7, 1973): 24.

Chapter Nine

1. Cobbett Steinberg, *Reel Facts: The Movie Book of Records* (New York: Vintage Books, 1978): 404.

2. "Kay Francis Heads Warners' Payroll," *The New York Times* (March 3, 1937): 37.

3. "Harold Lloyd, With Gems Worth $30,000, Heads Hollywood List," *Indianapolis News* (July 15, 1936): 10.

4. "Dave Loew Sets Joe E. Brown Pix on RKO Program," *The Hollywood Reporter* (April 30, 1936): 2.

5. Joe E. Brown (as told to Ralph Hancock), *Laughter Is a Wonderful Thing* (New York: A. S. Barnes, 1956): 259.

6. Richard Schickel, "The Slayer of False Values: Arthur Miller, 1915–2005," *Time* (February 21, 2005): 72.

7. James Robert Parish and William T. Leonard, *The Funsters* (New Rochelle, New York: Arlington House, 1979): 134.

8. John T. McManus, *Sons o' Guns* review, *The New York Times* (May 14, 1936): 29.

9. *Sons o' Guns* review, *Variety* (May 20, 1936).

10. William Gilmore, *Earthworm Tractors* review, *Brooklyn Daily Eagle* (July 25, 1936).

11. Eileen Creelman, "Joe E. Brown as That Super-Salesman, Alexander Botts, in *Earthworm Tractors*," *New York Sun* (July 27, 1936).

12. *Earthworm Tractors* review, *New York Evening Journal* (July 25, 1936).

13. *Earthworm Tractors* review, *New York American* (July 25, 1936).

14. *Earthworm Tractors* review, *The New York Post* (July 25, 1936).

15. "WB *Earthworm Tractors* Swell Comedy Thriller," *The Hollywood Reporter* (June 11, 1936): 3.

16. *Earthworm Tractors* review, *Variety* (July 29, 1936).

17. Brown, *Laughter Is a Wonderful Thing*: 246.

18. Rosalind Shaffer, "Film Beauty Has Own Reward," *Chicago Tribune* (July 12, 1936): "Drama Section": 1.

19. "Brown to See Peoria Premiere," (July 1936), uncredited article in the Joe E. Brown file, Margaret Herrick Library, Academy of Motion Picture Arts and Sciences (Beverly Hills, CA).

20. Leslie B. Ernst, "Joe E. Brown Is Truly Good Natured 'Boy,' He Shows at Peoria Reception," *Peoria Journal* (July 14, 1936): 1.

21. Leslie B. Ernst, "Crowds Cheer Joe E. Brown," *Peoria Journal* (July 15, 1936): 1; Ernst, "Joe E. Brown Is Truly Good Natured 'Boy,' He Shows at Peoria Reception."

22. Ernst, "Crowds Cheer Joe E. Brown."

23. Bosley Crowther, *Earthworm Tractors* review, *The New York Times* (July 25, 1936): 16.

24. Pauline Kael, *I Lost It at the Movies* (Boston: Little, Brown and Company, 1965): 206.

25. Brown, *Laughter Is a Wonderful Thing*: 211.

26. Marguerite Tazelaar, "*Polo Joe*— Criterion," *New York Herald Tribune* (November 4, 1936): 28.

27. "Hollywood Night Life Bit Bizarre," *Toledo Times* (November 18, 1934): 4-D.

28. William Boehnel, "Joe E. Brown Goes Horsey in *Polo Joe*," *New York World Telegram* (November 5, 1936): 21.

29. Wanda Hale, *Polo Joe* review, *New York Daily News* (November 5, 1936): 59.

30. "*Polo Joe* Joe E. Brown Par," *The Hollywood Reporter* (September 19, 1936): 3.

31. *Polo Joe* review, *Variety* (November 11, 1936).

32. Frank S. Nugent, *Polo Joe* review, *The New York Times* (November 5, 1936): 35.

33. Ibid.

34. Frederick L. Collins, "Old Brown Joe," *Liberty* (September 28, 1940): 25.

35. Joe E. Brown, "The Role I Liked Best...," *The Saturday Evening Post* (November 9, 1946).

36. Joyce Carol Oates, "Do You Love Me?," *The New York Times Book Review* (May 16, 2004).

Chapter Ten

1. "Foreign Legion Story for Joe E. Brown," *The Hollywood Reporter* (July 5, 1935): 2.

2. "David Loew Sets Joe E. Brown Pix on RKO Program," *The Hollywood Reporter* (April 30, 1936): 2; "Brown Ends *Fate* Role, Prepares for Operation," *The Hollywood Reporter* (September 7, 1938): 3.

3. Joe E. Brown (as told to Ralph Hancock), *Laughter Is a Wonderful Thing* (New York: A. S. Barnes, 1956): 259–61; Keith Monroe, "That Battling Buffoon Named Brown [Part 2]," *The Saturday Evening Post* (December 15, 1951): 130.

4. Joe E. Brown Press Release (1937), in the Joe E. Brown file, Margaret Herrick Library, Academy of Motion Picture Arts and Sciences, Beverly Hills, California.

5. Gary Giddins, *Bing Crosby: A Pocketful of Dreams: The Early Years, 1903–1940* (New York: Little, Brown, 2001): 405.

6. Mitchell Woodbury, "Strolling Around Hollywood," *Toledo Times* (September 30, 1934): 5-D.

7. Ibid.

8. Largely drawn from a 1930s "Inventory of Joe E. Brown's Trophy Cases," in the Joe E. Brown file, Margaret Herrick Library, Academy of Motion Picture Arts and Sciences, Beverly Hills, California.

9. Jack Holland, "Chumming With Champs

[rough draft]," (circa mid–1930s), in the Joe E. Brown file, Margaret Herrick Library, Academy of Motion Picture Arts and Sciences, Beverly Hills, California.

10. See the author's *Personality Comedians as Genre: Selected Players* (Westport, Connecticut: Greenwood, 1997).

11. Bosley Crowther, *The Gladiator* review, *The New York Times* (August 29, 1938): 10.

12. For example, see "Joe E. Brown: The Big Mouth," *Films of the Golden Age* (Winter 2004–05): 32.

13. *The Gladiator* review, *Variety* (August 31, 1938).

14. Irene Thirer, "Joe E. Brown as *Gladiator* Lures Laughs to the Globe," *The New York Post* (August 28, 1938).

15. Arthur Pollock, "Joe E. Brown, With a Brightly Written Movie Called *The Gladiator* Under Him, Gallops Hilariously Across Globe's Screen," *Brooklyn Eagle* (August 30, 1938).

16. *The Gladiator* review, *Motion Picture Herald* (August 13, 1938).

17. Wanda Hale, "Joe E. Brown Puts on Strong Farce," *New York Daily News* (August 28, 1938).

18. "The Critics Agree It's Joe E. Brown's Best Picture [ad]!," *The Hollywood Reporter* (September 9, 1938).

19. "*Gladiator* Best Joe Brown," *The Hollywood Reporter* (August 4, 1938): 3.

20. C. R. Greg, *The Gladiator* mini-review, *Motion Picture Herald* (October 29, 1938): 49.

21. C. W. Mills, *The Gladiator* mini-review, *Motion Picture Herald* (October 22, 1938): 53.

22. For example, see Richard Macaulay's Elmer Lane baseball short story: "Git Out O' T' Game!," *The Saturday Evening Post* (June 15, 1935): 18–19, 76.

23. See the author's *Seeing Red: The Skelton in Hollywood's Closet* (Davenport, Iowa: Robin Vincent, 2001): 205.

24. Bosley Crowther, *Fit for a King* review, *The New York Times* (October 15, 1937): 18.

25. Frank Capra, *Frank Capra: The Name Above the Title* (New York: Macmillan, 1971): 62–63.

26. Richard Macaulay, "Who's Who — and Why," *The Saturday Evening Post* (August 10, 1935): 78.

27. "*Wide Open Faces* Ok Brown," *The Hollywood Reporter* (April 23, 1938): 3.

28. *Riding on Air* review, *Variety* (June 30, 1937).

29. Joe E. Brown, "Post Toasties a Natural for Kiddies Air Show," *Rim Monthly* (December 1938): 18.

30. Ibid.

31. Harrison B. Summers (ed.), *A Thirty-Year History of Programs Carried on National Radio Networks in the United States, 1926–1956* (New York: Arno Press, 1971): 75.

32. "Joe E. Brown Pleads for Refugee Tots," *Los Angeles Daily News* (May 25, 1939).

33. Ibid.

34. "Actor Pleads For Refugees," *Los Angeles Times* (May 25, 1939).

35. "'Patriotic' Rally Has Anti-Semitic Tinge," *The New York Times* (May 25, 1939): 3.

36. Ibid.

37. "The Nizkor Project: Shofar FTP Archive File: places//usa/conspiracy. 101.

38. See the author's *Charlie Chaplin: A Bio-Bibliography* (Westport, Connecticut: Greenwood, 1983).

39. "Sees German Refugees As Boon to U. S.," *Des Moines Register* (May 25, 1939): 1.

40. "Many Make Pleas for Refugee Youth," *The New York Times* (May 25, 1939): 12.

41. Philip Roth, *The Plot Against America* (New York: Houghton Mifflin, 2004).

42. Frederick L. Collins, "Old Brown Joe," *Liberty* (September 28, 1940): 26.

43. Tom Brokaw, *The Greatest Generation* (1998; rpt. New York: Delta, 2001).

44. Hy Gardner, "We Need Better Grownups...," *Parade* (July 6, 1952): 13.

45. "Collision Is No Joke, But Has Joe E. Brown of Film in Stitches," *Chicago Tribune* (December 7, 1939): 8.

46. "Joe E. Brown Hurt in Auto Crash," *The New York Times* (December 7, 1939): 35.

47. Brown, *Laughter Is a Wonderful Thing*: 262.

48. Wanda Hale, "*$1,000 a Touchdown* Not Worth the Price," *New York Daily News* (October 5, 1939): 52.

49. Frank S. Nugent, *$1,000 a Touchdown* review, *The New York Times* (October 5, 1939): 27.

50. Brown, *Laughter Is a Wonderful Thing*: 265.

51. Joe E. Brown Press Release Questionnaire (ca. mid–1930s), in the Joe E. Brown file, Margaret Herrick Library, Academy of Motion Picture Arts and Sciences, Beverly Hills, California.

52. "Joe E. Brown Makes Speech," *The New York Times* (November 2, 1940): 32.

Chapter Eleven

1. Joe E. Brown (with Margaret Lee Runbeck), *Your Kids and Mine* (Garden City, New York: Doubleday, Doran, 1944): 32.

2. Joe E. Brown (as told to Ralph Hancock), *Laughter Is a Wonderful Thing* (New York: A. S. Barnes, 1956): 199.

3. "Joe E. Browns Wed Again on the 25th Anniversary," *The New York Times* (December 25, 1940): 32.

4. "Joe Brown's Son to Wed Tuesday," *Los Angeles Examiner* (September 20, 1940).

5. Joe E. Brown, "My Favorite Movie Scene," *The Saturday Evening Post* (March 31, 1945).

6. See "Joe Brown Makes Speech," *The New York Times* (November 1, 1940): 32; *Rio Rita* program (May 19, 1941), in the Joe E. Brown file, Margaret Herrick Library, Academy of Motion Picture Arts and Science, Beverly Hills, California.

7. For instance, see: *So You Won't Talk* review, *New York American* (October 17, 1940): 14.

8. *So You Won't Talk* review, *Variety* (October 23, 1940).

9. See the author's *Charlie Chaplin: A Bio-Bibliography* (Westport, Connecticut: Greenwood, 1983).

10. Alva Johnston, "Joe E. Brown Profile," *The New Yorker* (July 7, 1945): 26–30, 32, 34; Brown, *Laughter Is a Wonderful Thing*.

11. Joe Laurie, Jr., "A Thumbnose Sketch — Joe E. Brown," *Variety* (February 5, 1947).

12. "Actor Back from Alaska," *Hollywood Citizen-News* (June 4, 1942).

13. Will Rogers, *Letters of a Self-Made Diplomat to His President* (New York: Albert & Charles Boni, 1926).

14. Brown, *Your Kids and Mine*: 17.

15. "He Had to Open His Big Mouth," *Photoplay* (July 1942): 9.

16. Bob Hope, *I Never Left Home* (New York: Simon and Schuster, 1944): 198.

17. For instance, see "Joe E. Brown Will Tell of Dutch Harbor Trek," *The Hollywood Reporter* (June 10, 1942): 6.

18. "Joe E. Brown Scores Actor Wage Limits," Los Angeles newspaper (November 1, 1933), in the Joe E. Brown file, Margaret Herrick Library, Academy of Motion Picture Arts and Sciences, Beverly Hills, California; "Joe E. Brown Pleads for Refugee Tots," *Los Angeles Daily News* (May 25, 1939).

19. Lorrie Lynch, "Who's News" (syndicated), *USA Weekend* magazine (July 1–3, 2005): 2.

20. Brown, *Laughter Is a Wonderful Thing*: 269.

21. "Brown At Republic," *Hollywood Reporter* (April 16, 1942): 2.

22. Leonard Maltin, *The Great Movie Comedians: From Charlie Chaplin to Woody Allen* (New York: Crown, 1978): 129.

23. "*Joan of Ozark* Hit Teams Canova-Brown in Top Form," *The Hollywood Reporter* (July 15, 1942): 3.

24. *Joan of Ozark* review, *Variety* (July 15, 1942).

25. "Joe E. Brown Camp Tour," *The Hollywood Reporter* (June 30, 1942): 6.

26. Brown, *Your Kids and Mine*: 31.

27. Ibid.: 30.

28. Andrew Logue, "The 2002 Heisman Candidates: Brad Banks," *Des Moines Register* (December 14, 2002): 2-C.

29. "Brown In South Pacific," *New York Time* (February 25, 1943): 26.

30. "Joe E. Brown at Pacific Base," *The New York Times* (February 19, 1943): 5.

31. Carl Erskine, "Foreword," in the author's *Mr. Deeds Goes to Yankee Stadium: Baseball Films in the Capra Tradition* (Jefferson, North Carolina: McFarland, 2004): 10.

32. Brown, *Your Kids and Mine*: 100.

33. "Japanese Captives Wanted Baseball Talk, Says Joe E. Brown on Return from Pacific," *The New York Times* (April 25, 1943): Section 1: 13.

34. "Members of 37th May Be Home to Celebrate Joe E. Brown Day," *Toledo Times* (November 18, 1945).

35. "Japanese Captives Wanted Baseball Talk Says Joe E. Brown on Return from Pacific."

36. Cal York, "Inside Stuff," *Photoplay* (May 1944): 12.

37. Brown, *Your Kids and Mine*: 55.

38. Ibid.: 51.

39. "Brown in South Pacific."

40. "Joe E. Brown Finds Morale High," *The New York Times* (March 15, 1943): 5.

41. "Forces Want Fair Play to Nisei," *The New York Times* (June 24, 1945): Section 1:2.

42. Joe E. Brown 20th Century–Fox biography, August 31, 1943, in the Joe E. Brown files, Margaret Herrick Library, Academy of Motion Picture Arts and Sciences, Beverly Hills, California.

43. Ibid.

44. *Chatterbox* review, *Variety* (April 14, 1943).

45. "New Delhi," *The New York Times* (November 26, 1943): 7.

46. "Actors on China Tour," *The New York Times* (December 6, 1943): 3.

47. The mileage and number of shows varied from one period article to another. For widely conflicting figures see: "Joe E. Brown Gave 300 Shows at Front" *The Hollywood Reporter* (February 15, 1944); "Comedian Completes War Tour," *Hollywood Citizen-News* (February 24, 1944); "Joe E. Brown Comes Home," *Los Angeles Examiner* (February 25, 1944).

48. "Joe E. Brown Returns from Battle Line Tour," *Los Angeles Times* (February 25, 1944).

49. "Joe E. Brown Comes Home."

50. Joe E. Brown: Favorite Pin-Up Boy of the Army," *Look* (May 30, 1944): 55.

51. "Joe E. Brown Paid Tribute," *Los Angeles Examiner* (May 4, 1944).

52. "Joe E. Brown Honored for Entertaining G. I.'s," *Los Angeles Times* (May 4, 1944).

53. "Honor Joe E. Brown for Entertaining in War Theatres," *Daily Variety* (May 4, 1944).

54. "Bronze Star Presented to Joe E. Brown," *Los Angeles Times* (October 25, 1945).

55. "Wife Leaves for East to Greet Joe E. Brown," *Hollywood Citizen-News* (February 11, 1944).

56. For example, see: Sara Hamilton, "*Canteen Real Holiday Gift*," *Los Angeles Examiner* (December 21, 1944).

57. "Joe E. Brown Milestone Hailed," *Hollywood Citizen-News* (November 27, 1944).

58. "Forces Want Fair Play to Nisei."

59. Grant Reynard, "Joe E. on Headhunters, Taxes, and Hate," *PM* (November 5, 1944): 4.

60. Ibid.

61. Tom Brokaw, *The Greatest Generation* (1998; rpt. New York: Delta, 2001): xviii.

Chapter Twelve

1. "Joe E. Brown Paid Tribute," *Los Angeles Examiner* (May 4, 1944); Cal York, "Inside Stuff," *Photoplay* (May 1944): 10.

2. Arthur Gould, "Dreams Come True for Joe E. Brown," *Toledo Times* (December 8, 1945): 14.

3. "Comedian Expresses Love for All People; Many Leaders Attend," *Toledo Blade* (December 8, 1945): 12.

4. Joe E. Brown (as told to Ralph Hancock), *Laughter Is a Wonderful Thing* (New York: A. S. Barnes, 1956): 294.

5. "Friday Proclaimed Joe E. Brown Day; Mass Meeting Is Arranged," *Toledo Times* (December 2, 1945): 4.

6. Ibid.

7. "Joe E. Brown: Favorite Pin-Up Boy of the Army." *Look* (May 30, 1944): 55; "Bronze Star Presented to Joe E. Brown," *Los Angeles Times* (October 25, 1945).

8. "Joe E. Brown Is Top Toledoan for Today," *Toledo Times* (December 7, 1945): 11.

9. "War Tribute Given Brown," *Los Angeles Examiner* (May 4, 1946).

10. "Joe E. Brown Target of the Circus Saints," *The New York Times* (November 27, 1948): 11.

11. Ibid.

12. Mrs. Hobart Wagstaff, "10,000 Greet Joe E. Brown at Holgate," *Toledo Blade* (May 31, 1949): 13.

13. "Joe E. Brown Receives Bowling Green U. Honor," *The New York Times* (June 4, 1949): 8.

14. "Joe E. Brown's Killing of Japs on Luzon Told," *Los Angeles Times* (December 23, 1945).

15. "Joe E. Brown Describes Role as Fighter in Slaying 2 Japs," *Toledo Times* (December 23, 1945): 14.

16. Ibid.

17. "Screen Comedian Who Turned Serious," *The New York Times* (December 23, 1945): Section 1: 15.

18. "Joe E. Brown Asks Gold Star Group to Forgive," *Hollywood Citizen-News* (April 15, 1946).

19. Grant Reynard, "Joe E. on Headhunters, Taxes and Hate," *PM* (November 5, 1944): 4.

20. Robert C. Brownell, "Joe E. Brown Urges Solons to Assure Jobs for Vets," *Los Angeles Daily News* (March 22, 1945): 3.

21. "Joe E. Brown Tells What's Ailing G.I. Abroad," *Los Angeles Herald Express* (January 12, 1946).

22. Brown, *Laughter Is a Wonderful Thing*: 296.

23. Lowell Redelings, "Joe E. Brown Scores Smash Hit in *Harvey*," *Hollywood Citizen-News* (March 22, 1946).

24. Edwin Schallert, "*Harvey* Conjures Rare Spell of Laughter," *Los Angeles Times* (March 19, 1946): Section 2: 3.

25. Patterson Greene, "'Joe E.' Great in 'Harvey,'" *Los Angeles Examiner* (March 19, 1946).

26. "Harvey Makes 'Sage' Out of Joe E. Brown," *Indianapolis News* (February 16, 1948): Section 2: 1.

27. "Joe E. Brown, *Harvey* Back," *Indianapolis News* (February 16, 1948): Section 1: 14.

28. "*Harvey* Opens Return Engagement at English's," *Indianapolis News* (February 17, 1948): Section 2: 8.

29. "*Harvey* Makes 'Sage' Out of Joe E. Brown."

30. "Joe E. Brown And *Harvey* Return to English Tonight," *Indianapolis Star* (February 16, 1948): 18.

31. Corbin Patrick, "Keep Your Eyes on Brown and Bottle in *Harvey* This Week," *Indianapolis Star* (February 15, 1948): 37.

32. Harry Crocker, "Behind the Makeup," incomplete citation [circa early 1950s], in the Joe E. Brown files, Margaret Herrick Library, Academy of Motion Picture Arts and Sciences, Beverly Hills, California.

33. "Joe E. Brown, *Harvey* Back."

34. "Hollywood Should Study Trouping, Says Joe Brown," *Los Angeles Times* (April 25, 1948).

35. Brown, *Laughter Is a Wonderful Thing*: 299.

36. Laura Moser, *Bette Davis* (London: Haus, 2004): 88.

37. *The Tender Years* review, *Variety* (December 3, 1947).

38. Edwin Schallert, "*Tender Years* Genuinely Appealing," *Los Angeles Times* (January 31, 1948).

39. *The Tender Years* review, *Film Daily* (December 5, 1947).

40. Ann Helming, "Story of Protest Minister Well Done," *Hollywood Citizen News* (January 31, 1948).

41. *The Tender Years* review, *The Hollywood Reporter* (December 3, 1947).

42. "*The Tender Years* Is Fine Family Film," *Indianapolis News* (February 18, 1948): Section 2: 9.

43. "Joe E. Brown Ill, Opening Called Off," *Los Angeles Times* (March 1, 1949); "Joe E. Brown Again Stricken By Malaria," *Los Angeles Daily News* (March 8, 1949).

44. "Joe E. Brown's Malaria 'Licked' by New Drug Use," *Los Angeles Examiner* (March 9, 1949).

45. Harrison Carroll, "Joe E. Browns Are Re-Wed in Church," *Los Angeles Herald Express* (July 8, 1947).

46. "Joe E. Browns Donate Lodge in Memory of Son," *Los Angeles Daily News* (October 6, 1947).

47. Bosley Crowther, *Show Boat* review, *The New York Times* (July 20, 1951): 14; Edwin Schallert, "Musicals Look to Rich Future," *Los Angeles Times* (April 15, 1951): 3.

48. *Show Boat* review, *Saturday Review of Literature* (June 9, 1951): 26.

49. Edwin Schallert, "Gala *Show Boat* Premiere Restores Old-Time Glamour," *Los Angeles Times* (June 18, 1951).

50. Keith Monroe, "That Battling Buffoon Named Brown," *The Saturday Evening Post* (December 8, 1951): 23.

51. Ibid.: 107.

52. Val Adams, "Adjusting to the Television Art," *The New York Times* (November 9, 1952): Section 2: 13.

53. Ibid.

54. Tim Brooks and Earle Marsh, *The Complete Directory to Prime Time Network TV Shows, 1946–Present* (New York: Ballantine Books, 1979): 802.

55. Ibid.: 39.

56. *Buick Circus Hour* review, *Variety* (October 15, 1952).

57. "Joe E. Brown TV's Baseball," *Los Angeles Examiner* (May 3, 1953).

58. "Sporting Life," *Time* (April 27, 1953).

59. "Baseball Post to Joe E. Brown," *The New York Times* (April 1, 1953): 38.

60. "Rickey Successor Pledges Pennant," *The New York Times* (October 26, 1955): 36.

61. Wanda Henderson, "Joe E. Brown's Daughters Choose Double Wedding," *Hollywood Citizen-News* (February 16, 1953).

62. Joseph Finnigan, "Joe E. Brown Just Misses," *Los Angeles Mirror* (July 19, 1961): Section 1: 12.

63. Louella Parsons, "Joe E. Brown Stops Work to Be Grandpa" (syndicated column), *Los Angeles Examiner* (January 10, 1954).

64. "Joe E. Brown's Daughters Nearly Tie in Stork Race," *Los Angeles Times* (January 14, 1954).

65. Abe Greenberg, "Joe E. Brown to Turn Night Club Performer," *Los Angeles Examiner* (November 1, 1959).

66. Cobbett Steinberg, *Reel Facts: The Movie Book of Records* (New York: Vintage Books, 1978): 348.

67. "Toledo Figures Prominently in Joe E. Brown Biography," *Toledo Times* (October 30, 1956): 20; A. H. Weiler, "A Fortune in His Face," *The New York Times* (March 24, 1957): Section 7: 18.

68. Abel Green, "A Book by Ex-Kinker Kid Joe E. Brown, Who Made It With a Grand Canyon Grin," *Variety* (November 21, 1956).

69. "Books-Authors," *The New York Times* (November 17, 1956): 19.

70. Charles Davis, Jr., "Joe E. Brown Celebrates His 72nd Birthday as Past Meets Present," *Los Angeles Times* (July 28, 1963): 1.

Afterword

1. For example, see Sara Hamilton's "Whooie! Here Comes Joe E.," *Photoplay* (November 1932).

2. "Joe E. Brown, Held Up, Yields $5," *The New York Times* (July 3, 1938): Section 2: 5.

3. Hedda Hopper, "The Ten Best Husbands," *Photoplay* (May 1943): 26.

4. Ibid.: 79.

5. Cameron Crowe, *Conversations with Wilder* (New York: Knopf, 2001): 42.

6. Ed Sikov, *On Sunset Boulevard: The Life and Times of Billy Wilder* (New York: Hyperion, 1998): 422.

7. *Some Like It Hot* review, *Motion Picture Herald* (February 28, 1959); Jack Moffitt, "Billy Wilder Pic Distills Laughs from Dry Era," *The Hollywood Reporter* (February 25, 1959).

8. *Some Like It Hot* review, *Boxoffice* (March 16, 1959).

9. Sikov, *On Sunset Boulevard: The Life and Times of Billy Wilder*: 422.

10. Bernard F. Dick, *Billy Wilder* (New York: Da Capo Press, 1996): 91.

11. Cliff Rothman, "A 40-Year-Old Comedy

That Hasn't Grown Stale," *The New York Times* (August 1, 1999): Entertainment Section: 24.

12. Francine Prose, "Not Just at the P. O.," *The New York Times* (August 14, 2005): Book Review Section: 21.

13. Jane Leavy, "Tape from 1965 Easier to Find Than Ill Will Toward Koufax," *The New York Times* (September 1, 2002): Spots Section: 6.

14. Hal Bodley, "Dream Comes True for Duo," *USA Today* (August 1, 2005): 6-C.

Bibliography

Books

Blair, Walter. *Native American Humor.* 1937; rpt. Scranton, Pennsylvania: Chandler, 1960.

Bowman, John, and Zoel Zoss. *Diamond in the Rough: The Untold History of Baseball.* New York: Macmillan, 1989.

Brooks, Tim, and Earle Marsh. *The Complete Directory to Prime Time Network TV Shows, 1946–Present.* New York: Ballantine Books, 1979.

Brokaw, Tom. *The Greatest Generation.* 1998; rpt. New York: Delta, 2001.

Brown, Joe E. (as told to Ralph Hancock). *Laughter Is a Wonderful Thing.* New York: A. S. Barnes, 1956.

_____ (with Margaret Lee Runbeck). *Your Kids and Mine.* Garden City, New York: Doubleday, Doran, 1944.

Capra, Frank. *Frank Capra: The Name Above the Title.* New York: Macmillan, 1971.

Cavell, Stanley. *Pursuits of Happiness: The Hollywood Comedy of Remarriage.* Cambridge, Massachusetts: Harvard University Press, 1981.

Chabon, Michael. *Wonder Boys.* New York: Picador, 1995.

Crowe, Cameron. *Conversations with Wilder.* New York: Knopf, 2001.

Dawidoff, Nicholas (ed.). *Baseball: A Literary Anthology.* New York: Library of America, 2002.

Dent, Jim. *Monster of the Midway.* New York: St. Martin's, 2003.

Dick, Bernard F. *Billy Wilder.* New York: Da Capo Press, 1996.

Frye, Northrop. *Anatomy of Criticism: Four Essays.* 1957; rpt. Princeton, New Jersey: Princeton University Press, 1973.

_____. *A Natural Perspective.* New York: Columbia University Press, 1965.

Gehring, Wes D. *Charlie Chaplin: A Bio-Bibliography.* Westport, Connecticut: Greenwood, 1983.

_____. *Groucho & W. C. Fields: Huckster Comedians.* Jackson: University Press of Mississippi, 1994.

_____. *Laurel & Hardy: A Bio-Bibliography.* Westport, Connecticut: Greenwood, 1990.

_____. *Leo McCarey: From Marx to McCarthy.* Lanham, Maryland: Scarecrow, 2005.

_____. *The Marx Brothers: A Bio-Bibliography.* Westport, Connecticut: Greenwood, 1987.

_____. *"Mr. B" or Comforting Thoughts About the Bison: A Critical Biography of Robert Benchley.* Westport, Connecticut: Greenwood, 1992.

_____. *Mr. Deeds Goes to Yankee Stadium: Baseball Films in the Capra Tradition.* Jefferson, North Carolina: McFarland, 2004.

_____. *Parody as Film Genre: "Never Give a Saga an Even Break."* Westport, Connecticut: Greenwood, 1999.

_____. *Personality Comedians As Genre: Selected Players.* Westport, Connecticut: Greenwood, 1997.

_____. *Populism and the Capra Legacy.* Westport, Connecticut: Greenwood, 1995.

_____. *Romantic vs. Screwball Comedy: Charting the Difference.* Lanham, Maryland: Scarecrow, 2002.

_____. *Screwball Comedy: A Genre of Madcap Romance.* Westport, Connecticut: Greenwood, 1986.

_____. *Seeing Red: The Skelton in Hollywood's Closet: An Analytical Biography.* Davenport, Iowa: Robin Vincent, 2001.

_____. *W. C. Fields: A Bio-Bibliography.* Westport, Connecticut: Greenwood, 1984.

Giddins, Gary. *Bing Crosby: A Pocketful of Dreams: The Early Years, 1903–1940*. New York: Little, Brown, 2001.

Goddard, Harold C. *The Meaning of Shakespeare, Volume 1*. 1951; rpt. Chicago: University of Chicago Press, 1970.

Hope, Bob. *I Never Left Home*. New York: Simon and Schuster, 1944.

Jenkins, Henry. *What Made Pistachio Nuts? Early Sound Comedy and the Vaudeville Aesthetic*. New York: Columbia University Press, 1992.

Kael, Pauline. *I Lost It at the Movies*. Boston: Little, Brown, 1965.

Kahn, Roger. *A Flame of Pure Fire: Jack Dempsey and the Roaring '20s*. New York: Harcourt Brace, 1999.

Kelly, Fred C. *The Life and Times of Kin Hubbard: Creator of Abe Martin*. New York: Farrar, Straus and Young, 1952.

Knipfel, Jim. *Slackjaw: A Memoir*. 1999; rpt. New York: Berkley Books, 2000.

Lahr, John. *Notes on a Cowardly Lion: The Biography of Bert Lahr*. 1969; rpt. New York: Ballantine Books, 1970.

McGilligan, Patrick. *Cagney: The Actor as Auteur*. 1975; rpt. New York: Da Capo Press, 1979.

Maltin, Leonard. *The Great Movie Comedians from Charlie Chaplin to Woody Allen*. New York: Crown, 1978.

Manlove, Donald C. (ed). *The Best of James Whitcomb Riley*. Bloomington: Indiana University Press, 1982.

Mast, Gerald. *Howard Hawks, Storyteller*. New York: Oxford University Press, 1982.

Moser, Laura. *Bette Davis*. London: Haus, 2004.

Parish, James Robert, and William T. Leonard. *The Funsters*. New Rochelle, NY: Arlington House, 1979.

Robinson, David. *Chaplin: His Life and Art*. New York: McGraw-Hill, 1985.

Rogers, Will. *Letters of a Self-Made Diplomat to His President*. New York: Albert & Charles Boni, 1926.

Roth, Philip. *The Plot Against America*. New York: Houghton Mifflin, 2004.

Schelly, William. *Harry Langdon*. Metuchen, New Jersey: Scarecrow, 1982.

Sikov, Ed. *On Sunset Boulevard: The Life and Times of Billy Wilder*. New York: Hyperion, 1998.

Staten, Vince. *Ol' Diz: A Biography of Dizzy Dean*. New York: HarperCollins, 1992.

Steinberg, Cobbett. *Reel Facts: The Movie Book of Records*. New York: Vintage Books, 1978.

Summers, Harrison B. (ed.). *A Thirty-Year History of Programs Carried on National Radio Networks in the United States, 1926–1956*. New York: Arno Press, 1971.

Twain, Mark. *A Connecticut Yankee in King Arthur's Court*. 1889; rpt. New York: Berkley Books, 2000.

Van Pelt, Lori. *Amelia Earhart: The Sky's No Limit*. New York: Tom Doherty Associates Book, 2005.

Articles

"Actor Back from Alaska." *Hollywood Citizen-News* (June 4, 1942).

"Actor Pleads for Refugees." *Los Angeles Times* (May 25, 1939).

"Actors on China Tour." *The New York Times* (December 6, 1943): 3.

Adams, Roy W. *Alibi Ike* mini-review. *Motion Picture Herald* (December 21, 1935): 67.

Adams, Val. "Adjusting to the Television Art." *The New York Times* (November 9, 1952): Section 2: 13.

Agee, James. "Comedy's Greatest Era" (1949). In *Agee on Film, Volume 1*. 1969; rpt. New York: Grosset & Dunlap, 1972.

"*Alibi Ike* Comedy Home Run." *The Hollywood Reporter* (June 8, 1935): 3.

Alibi Ike review. *Los Angeles Times* (June 7, 1935).

"Anna Brown: Actor's Mother Active in Social, Civic Life." *Toledo Times* (July 11, 1961).

"Anna M. Brown [obituary]." *Toledo Blade* (July 10, 1961).

"An Aquatic Hero." *The New York Times* (November 18, 1932): 23.

"Baseball Post to Joe E. Brown." *The New York Times* (April 1, 1953): 38.

Bazin, André. "The Virtues and Limitations of Montage." In *What Is Cinema?*, vol. 1, ed/trans. Hugh Gray. 1958; rpt. Los Angeles, CA: University of California Press, 1967.

Beebo, Lucius. "*Elmer the Great*— Radio City Music Hall." *New York Herald Tribune* (May 26, 1933): 18.

"*Betty Lee* Premiere." *The New York Times* (December 26, 1924): 18.

"*Betty Lee* Tuneful, Gay, Speedy Musical Comedy." *New York Herald Tribune* (December 26, 1924): 8.

Bodley, Hal. "Dream Comes True for Duo," *USA Today* (August 1, 2005): 6-C.

Boehnel, William. "At the Strand [*The Tenderfoot*]." *New York World-Telegram* (May 21, 1932): 19.

_____. "*Fireman, Save My Child* Called Joe Brown's Best." *New York World Telegram* (February 19, 1932): 24.

_____. "Joe Brown Amusing in *The Circus Clown*." *New York World Telegram* (July 3, 1934): 4.

_____. "Joe E. Brown Goes Horsey in *Polo Joe*." *New York World Telegram* (November 5, 1936): 21.

_____. "Joe Brown Sets New Mark in Slapstick." *New York World Telegram* (December 1, 1933): 34.

_____. *Local Boy Makes Good* review. *New York World Telegram* (November 28, 1931): 21.

_____. *You Said a Mouthful* review. *New York World Telegram* (November 18, 1932): 28.

"Books — Authors." *The New York Times* (November 17, 1956): 19.

"*Bright Lights* at Strand." *New York World Telegram* (August 15, 1935): 14.

Bright Lights review. *New York Sun* (August 15, 1935): 15.

Bright Lights review. *The New York Times* (August 15, 1935): 15.

Bright Lights review. *Time* (August 26, 1935).

Bright Lights review. *Variety* (August 21, 1935).

Broad Minded review. *Variety* (July 7, 1931).

"Bronze Star Presented to Joe E. Brown." *Los Angeles Times* (October 25, 1945).

Brooks, Bob. "'Circus Is Greatest' Says Joe E. Brown." *Los Angeles Mirror* (March 20, 1961).

"Brown and Keaton in Ball Game Sunday." *The Hollywood Reporter* (February 27, 1932): 2.

"Brown at Republic." *The Hollywood Reporter* (April 16, 1942): 2.

"Brown Ends *Fate* Role, Prepares for Operation." *The Hollywood Reporter* (September 7, 1938): 3.

Brown, Herman J. *You Said a Mouthful* mini-review. *Motion Picture Herald* (May 19, 1934): 87.

"Brown in South Pacific." *The New York Times* (February 25, 1943): 26.

Brown, Joe E. "My Favorite Movie Scene." *The Saturday Evening Post* (March 31, 1945).

_____. "Post Toasties a Natural for Kiddies' Air Show." *Rim Monthly* (December 1938): 17.

_____. "The Role I Liked Best..." *The Saturday Evening Post* (November 9, 1946).

"Brown, LeRoy and Story Highlights." *The Hollywood Reporter* (March 23, 1933): 3.

"Brown to See Peoria Premiere." Uncredited article (July 1936). In the Joe E. Brown files, Margaret Herrick Library, Academy of Motion Picture Arts and Sciences, Beverly Hills, California.

Brownell, Robert C. "Joe E. Brown Urges Solons to Assure Jobs for Vets." *Los Angeles Daily News* (March 22, 1945): 3.

Buick Circus Hour review. *Variety* (October 15, 1952).

Bylsma, Peter. *Son of a Sailor* mini-review. *Motion Picture Herald* (March 31, 1934): 61.

"*Captain Jinks* Comes to Town and Charms Everybody." *The New York Post* (September 9, 1925): 14.

Carroll, Harrison. "Joe E. Browns Are Re-Wed in Church." *Los Angeles Herald Express* (July 8, 1947).

Casanova in Burlesque review. *Variety* (January 26, 1944).

"Celebrities to Join Fourth Ward Group, City in Dedicating Field to Joe E. Brown." *Toledo Blade* (May 18, 1958).

"Chaplin to Play in Shakespeare at Bowl." *The Hollywood Reporter* (June 27, 1934): 4.

Chatterbox review. *Variety* (April 14, 1943).

"Cinema Stars' Homes Under Heavy Guard." *Los Angeles Examiner* (May 12, 1934).

"*Circus Clown* Grand Fun." *The Hollywood Reporter* (May 5, 1934): 3.

"*The Circus Clown*: Romance, Comedy, Drama." *Motion Picture Herald* (May 13, 1934).

The Circus Kid review. *Variety* (December 19, 1928).

Cohen, John S., Jr., "*Let's Go Native*, Wherein Jack Oakie and Others Spread Mirth on a Tropical Island." *New York Sun* (August 30, 1930): 4.

_____. *Local Boy Makes Good* review. *New York Sun* (November 27, 1931): 43.

_____. "The Warners' Hollywood Theater Opens with *Hold Everything*." *New York Sun* (April 23, 1930): 23.

Collins, Frederick L. "Old Brown Joe." *Liberty* (September 28, 1940): 25.

"Collision Is No Joke, But Has Joe E. Brown of Film in Stitches." *Chicago Tribune* (December 7, 1939): 8.

"Colorful *Captain Jinks* Here With Wit and Song." *New York Herald Tribune* (September 9, 1925): 14.

"Comedian Completes War Tour." *Hollywood Citizen-News* (February 24, 1944).

"Comedian Expresses Love for All People; Many Leaders Attend." *Toledo Blade* (December 8, 1945): 12.

Cook, Louis. "Who Said Joe's Mouth Was Big? You Can Blame It All on Lester..." *Detroit Free Press* (July 12, 1964): 10-D.

Creelman, Eileen. *Bright Lights* review. *New York Sun* (August 15, 1935): 9.

____. *The Circus Clown* review. *New York Sun* (June 2, 1934): 15.

____. "Joe E. Brown as a Ring Lardner Ball Player in *Alibi Ike*." *New York Sun* (July 17, 1935).

____. "Joe E. Brown as That Super-Salesman, Alexander Botts, in *Earthworm Tractors*." *New York Sun* (July 27, 1936).

Crewe, Regina. "*Alibi Ike*, Amusing Ring Lardner Tale, Stars Joe Brown." *New York American* (July 17, 1935).

____. "*Elmer the Great* Is Hilarious Film of Lardner-Cohan Play." *New York American* (May 26, 1933): 13.

____. "*Going Wild* Hits High Laugh Mark; Joe E. Brown Star." *New York American* (January 27, 1931): 17.

____. "*Hold Everything* Marvel in Comedy as Seen on Screen." *New York American* (April 23, 1930): 17.

____. "Joe E. Brown Climbs to New Heights in Picture Hilarity." *New York American* (November 27, 1931): 15.

____. "*6-Day Bike Rider* Hilarious Comedy." *New York American* (November 3, 1934): 9.

"The Critics Agree It's Joe E. Brown's Best Picture [ad]!" *The Hollywood Reporter* (September 9, 1938).

Crocker, Harry. "Behind the Makeup." Incomplete citation [circa early 1950s]. In the Joe E. Brown files, Margaret Herrick Library, Academy of Motion Picture Arts and Sciences, Beverly Hills, California.

Crooks Can't Win review. *Variety* (May 30, 1928).

Crowther, Bosley. *Earthworm Tractors* review. *The New York Times* (July 25, 1936): 16.

____. *Fit For a King* review. *The New York Times* (October 15, 1937): 18.

____. *The Gladiator* review. *The New York Times* (August 29, 1938): 10.

____. *Show Boat* review. *The New York Times* (July 20, 1951): 14.

____. *Wide Open Faces* review. *The New York Times* (April 15, 1938): 23.

Dabb, William. *Elmer the Great* mini-review. *Motion Picture Herald* (May 13, 1933): 53.

"Dave Loew Sets Joe E. Brown Pix on RKO Program." *The Hollywood Reporter* (April 30, 1936): 2.

Davis, Charles Jr. "Joe E. Brown Celebrates His 72nd Birthday as Past Meets Present." *Los Angeles Times* (July 28, 1963): 1.

Delehanty, Thornton. "*A Midsummer Night's Dream* Has Premiere on Broadway." *The New York Post* (October 10, 1935): 21.

"Dizzy Calls Self 'Lousy' But Paul Will Thump 'Em." *Toledo Times* (October 4, 1934): 1.

Dunkley, Charles W. "Cards Go Wild in Dressing Room." *Toledo Times* (October 10, 1934): 7.

Earthworm Tractors review. *New York American* (July 25, 1936).

Earthworm Tractors review. *New York Evening Journal* (July 25, 1936).

Earthworm Tractors review. *New York Post* (July 25, 1936).

Earthworm Tractors review. *Variety* (July 29, 1936).

Edgren, Robert. "Miracles of Sport." *Toledo Times* (August 13, 1934): 6.

"*Elmer the Great* Gives Plenty of Belly-Laughs." *The Hollywood Reporter* (March 23, 1933): 3.

Elmer the Great review. *New York Sun* (May 27, 1933): 27.

"Engagement of Joe E. Brown to Be Limited." *Los Angeles Times* (November 24, 1932).

Ernst, Leslie B. "Crowds Cheer Joe E. Brown." *Peoria Journal* (July 15, 1936): 1.

____. "Joe E. Brown Is Truly Good Natured *Boy*, He Shows at Peoria Reception." *Peoria Journal* (July 14, 1936): 1, 14.

Erskine, Carl. "Foreword." In *Mr. Deeds Goes to Yankee Stadium: Baseball Films in the Capra Tradition*. Jefferson, North Carolina: McFarland, 2004.

Ferguson, Otis. "Shakespeare in Hollywood." *The New Republic* (October 16, 1935).

Finnigan, Joseph. "Joe E. Brown Just Misses." *Los Angeles Mirror* (July 19, 1961): Section 1: 12.

"*Fireman* Corking Comedy." *The Hollywood Reporter* (January 27, 1932): 3.

Fireman, Save My Child review. *Film Daily* (February 21, 1932).

Fireman, Save My Child review. *New York Sun* (February 20, 1932): 6.

Fireman, Save My Child review. *Variety* (February 23, 1932).

"Forces Want Fair Play to Nisei." *The New York Times* (June 24, 1945): Section 1: 2.

"Foreign Legion Story for Joe E. Brown." *The Hollywood Reporter* (July 5, 1935): 2.

"Free $50,000 Worth of Bicycles" (ad). *Toledo Times* (September 23, 1934).

"Friday Proclaimed Joe E. Brown Day; Mass Meeting Is Arranged." *Toledo Times* (December 2, 1945): 4.

Gardner, Hy. "'We Need Better Grownups...' So Says Joe E. 'Grin,' Who Defends Our Kids." *Parade* (July 6, 1952): 13.

Gehring, Wes D. "The Comic Anti-Hero in American Fiction: Its First Full Articulation." *Thalia: Studies in Literary Humor* (Winter 1979–80): 11–14.

_____. "John Bunny: America's First Important Screen Comedian." *Literature/Film Quarterly* (vol. 23, no. 2, 1995): 120–24.

_____. "The Last William Wellman Interview." *Paper Cinema* (vol. 1, no. 1, 1982): 9–13.

_____. "The Many Faces of Movie Comedy." *USA Today Magazine* (July 1998): 80–89.

_____. "W. C. Fields: The Copyrighted Sketches." *Journal of Popular Film & Television* (Summer 1986): 65–75.

_____. William Wellman interview. Los Angeles (June 1975). Author's files.

Gilmore, William. *Earthworm Tractors* review. *Brooklyn Daily Eagle* (July 25, 1936).

"*Gladiator* Best Joe Brown." *The Hollywood Reporter* (August 4, 1938): 3.

The Gladiator review. *Motion Picture Herald* (August 13, 1938).

The Gladiator review. *Variety* (August 31, 1938).

Glassburn, Col. Robert P. (retired). "War Law Violation Is Seen [letter to the editor]." *The New York Times* (January 7, 1946): 18.

"Going to Movies Is Social Obligation in Hollywood." *Toledo Times* (September 2, 1934): 4-D.

Going Wild review. *The New York Times* (January 26, 1931): 21.

Gould, Arthur. "Dreams Come True for Joe E. Brown." *Toledo Times* (December 8, 1945): 14.

Green, Abel. "A Book by Ex-Kinker Kid Joe E. Brown, Who Made It with a Grand Canyon Grin." *Variety* (November 21, 1956).

Greenberg, Abe. "Joe E. Brown to Turn Night Club Performer." *Los Angeles Examiner* (November 1, 1959).

Greene, Patterson. "'Joe E.' Great in *Harvey*." *Los Angeles Examiner* (March 19, 1946).

Greenwich Village Follies review. *The New York Times* (September 21, 1923): 4.

Greg, C. R. *The Gladiator* mini-review. *Motion Picture Herald* (October 29, 1938): 49.

Hale, Wanda. "*Alibi Ike* Cheers Joe E. Brown Fans." *New York Daily News* (July 17, 1935).

_____. "Joe E. Brown Puts on Strong Farce." *New York Daily News* (August 28, 1938).

_____. "New Brown Musical Is Field Day for Star." *New York Daily News* (August 16, 1935): 43.

_____. "*$1,000 a Touchdown* Not Worth the Price." *New York Daily News* (October 5, 1939): 52.

_____. *Polo Joe* review. *New York Daily News* (November 5, 1936): 59.

Hall, Mordaunt. "*Hold Everything* Opens New Theatre." *The New York Times* (April 23, 1930): 24.

_____. "Joe E. Brown and Patricia Ellis in a Film of a Baseball Comedy by Ring Lardner." *The New York Times* (May 26, 1933): 24.

_____. "Joe E. Brown in a Boisterous Film Conception of the Stage Comedy, *The Butter and Egg Man*." *The New York Times* (May 25, 1932): 23.

_____. "Joe E. Brown in Comedy: Laura Lee Also Amuses in *Top Speed* at the Strand." *The New York Times* (August 30, 1930): 7.

_____. *On with the Show* review. *The New York Times* (May 29, 1929): 28.

_____. *Son of a Sailor* review. *The New York Times* (November 30, 1933): 38.

Hamilton, Sara. "*Canteen* Real Holiday Gift." *Los Angeles Examiner* (December 21, 1944).

_____. "Whooie! Here Comes Joe E." *Photoplay* (November 1932).

"Harold Lloyd, with Gems Worth $30,000, Heads Hollywood List." *Indianapolis News* (July 15, 1936): 10.

"*Harvey* Makes 'Sage' Out of Joe E. Brown." *In-*

dianapolis News* (February 16, 1948): Section 2: 1.

"*Harvey* Opens Return Engagement at English's." *Indianapolis News* (February 17, 1948): Section 2: 8.

"He Had to Open His Big Mouth." *Photoplay* (July 1942): 10.

Helming, Ann. "Story of Protest Minister Well Done." *Hollywood Citizen News* (January 31, 1948).

Henderson, Wanda. "Joe E. Brown's Daughters Choose Double Wedding." *Hollywood Citizen-News* (February 16, 1953).

Hensley, Dennis E. "Foreword." In *Personality Comedians As Genre: Selected Players*, Wes D. Gehring. Westport, Connecticut: Greenwood, 1997.

Hewitt, Joe E. *Bright Lights* mini-review. *Motion Picture Herald* (October 26, 1935): 89.

Hickman, R. W. *Elmer the Great* mini-review. *Motion Picture Herald* (May 27, 1933): 39.

Hit of the Show review. *Variety* (July 11, 1928).

Hold Everything review. *Variety* (March 26, 1930).

Holland, Jack. "Chumming with Champs [rough draft]" [circa mid–1930s]. In the Joe E. Brown files, Margaret Herrick Library, Academy of Motion Picture Arts and Sciences, Beverly Hills, California.

"Hollywood Night Life Bit Bizarre." *Toledo Times* (November 18, 1934): 4-D.

"Hollywood Should Study Trouping, Says Joe Brown." *Los Angeles Times* (April 25, 1948).

"Honor Joe E. Brown for Entertaining in War Theatres." *Daily Variety* (May 4, 1944).

Hopper, Hedda. "The Ten Best Husbands." *Photoplay* (May 1943): 26–27, 78–79.

"Inventory of Joe E. Brown's Trophy Cases" [ca. 1930s]. In the Joe E. Brown files, Margaret Herrick Library, Academy of Motion Picture Arts and Sciences, Beverly Hills, California.

"Invoking the Gag Rule." *The New York Times* (November 3, 1934): 20.

Jackson, Sammie. *Son of a Sailor* mini-review. *Motion Picture Herald* (June 23, 1934): 131.

"Japanese Captives Wanted Baseball Talk, Says Joe E. Brown on Return from Pacific." *The New York Times* (April 25, 1943): Section 1: 13.

"*Jim Jam Jems* Noisy But Funny." *New York Herald* (October 5, 1920): 11.

"*Jim Jam Jems* Takes Front Ranks on Broadway." *New York Tribune* (October 5, 1920): 8.

"*Joan of Ozark* Hit Teams Canova-Brown in Top Form." *The Hollywood Reporter* (July 15, 1942): 3.

Joan of Ozark review. *Variety* (July 15, 1942).

"Joe Brown Comedy at Rivoli." *Toledo Times* (November 3, 1934): 6.

"Joe Brown Makes Speech." *The New York Times* (November 1, 1940): 32.

"Joe Brown to Hawaii." *The Hollywood Reporter* (May 26, 1934): 3.

"Joe Brown Wants to Play Rube Waddell." *The Hollywood Reporter* (December 28, 1942): 3.

"Joe E. Brown Again Stricken by Malaria." *Los Angeles Daily News* (March 8, 1949).

"Joe E. Brown and *Harvey* Return to English Tonight." *Indianapolis Star* (February 16, 1948): 18.

"Joe E. Brown Arrives; Gets Auto from Missus." *The Hollywood Reporter* (October 14, 1931): 3.

"Joe E. Brown Asks Gold Star Group to Forgive." *Hollywood Citizen-News* (April 15, 1946).

"Joe E. Brown at Pacific Base." *The New York Times* (February 19, 1943): 5.

"Joe E. Brown Camp Tour." *The Hollywood Reporter* (June 30, 1942): 6.

"Joe E. Brown, Comedian of Movies and Stage, Dies." *The New York Times* (July 7, 1973): 24.

"Joe E. Brown Comes Home." *Los Angeles Examiner* (February 25, 1944).

"Joe E. Brown Describes Role as Fighter in Slaying 2 Japs." *Toledo Times* (December 23, 1945): 14.

"Joe E. Brown: Favorite Pin-Up Boy of the Army." *Look* (May 30, 1944): 55.

"Joe E. Brown Finds Morale High." *The New York Times* (March 15, 1943): 5.

"Joe E. Brown Gave 300 Shows at Front." *The Hollywood Reporter* (February 15, 1944).

"Joe E. Brown, *Harvey* Back." *Indianapolis News* (February 16, 1948): Section 1: 14.

"Joe E. Brown, Held Up, Yields $5." *The New York Times* (July 3, 1938): Section 2: 5.

"Joe E. Brown Here for World Premier Tomorrow." *Peoria Journal* (July 13, 1936): 1.

"Joe E. Brown Honored for Entertaining G. I.'s." *Los Angeles Times* (May 4, 1944).

"Joe E. Brown Hurt in Auto Accident." *Indianapolis Star* (December 7, 1939): 4.

"Joe E. Brown Hurt in Auto Crash." *The New York Times* (December 7, 1939): 35.

"Joe E. Brown Ill, Opening Called Off." *Los Angeles Times* (March 1, 1949).

"Joe E. Brown in *Fireman, Save My Child.*" *Film Daily* (February 21, 1932).

"Joe E. Brown in Hospital." *The New York Times* (May 8, 1936): 21.

"Joe E. Brown in Hospital Role." Uncredited Los Angeles newspaper (May 11, 1932). In the Joe E. Brown files, Margaret Herrick Library, Academy of Motion Picture Arts and Sciences, Beverly Hills, California.

"Joe E. Brown Is Top Toledoan for Today." *Toledo Times* (December 7, 1945): 11.

"Joe E. Brown Makes Speech." *The New York Times* (November 2, 1940): 32.

"Joe E. Brown Milestone Hailed." *Hollywood Citizen-News* (November 27, 1944).

"Joe E. Brown on Hop to Fulfill Radio Spots." *The Hollywood Reporter* (April 14, 1937): 4.

"Joe E. Brown Operated Upon." Uncredited Los Angeles newspaper (May 26, 1932). In the Joe E. Brown files, Margaret Herrick Library, Academy of Motion Picture Arts and Sciences, Beverly Hills, California.

"Joe E. Brown Paid Tribute." *Los Angeles Examiner* (May 4, 1944).

"Joe E. Brown Pleads for Refugee Tots." *Los Angeles Daily News* (May 25, 1939).

Joe E. Brown Press Release. Paramount studio biography (July 5, 1939). In the Joe E. Brown files, Margaret Herrick Library, Academy of Motion Picture Arts and Sciences, Beverly Hills, California.

Joe E. Brown Press Release. RKO Studio biography [ca. 1937]. In the Joe E. Brown files, Margaret Herrick Library, Academy of Motion Picture Arts and Sciences, Beverly Hills, California.

Joe E. Brown Questionnaire, circa 1930s. In the Joe E. Brown files, Margaret Herrick Library, Academy of Motion Picture Arts and Sciences, Beverly Hills, California.

"Joe E. Brown Raisin King." *The Hollywood Reporter* (September 8, 1934): 4.

"Joe E. Brown Receives Bowling Green U. Honor." *The New York Times* (June 4, 1949): 8.

"Joe E. Brown Returns from Battle Line Tour." *Los Angeles Times* (February 25, 1944).

"Joe E. Brown Returns from Milking Ball Games." *The Hollywood Reporter* (May 22, 1937): 5.

"Joe E. Brown Returns in a Merry Film Version of Ring Lardner's *Alibi Ike*, at the Cameo." *The New York Times* (July 17, 1935): 22.

"Joe E. Brown Scores Actor Wage Limits." Uncredited Los Angeles newspaper (November 1, 1933). In the Joe E. Brown files, Margaret Herrick Library, Academy of Motion Picture Arts and Sciences, Beverly Hills, California.

"Joe E. Brown Target of the Circus Saints." *The New York Times* (November 27, 1948): 11.

"Joe E. Brown Tells What's Ailing G. I. Abroad." *Los Angeles Herald Express* (January 12, 1946).

"Joe E. Brown to Report Baseball on Radio at Chicago. *The Hollywood Reporter* (January 29, 1937): 2.

"Joe E. Brown TV's Baseball." *Los Angeles Examiner* (May 3, 1953).

Joe E. Brown 20th Century–Fox biography (August 31, 1943). In the Joe E. Brown files, Margaret Herrick Library, Academy of Motion Picture Arts and Sciences, Beverly Hills, California.

Joe E. Brown untitled essay in uncited Los Angeles newspaper (March 3, 1934). In the Joe E. Brown files, Margaret Herrick Library, Academy of Motion Picture Arts and Sciences, Beverly Hills, California.

"Joe E. Brown Visits Toledo." *Toledo Blade* (April 19, 1940).

Joe E. Brown Warners biography (circa 1932). In the Joe E. Brown files, Margaret Herrick Library, Academy of Motion Picture Arts and Sciences, Beverly Hills, California.

"Joe E. Brown Will Tell of Dutch Harbor Trek." *The Hollywood Reporter* (June 10, 1942): 6.

"Joe E. Brown's Daughters Nearly Tie in Stork Race." *Los Angeles Times* (January 14, 1954).

"Joe E. Browns Donate Lodge in Memory of Son." *Los Angeles Daily News* (October 6, 1947).

"Joe E. Brown's Killing of Japs on Luzon Told." *Los Angeles Times* (December 23, 1945).

"Joe E. Brown's Malaria 'Licked' by New Drug Use." *Los Angeles Examiner* (March 9, 1949).

"Joe E. Brown's Son to Wed Tuesday." *Los Angeles Examiner* (September 20, 1940).

"Joe E. Browns Wed Again on the 25th Anniversary." *The New York Times* (December 25, 1940): 32.

"Joe Evan Brown." In *Current Biography 1945*, Anne Rothe, ed. New York: H. W. Wilson Company, 1946.

Johnson, H. M. *Son of a Sailor* mini-review. *Motion Picture Herald* (March 31, 1934): 61.

Johnston, Alva. "Joe E. Brown Profile." *The New Yorker* (July 7, 1945): 26–30, 32, 34.

Jones, Carlisle. Most of Filmdom's Biggest Stars Have Lived Horatio Alger Stories" (syndicated). *Toledo Times* (October 21, 1934): 5-D.

"Kay Francis Heads Warners' Payroll." *The New York Times* (March 3, 1937): 37.

Kingsley, Grace. "Screen's Comedians Make Best Fathers." *Los Angeles Times* (May 27, 1934): Part 2: 1.

Lahr, Bert (letter). "Bert Lahr Labels Joe Brown 'Lifter.'" *Variety* (March 28, 1930).

Lane, Anthony. "The Disappearing Poet." *The New Yorker* (July 4, 2005): 76.

Lardner, Ring. *You Know Me Al: A Busher's Letters.* 1914; rpt. New York: Collier Books, 1991.

"Latest 'Joe E.' Typical." *The Hollywood Reporter* (November 1, 1933): 3.

Laurie, Joe, Jr. "A Thumbnose Sketch — Joe E. Brown." *Variety* (February 5, 1947).

Leavy, Jane. "Tape from 1965 Easier to Find Than Ill Will Toward Koufax." *The New York Times* (September 1, 2002): Sports Section: 6.

"Leo McCarey Is Guarded After Kidnapping Attempt." *Los Angeles Evening Herald* (May 29, 1934).

"Lion Claws Film Comic Joe Brown." Uncredited Los Angeles newspaper (February 25, 1934). In the Joe E. Brown files, Margaret Herrick Library, Academy of Motion Picture Arts and Sciences, Beverly Hills, California.

Lloyd, Harold (with Wesley W. Stout). *An American Comedy.* 1928; rpt. New York: Dover, 1971.

Local Boy Makes Good review. *New York Herald Tribune* (November 27, 1931): 21.

Local Boy Makes Good review. *The New York Post* (November 27, 1931): 21.

Logue, Andrew. "The 2002 Heisman Candidates: Brad Banks." *Des Moines Register* (December 14, 2002): 2-C.

The Lottery Bride review. *New York Evening Journal* (November 29, 1930): 9.

The Lottery Bride review. *Variety* (December 3, 1930).

"Lusty Shake: Joe Brown's Grip May Have Cost Game." *Toledo Times* (October 9, 1934): 2.

Lynch, Lorrie. "Who's News" (syndicated). *USA Weekend* magazine (July 1–3, 2005): 2.

Macaulay, Richard. "Git Out o' T' Game!" *The Saturday Evening Post* (June 15, 1935).

_____. "Who's Who — And Why." *The Saturday Evening Post* (August 10, 1935): 78.

McArdle, Gladys E. *Elmer the Great* mini-review. *Motion Picture Herald* (July 15, 1933): 79.

Mclurg, E. J. *Bright Lights* mini-review. *Motion Picture Herald* (October 5, 1935): 59.

McManus, John T. *Sons o' Guns* review. *The New York Times* (May 14, 1936): 29.

"Many Make Pleas for Refugee Youth." *The New York Times* (May 25, 1939): 12.

Maybe It's Love review. *Variety* (October 22, 1930).

"Me 'n Paul" (cover story). *Time* (April 15, 1935): 52.

"Members of 37th May Be Home to Celebrate Joe E. Brown Day." *Toledo Times* (November 18, 1945).

A Midsummer Night's Dream review. *Screenland* (October 1935).

A Midsummer Night's Dream review. *Variety* (October 16, 1935).

"*Midsummer Night's Dream* Triumph for All Concerned." *The Hollywood Reporter* (October 9, 1935): 3.

Mills, C. W. *The Gladiator* mini-review. *Motion Picture Herald* (October 22, 1938): 53.

"Mr. Brown Goes to Australia." *The New York Times* (April 12, 1943): 6.

Moffitt, Jack. "Billy Wilder Pic Distills Laughs from Dry Era." *The Hollywood Reporter* (February 25, 1959).

Monroe, Keith. "The Battling Buffoon Named Brown." *The Saturday Evening Post* (two parts, December 8 & 15, 1951).

"Music by Mr. Frimi." *The New York Times* (November 29, 1930): 21.

"New Delhi." *The New York Times* (November 26, 1943): 7.

"9 Hurt in Film Crash." *Los Angeles Examiner* (August 8, 1934): 1.

"The Nizkov Project: Shofar FTP Archive File: places 11 usa/conspiracy. 101.

"Notable Audience Views Picture of *Hold Everything*." *New York American* (April 23, 1930): 17.

"Notre Dame Grid Banquet Done Up Good and Brown." *Indianapolis News* (December 13, 1938): Section 2: 2.

Nugent, Frank S. *$1,000 a Touchdown* review. *The New York Times* (October 5, 1939): 27.

_____. *Polo Joe* review. *The New York Times* (November 5, 1936): 35.

Oates, Joyce Carol. "Do You Love Me?" *The New York Times Book Review* (May 16, 2004).

O'Brien, W. E. *Son of a Sailor* mini-review. *Motion Picture Herald* (March 3, 1934): 57.

On With the Show review. *Variety* (June 5, 1929).

"One of Best Joe E. Brown Films." *The Hollywood Reporter* (July 24, 1935): 3.

"The Palladium: Mr. Joe E. Brown in Person." *London Times* (August 19, 1936): 8.

Parsons, Louella. "Joe E. Brown Stops Work to Be Grandpa" (syndicated column). *Los Angeles Examiner* (January 10, 1954).

_____. "Joe E. to Do Song, Dance" (syndicated). *Toledo Times* (August 11, 1934): 6.

_____. "'Puck' Found By Producer" (syndicated). *Toledo Times* (September 13, 1934): 6.

Patrick, Corbin. "Keep Your Eyes on Brown and Bottle in *Harvey* This Week." *Indianapolis Star* (February 15, 1948): 37.

_____. "Victor Varies Musical Output with Joe Brown Baseball Album." *Indianapolis Star* (May 16, 1947): 25.

"'Patriotic Rally Has Anti-Semitic Tinge." *The New York Times* (May 25, 1939): 3.

Pelswick, Rose. "Baseball Hero Wins." *New York Evening Journal* (May 26, 1933): 20.

_____. "Delight Picture." *New York Evening Journal* (May 21, 1932): 10.

_____. "Joe E. Brown Amusingly Plays Goofy Pitcher in Baseball Classic." *New York Evening Journal* (July 17, 1935).

_____. "Joe E. Brown Has Amusing Gags." *New York Evening Journal* (November 3, 1934): 15.

_____. *Local Boy Makes Good* review. *New York Evening Journal* (November 27, 1931): 29.

_____. "*Midsummer Night's Dream*: Shakespearean Fantasy Molded by Reinhardt Makes Film History." *New York Evening Journal* (October 10, 1935): 25.

Phelps, Donald. "Golden Boy: The Life, Times, and Comedic Genius of Joe E. Brown." *Film Comment* (November-December 1994).

"Pleasing Bill at Palace." *The New York Times* (October 23, 1923): 18.

Polito, Sol. *Fireman, Save My Child* review. *International Photographer* (March 1932).

Pollock, Arthur. "Joe E. Brown, with a Brightly Written Movie Called *The Gladiator* Under Him, Gallops Hilariously Across Globe's Screen." *Brooklyn Eagle* (August 30, 1938).

"*Polo Joe* Joe E. Brown Par." *The Hollywood Reporter* (September 19, 1936): 3.

Polo Joe review. *Variety* (November 11, 1936).

Prose, Francine. "Not Just at the P. O." *The New York Times* (August 14, 2005): Book Review Section: 21.

Rathbun, Stephen. "Joe Brown Plays a Texan in *The Tenderfoot*." *New York Sun* (May 23, 1932): 29.

Redelings, Lowell. "Joe E. Brown Scores Smash Hit in *Harvey*." *Hollywood Citizen-News* (Marcy 22, 1946).

Reeve, Henry. *Son of a Sailor* mini-review. *Motion Picture Herald* (June 2, 1934): 59.

Reidenbaugh, Lowell. *Baseball's Hall of Fame: Coopertown, Where the Legends Live.* 1983; rpt. New York: Crescent Books, 1937.

"Reinhardt's Production of *Dream* Superbly Beautiful." *The Hollywood Reporter* (September 18, 1934): 2.

Reynard, Grant. "Joe E. on Headhunters, Taxes, and Hate." *PM* (November 5, 1944): 4.

Reynolds, E. A. *Elmer the Great* mini-review. *Motion Picture Herald* (September 30, 1933): 50.

Rich, S. H. *Son of a Sailor* mini-review. *Motion Picture Herald* (February 24, 1934): 51.

_____. *You Said a Mouthful* mini-review. *Motion Picture Herald* (April 29, 1933): 37.

"Ricky Successor Pledges Pennant." *The New York Times* (October 26, 1955): 36.

Riding on Air review. *Variety* (June 30, 1937).

"Ring Lardner Story Offers Joe Brown Familiar Material." *The New York Post* (July 17, 1935).

Rio Rita program (May 19, 1941). In the Joe E. Brown files, Margaret Herrick Library, Academy of Motion Picture Arts and Sciences, Beverly Hills, California.

Roberts, John. "Joe E. Brown: The Big Mouth." *Films of the Golden Age* (Winter 2004–2005).

Rogers, Will. "Mr. Rogers Makes His Official Report on World Series Finale and the Riot" (October 10, 1934, syndicated daily newspaper telegram). In *Will Rogers' Daily Telegrams, vol. 4, The Roosevelt Years: 1933–1935*, James M. Smallwood, ed. Stillwater: Oklahoma State University Press, 1979.

Rothman, Cliff. "A 40-Year-Old Comedy That Hasn't Grown Stale." *The New York Times* (August 1, 1999): Entertainment Section: 24.

"Rowe's Hand Mashed by Joe Brown." *New York Herald Tribune* (October 9, 1934): 20.

"St. Louis Acclaims Cardinals on Return Home." *Toledo Times* (October 11, 1934): 7.

Sally review. *Variety* (December 25, 1929).

"Scared Lion Scares Brown." Uncredited newspaper (February 16, 1934). In the Joe E. Brown files, Margaret Herrick Library, Academy of Motion Picture Arts and Sciences, Beverly Hills, California.

Schallert, Edwin. "Gala *Show Boat* Premiere Restores Old-Time Glamour." *Los Angeles Times* (June 18, 1951).

_____. "*Harvey* Conjures Rare Spell of Laughter." *Los Angeles Times* (March 19, 1946): Section 2: 3.

_____. "Musicals Look to Rich Future." *Los Angeles Times* (April 15, 1951): 3.

_____. "*Tender Years* Genuinely Appealing." *Los Angeles Times* (January 31, 1948).

Schickel, Richard. "The Slayer of False Values: Arthur Miller, 1915–2005." *Time* (February 21, 2005): 72.

"Screen Comedian Who Turned Serious." *The New York Times* (December 23, 1945): Section 1: 15.

"Sees German Refugees as Boon to U. S." *Des Moines Register* (May 25, 1939): 1.

Sennwald, Andre. *A Midsummer Night's Dream* review. *The New York Times* (October 10, 1935): 31.

Shaffer, Rosalind. "Film Beauty Has Own Reward." *Chicago Tribune* (July 12, 1936): Drama Section: 1.

Shapiro, Michael. "It's 1942: The Bronx Bombers Play and U. S. Bombers Attack." *The New York Times* (March 30, 2003): Section 4: 1.

Show Boat review. *Saturday Review of Literature* (June 9, 1951): 26.

Shut My Big Mouth review. *Variety* (February 25, 1942).

"Sidelights of the Week." *The New York Times* (December 29, 1940): Section 4: 2.

Silver, Bert. *Son of a Sailor* mini-review. *Motion Picture Herald* (January 27, 1934): 59.

Simon, Henry W., Ph. D. "Supplement to *Photoplay* Studies: for *Midsummer Night's Dream*." *Photoplay* [and Warner Brothers] (September 1935): 9.

"*Sit Tight* a Sad Film." *The New York Times* (February 19, 1931): 20.

Sit Tight review. *Variety* (February 25, 1931).

"*Six-Day Bike Race* Amusing Farce." *The Hollywood Reporter* (September 28, 1934): 2.

"Skylarking." *The New York Times* (January 26, 1931): 21.

So You Won't Talk review. *New York American* (October 17, 1940): 14.

So You Won't Talk review. *Variety* (October 23, 1940).

Some Like It Hot review. *Boxoffice* (March 16, 1959).

Some Like It Hot review. *Motion Picture Herald* (February 28, 1959).

Sons o' Guns review. *Variety* (May 20, 1936).

"Sporting Life." *Time* (April 27, 1953).

"Strand Shows Joe E. Brown in Gay Film." *New York Evening Journal* (August 15, 1935): 14.

Take Me Home review. *Variety* (October 24, 1928).

Tazelaar, Marguerite. "*Hold Everything* Opens New Hollywood Theater." *New York Herald Tribune* (April 23, 1930): 16.

_____. "*Polo Joe*—Criterion." *New York Herald Tribune* (November 4, 1936): 28.

_____. *Sit Tight* review. *The New York Times* (February 19, 1931): 17.

_____. "*You Said a Mouthful*—Winter Garden." *New York Herald Tribune* (November 18, 1932): 16.

"*The Tender Years* Is Fine Family Film." *Indianapolis News* (February 18, 1948): Section 2: 9.

The Tender Years review. *Film Daily* (December 5, 1947).

The Tender Years review. *The Hollywood Reporter* (December 3, 1947).

The Tender Years review. *Variety* (December 3, 1947).

The Tenderfoot opening announcement. *The New York Times* (May 22, 1932): Section 8: 4.

The Tenderfoot review. *Variety* (May 24, 1932).

"Their Boys Made Good." *Toledo News* (November 12, 1930).

Thirer, Irene. "*Hold Everything* Opens Hollywood." *New York Daily News* (April 23, 1930): 38.

_____. "Joe E. Brown as *Gladiator* Lures Laughs to the Globe." *New York Post* (August 28, 1938).

Thorn, John, and Pete Palmer, ed. *Total Baseball*. New York: Warner Books, 1989.

Tinée, Mae. "Sparkling Role Helps Joe Brown in Film Comeback." *Chicago Tribune* (January 31, 1932): Part 9: 1.

"Toledo Figures Prominently in Joe E. Brown Biography." *Toledo Times* (October 30, 1956): 20.

Top Speed review. *Variety* (September 3, 1930).

"*Top Speed* with Joe Brown." *Harrison's Reports* (September 6, 1930).

"A Tragic Comedian." *The New York Times* (July 9, 1928): 25.

Troyer, G. A. *Bright Lights* mini-review. *Motion Picture Herald* (October 12, 1935): 55.

Twinkle Twinkle review. *The New York Times* (November 17, 1926): 22.

"*Twinkle Twinkle* Sparks at the Liberty Theatre." *The New York Post* (November 17, 1926): 8.

Veseth, Carl. *Elmer the Great* mini-review. *Motion Picture Herald* (July 22, 1933): 69.

Wagstaff, Mrs. Hobart. "10,000 Greet Joe E. Brown at Holgate." *Toledo Blade* (May 31, 1949): 13.

"War Tribute Given Brown." *Los Angeles Examiner* (May 4, 1946).

Watts, Richard, Jr. *Alibi Ike* review. *New York Herald Tribune* (July 17, 1935): 10.

_____. *Fireman, Save My Child* review. *New York Herald Tribune* (February 19, 1932): 12.

_____. *A Midsummer Night's Dream* review. *New York Herald Tribune* (October 10, 1935): 17.

_____. "*Twinkle Twinkle* Tells of Film Star And Hollywood 'Sin.'" *New York Herald Tribune* (November 17, 1926): 21.

"WB *Earthworm Tractors* Swell Comedy Thriller." *The Hollywood Reporter* (June 11, 1936): 3.

Weber, L. *Elmer the Great* mini-review. *Motion Picture Herald* (July 8, 1933): 47.

Weiler, A. H. "A Fortune in His Face." *The New York Times* (March 24, 1957): Section 7: 18.

"*Wide Open Faces* OK Brown." *The Hollywood Reporter* (April 23, 1938): 3.

"Wife Leaves for East to Greet Joe E. Brown." *Hollywood Citizen-News* (February 11, 1944).

Wile, Robert. *Bright Lights* mini-review. *Motion Picture Herald* (November 16, 1935): 68.

"Winter and the Circus." *The New York Times* (December 17, 1928): 23.

Wolfe, Sheila. "Joe E. Brown Grins, Waits for Surgery." *Chicago Tribune* (April 16, 1965): Section 1: 3.

Woodbury, Mitchell. "Strolling Around: Cup o' Chatter." *Toledo Times* (August 12, 1934): 5-D.

_____. "Strolling Around Hollywood." *Toledo Times* (September 15, 1934): 6.

_____. "Strolling Around Hollywood." *Toledo Times* (September 16, 1934): 5-D.

_____. "Strolling Around Hollywood." *Toledo Times* (September 30, 1934): 5-D.

_____. "Strolling Around [Note Book]." *Toledo Times* (August 5, 1934): 5-D.

_____. "Strolling Around [:Series Trophies Given Joe Brown]." *Toledo Times* (October 14, 1934): 5-D.

Woodward, C. Wann. "Political Stalemate and Agrarian Revolt, 1877–1896." In *The National Experience: A History of the United States*, John M. Blum, ed. New York: Harcourt Brace, 1968.

Yardley, Jonathan. *Ring: A Biography of Ring Lardner*, 1977; rpt. New York: Rowman & Littlefield, 2001.

York, Cal. "Inside Stuff." *Photoplay* (May 1944).

You Said a Mouthful ad. *The Hollywood Reporter* (November 23, 1932): 4.

"*You Said a Mouthful* Funny." *New York Daily News* (November 18, 1932): 54.

You Said a Mouthful review. *Variety* (November 22, 1932).

Index

Numbers in **_bold italics_** indicate pages with photographs.